ISRAEL'S SACRED SONGS

A Study of Dominant Themes

ISRAEL'S SACRED SONGS

A STUDY OF DOMINANT THEMES

Harvey H. Guthrie, Jr.

A CROSSROAD BOOK • THE SEABURY PRESS • NEW YORK

Acknowledgments

Thankful acknowledgment is made to the following publishers for permission to reprint copyrighted material from the titles listed:

UNIVERSITY OF CHICAGO PRESS, which permitted quotation of material by Thorkild Jacobsen in *The Intellectual Adventure of Ancient Man*, by H. and H. A. Frankfort, John A. Wilson, Thorkild Jacobsen, and William A. Irwin. Copyright 1946 by The University of Chicago. Published 1946. Third Impression 1950.

PRINCETON UNIVERSITY PRESS, which permitted quotation of texts translated by E. A. Speiser, A. Sachs, Ferris J. Stephens, and John A. Wilson in *Ancient Near Eastern Texts*, edited by James B. Pritchard. Copyright 1950, 1955, by Princeton University Press. Second Edition, 1955.

1978
The Seabury Press
815 Second Avenue
New York, N.Y. 10017

Library of Congress Catalog Card Number: 66-10833
ISBN: 0-8164-2178-1
Printed in the United States of America

To the Memory of My Father
And to My Mother
In Grateful Appreciation

Preface

This book is primarily concerned with the way in which Israel adopted certain cultural idioms as means of praising and addressing her God, and with how these idioms were transformed by the content they were made to carry. The final chapter shows how I take this, and not specific items of their content, to be the source of the relevance of the songs of Israel for us today.

My own experience in teaching, in theological school and elsewhere, has convinced me that what I have tried to do fulfills a need. The kind of interpretation of Israel's poetry given here finds expression, for the most part, either in scattered works on various subjects or in larger, more technical works. In one sense there is nothing new here, and my debt to scholars who have worked in the field is apparent. I believe, however, that I do offer an approach to the subject and a framework for it that are my own. Other smaller books interpreting the psalms in the light of factors stressed here are Helmer Ringgren's *The Faith of the Psalmists* and Claus Westermann's *The Praise of God in the Psalms*. (The English edition of the latter appeared after I had finished writing, therefore I used the German original.)

Not all of Israel's songs are treated here, samples being used to illustrate things found more extensively in the Old Testament. Nor has space permitted more than reference to samples of extrabiblical ancient Near Eastern literature. I have indicated where others can be found. A treatment of the structure and form of Hebrew poetry is not within the scope of this book. The reader may be referred to the various commentaries on the psalter as well as to T. H. Robinson's *The Poetry of the Old Testament*. The Introduction provides background for the present study in significant contemporary discussion of the poetry of the Old Testament. Although it provides a necessary perspective, some readers may want to pass over it directly to the first chapter. Translations of the biblical material and of the Ugaritic literature are my own, and are fairly free. I have not given detailed justification for them, but their basis should be clear from consultation of text and commentaries. Because the word "myth" means so many things, popularly an ancient story that is not true, I have made use of its transliterated Greek original, *mythos*, as a term for an over-all view of the nature and meaning of life. Some such term has had to be used in order to convey a more precise meaning as there is none readily available in English.

This book had its beginnings in a course offered biennially for the past several years at the Episcopal Theological School in Cambridge, Massachusetts, as well as in lectures given at Grace Church, New Bedford, Massachusetts; the Faculty Conference in Theology at Trinity College, Hartford, Connecticut; and the Lay School of Theology at the Episcopal Theological School. To all who listened, questioned, and commented, I am most grateful. That the original spadework was done is due to the generosity of the Episcopal Theological School's trustees, who granted me leave during the fall semester of 1961-62; to the American Association of Theological Schools for a faculty fellowship; and to the Georg-August University in Göttingen for its hospitality during that period. That all has finally been written down is due to the trustees' grant of a leave in the spring of 1965 and to the Yale Divinity School for the privilege of working there as a research fellow. I should also like to express my gratitude to Mr. Arthur R. Buckley of The Seabury Press and to his associates for their interest and invaluable assistance.

HARVEY H. GUTHRIE, JR.

Cambridge, Massachusetts
October 11, 1965

Preface to the Paperback Edition

The reprinting of this book more than a decade since it was first published provides me with the opportunity to write a new preface. I wish simply to say three things.

First, while I would obviously like to redo a number of detailed things, I think that the main lines of what the book has to say are still valid. Study since the book was originally published would not lead to my making substantial changes in what is said. I stand by my main lines of argument.

Second, I have provided a very short supplement to the bibliography. It lists general works on the psalms published through the last eleven years which I have found helpful. It also lists one or two more technical articles that have helped my own thinking. Of course, a tremendous amount of material has been published during that time. Again, however, the main lines of what this book has to say are not substantially affected, and the short supplement seems to me sufficient.

Third, if it were possible to redo the text of the book, I would want to make the references both to the human community and to God much less blatantly and exclusively masculine than they are. My consciousness on that set of issues has been sharpened in the years since the book was originally published. Every time I look at it I am painfully aware of the need for revision along these lines, and want to record that awareness here. I also want to record my gratitude to the ministry of women who have sharpened that awareness.

I continue to be indebted to students and others who have used the book and with whom I have worked in courses and lectures. I both learn much from them and am inspired by them to continue my own research.

HARVEY H. GUTHRIE, JR.

Cambridge, Massachusetts
St. Nicholas' Day, 1977

Contents

ISRAEL'S SACRED SONGS

A Study of Dominant Themes

INTRODUCTION:
Method and Approach

The sacred songs of ancient Israel, particularly the psalms, are perhaps the most familiar texts of the Old Testament. Extensive quotation of the psalms in the New Testament indicates how readily they came to the minds even of the early Christians. This was a natural consequence of the wide use of the psalms in the liturgy of the Jewish synagogue. They have been used widely, also, in the classical liturgies of Christendom, constituting the backbone of the daily offices in the Orthodox churches, in the Roman Breviary, and in the Book of Common Prayer. In metrical paraphrase in the Scottish and Swiss Reformed churches, or in substance in Luther's "Ein' Feste Burg," they are the source of much of the hymnody of the Reformation. They have provided material for the prayers and praise of Jewish and Christian people down through the ages.[1]

In recent times, however, the application of new methods of historical research to the Bible has raised the question of what Israel's poetry is in terms of the cultural context from which it arose. This question received no significant attention before the nineteenth century. The writers of the New Testament and their Christian successors through many centuries assumed that the psalms, as tradition and many of their titles had it, were written by King David. It was an unquestioned assumption that the psalms, and other poems

1

of the Old Testament as well, were written by individual poets in response to individual experiences, thoughts, and inspirations. It was further assumed without question that the psalms and other poems of the Old Testament, indeed the whole Bible, contained unchangeable, eternal, propositional truth.

Probably because the psalms were so precious to Christians, both in public worship and in private devotion, they were not subjected to the new methods of historical research as early as were some other parts of the Old Testament. Even when Davidic authorship of the psalms was challenged in favor of later dates of origin, the two basic assumptions inherited from the past continued to operate. For most radical critics of the nineteenth and early twentieth centuries, the study of a given psalm, or other poem in the Old Testament, once the conclusion was reached that it must come from a time later than that of David, focused upon the circumstances in which some other individual poet might have composed the poem.[2] Although the tradition of Davidic authorship gradually withered, the basic assumption that the psalms were a result of individual literary activity was retained. Furthermore, once the authentic nucleus, probable date, and authorship had been decided, a given psalm was discussed in terms of its ideas, the theological concepts it expressed, the profundity of the thought behind it, and the individual religious experience and inspiration that had produced it. Although older theories of inspiration and revelation might be called into question, the psalms were nevertheless expounded in terms of abstract, conceptual truths considered to be inherent in them.[3]

Study of Israel's poetry, as of other areas of scripture, has recently taken a radically new historical and critical approach. The application of more sophisticated methods of research, and the wealth of material from the ancient Near

East uncovered in the last half-century, have indeed placed the psalms and other Old Testament poetry in a new perspective. Despite many specific disagreements among experts in the field, there is no doubt that we are in a position today to hear this poetry on its own terms in a way that our predecessors were not. This new understanding of Israel's poetry has challenged the two standard assumptions accepted uncritically by conservative and liberal readers of this poetry even in recent times. No longer may we responsibly read into the poetry the attitudes and point of view of our own culture. Rather must we let Israel's sacred songs speak for themselves and for the complex culture out of which they were shaped.

Israel's songs may no longer be thought of as the work of individual poets; they are clearly expressions of the devotion of a total worshiping community. As it is not possible to speak of the "author" of the Roman liturgy or of the Book of Common Prayer, so it is not possible to speak of "authorship" of the poems of the Old Testament. The psalms, like the classic eucharistic prayers and collects of Christendom, are cast in certain established "forms" or "shapes." Individual poets or singers must have been responsible, of course, for the actual writing or the original oral composition, but they merely followed patterns and traditions common to the given culture and religious tradition. Even if information identifying the original writer or singer of a given psalm or other poem in the Old Testament were available (and it almost never is), that identification would contribute little of substance to a full understanding of the poem. An understanding of the patterns and traditions underlying the songs of ancient Israel has been the emphasis of recent research and study. This study has led us into the world and culture Israel shared with her neighbors in the ancient Near East.

This has made it necessary to revise our assumptions about the way the content of Israel's poetry may be interpreted. Whatever meaning familiar psalms such as "The Lord is my shepherd" or "O come, let us sing unto the Lord" may have for modern readers and worshipers in terms of the world view of the nineteenth and twentieth centuries, their original allusions and terminology derive from a time and a culture far removed from our own. Advances in archaeology and philology and the history of religions and related disciplines in the last half-century enable us to reconstruct how Israel's sacred poetry was used in its own time and to recognize the connotations of its language in terms of the culture of that time. Ancient Babylon, Nineveh, Ugarit, and Egypt produced sacred poems parallel to those of the Old Testament in form and content. Israel was part of a much larger culture, and our ever-increasing knowledge of that culture sheds light on what is said in Israel's poetry and in her other literature. The anti-Canaanite sentiments of such Old Testament books as Deuteronomy do not gainsay the evidence we have that the language in which Israel sang her sacred songs and the poetic patterns in which she framed them were borrowed from the Canaanites.[4] Our new knowledge compels realization that Israel was profoundly affected by the culture surrounding her along with the recognition that her faith and point of view were unique within that culture.

If the Bible, especially the much-loved and much-used poetry of the psalms and the prophets, comes from a pre-scientific world in which mythology, and not rational philosophy, served to interpret reality, what has the Bible really to say to men and women of this very different world of the twentieth century? If advances in our knowledge of the biblical world challenge the meanings we have laid upon biblical literature, meanings so dear to so many, and replace them with meanings native to a far-removed, prephilosophical, and prescientific culture, can the Bible be normative for and creative of faith in the modern world? If, to borrow biblical terminology, the sacred songs were originally sung in so foreign a land, how can we effectively and validly use them to sing to the Lord in our land and time? It is with such questions that this book is essentially concerned. However uncomfortable and disconcerting these questions may be, they have been inexorably raised by the passage of history and the pursuit of historical investigation, and they must be faced if the community of faith in which the Bible is read and heard and used to sing the Lord's praises is to substantiate its claim that the God it worships and proclaims is truly God.

To these questions, therefore, we shall return in our conclusion.

FORM CRITICISM:
THE TRACING OF TYPICAL PATTERNS

Discussion of the basic motifs of Israel's sacred songs requires a brief introduction to the methods by which these motifs have been uncovered. Such an introduction necessarily begins with "form criticism," the English name for study of the literature of the Bible that distinguishes its literary units and classifies them according to form and content. Actually, the German name for this approach to biblical literature, *Gattungsgeschichte* (literally: "the history of species"), is more descriptive of what is involved.

As there are various species and classes of plants and animals, so there are various species and classes—genres—of literature. Whatever a writer has to say, he usually will express it in a form available to him in his tradition and culture. We all distinguish prose from poetry, novels from essays, editorials from short stories, sonnets from folk songs.

When we make such distinctions, we are functioning as form critics. When we thumb through a magazine or browse among the paperbacks at the corner drugstore in order to find reading that suits our mood, we are practicing form criticism.

Classification of literature involves not only the *form* of what has been written (or of its recitation if it is oral) but also its *content*. An essay or an editorial or a poem may also, depending on its content and purpose, be a eulogy or an exhortation or a fantasy. Classifying literature cannot, therefore, ever be an exact science. No universally applicable and agreed-upon set of classifications can ever be set forth, because the forms of human expression are as manifold as the reaches of human imagination and as changeable as the history of human thought and action. Yet, attempts at classification are useful, and we all employ and learn from them. A course in English literature in which various types of literature are analyzed and evaluated, or a course in music appreciation in which the structure of the symphony or the cantata is investigated, cannot capture the genius of a particular writer or composer or the effect of specific literature or music on the reader or auditor. It can, however, increase the capacity to see and hear and appreciate, and it may cultivate and sharpen taste and discrimination.

Furthermore, identification of literary form is indispensable if a given piece of writing is not to be misunderstood and misapplied. Allen Drury's *Advise and Consent* and *A Shade of Difference* are popular and relevant investigations of issues and human reactions in twentieth-century politics and diplomacy as they transpire in the United States Senate and in the functioning of the United Nations. The literary form employed is the novel. Five or ten centuries hence a student of history might well use these novels in a reconstruction of the issues and attitudes and events of the mid-twentieth century. If, however, that hypothetical student fails to recognize that he is studying novels and regards them as reports on actual events, he will err in a most disastrous way, and his history will be false. The same situation applies to the little book of Jonah in the Old Testament. Whether it is an actual report on the words and actions of the prophet mentioned in II Kings 14:25, or a story composed in the late fourth century B.C. to condemn postexilic Jewish exclusivism, is a matter of considerable importance.

Study of various forms of literature, particularly how newer forms evolved from older ones, also illuminates for us related changes in human culture and attitudes, not least the development of methods and techniques. Thus, comparison of a premedieval epic poem with a modern, critical, historical essay will disclose many changes in points of view, methods of transmission, and techniques of investigation: for example, there will have intervened the invention and development of the typographical arts. What is composed to be recited orally from memory will differ markedly from what is written to be disseminated in so many printed copies. There will also be differences in the way of looking at the universe and evaluating the causes of actions and events. Conversely, of course, what we know from other data of the differences between the eras in which two documents are composed will shed much light upon differences discerned between the documents.

Literature, read and analyzed critically, can help us to reconstruct the culture from which it came. On the other hand, our knowledge of that culture can help to explain the form and the content of the literature. *Gattungsgeschichte* serves as a technical designation of form criticism's attempt to analyze and trace the history of various species of literature; *Sitz im Leben* ("seat in life") is the technical designation for the placing in human life and culture of a literary unit.

Reconstruction of the *Sitz im Leben* of the various types of literature found in the Bible requires imaginative analysis of these types and imaginative application to them of knowledge of the biblical culture obtained from other sources.

Form criticism is no esoteric exercise for learned exegetes. It is a practical attempt, justified by fruitful results, to get at what biblical literature is saying on its own terms. Its aim is threefold: to classify the literature into types; to trace the history of those types; and to reconstruct the *Sitz im Leben*, the situation in life and culture which influenced the various types.[5]

FORM CRITICISM AND ISRAEL'S SACRED SONG

The German scholar Hermann Gunkel pioneered the use of form criticism to shed light on the psalms and other poetry in the Old Testament.[6] Subsequent study of Israel's poetry, unless it rejects or ignores the form-critical method entirely, has started from Gunkel's classification of that poetry into certain types.[7] Proceeding from the premise that "literary material must above all be classified according to laws befitting its peculiar character, i.e., laws arising from the history of the literature," [8] Gunkel's pivotal work is erected upon four basic principles.

1. Poetry in a given classification (type or genre) arose out of specific occasions in Israel's history. Her sacred songs originated in actual situations in the cultic life of the Israelite community, and acquired their characteristic form and content because that form and content were appropriate to those concrete situations. Because the form and content of the various types of sacred songs were appropriate to the occasions on which they were used, it is possible to reconstruct by study something of the *Sitz im Leben* of the sacred songs.

2. The recurrence of certain types of poetry implies the

existence of a common treasury of thought and expression. In other words, the types were not invented by individual writers, and the poems themselves are not to be considered primarily as creations of individuals. Exegesis of Israel's poetry, if it is to be significant, must take account of this heritage of a worshiping community.

3. Discernment of the common forms of expression which bind individual poems to a particular type requires aesthetic sensitivity. In his discussion of individual psalms, for example, Gunkel often speaks of the "democratizing" of a given form: a form originally purely cultic became so much a part of the unconscious heritage of the people that it would later serve as a vehicle for creations by many diverse poets. Indeed, sometimes structures arising from different types in the common heritage were combined in a single composition.

4. Classification of Old Testament poetry into species (types or genres) and location of those species in particular cultural situations cannot proceed with reference to the Old Testament alone. Israel did not live and worship in a cultural vacuum, but was part of a wider society and culture. Parallels to the various types of poetry in the Old Testament from the recovered literatures of the Sumerians, Babylonians, Assyrians, and Egyptians must be considered. Archaeological research has subsequently added to our knowledge of ancient Near Eastern literature and has uncovered literature in previously unknown languages,[9] but it was Gunkel's use of such material that established the pattern for later work on Israel's poetry and other literature.[10]

Proceeding from his four principles, Gunkel identified in the Old Testament six major types of poetry, six minor types, and two special types. Subsequent classification, including that used in this book, derives from Gunkel, so it will be helpful to list his types and briefly to describe them.[11]

1. *The Hymn* is a song of praise in which God is simply glorified as God. Typically, it consists of an introduction in which the people or the nations or the world or the heavenly host is called upon to praise God, a body in which the power and activity of God are recounted, and a conclusion in which elements of the introduction are rehearsed and/or concluding petitions recited. The original setting of the hymn was any occasion of common worship where it was sung by a choir or by individual "professional" singers. Psalms 29 and 104, and Exodus 15:1-18, are examples of the hymn.

The form of the hymn may sometimes be discerned in psalms and poems classified also under other types (cf. the enthronement songs below) and in other expressions of Israel's literature. A special subtype within the hymn type consists of poems praising God for his presence in the Jerusalem sanctuary. Called "songs of Zion," Psalms 46, 48, 76, 84, and 87 are examples.

2. *Songs of Yahweh's Enthronement,* hymns in form, are distinguishable as a separate type in terms of content. "Eschatological hymns," they acclaim Israel's God, Yahweh, as sovereign over the world and history, employing the coronation acclamation, "Yahweh is (or has become) king!" (Revised Standard Version: "The Lord reigns.") Examples include Psalms 93, 97, and 99, and, although it lacks a specific formula, Psalm 47. Psalms 96 and 98 are closely related to the songs of enthronement.

3. *The Community Lament,* a corporate cry to God in time of need, is distinguished by the vocative exclamation of Yahweh's name at its outset, and by its use of the plural "we" rather than the "I" characteristic of individual laments. It consists of a description of the misfortune in which the community finds itself (often, oppression by political enemies) and a petition for relief. The aim is to excite God's pity and to move him to action. The occasion was probably

the fast days referred to in the Old Testament in connection with times of special community need.

Except for the use of "we," community laments closely resemble individual laments (cf. below), and share two distinctive elements with them. It is a presupposition of all laments that they will be heard, that a response will come from God. Gunkel expressed this element as the "certainty of a hearing." The second element, responding to the first, constituted an oracle, pronounced by a cultic official immediately following delivery of the lament. It proclaimed that the lament had indeed been heard by God. Psalms 44 and 80, and the Book of Lamentations, provide examples of community laments.

4. *The Royal Psalm,* cast in various forms, is distinguished by its content, always having to do with activities of the king. It was employed on a variety of occasions: a coronation, a royal banquet, a particular religious occasion in which the king had an official part. There are other royal psalms celebrating the promise of God to establish the Davidic dynasty, a victory to which a king has led his armies, and a royal marriage. Royal psalms probably originated with court singers and poets resident in a royal sanctuary. They date, according to Gunkel's reckoning, from the time of the pre-exilic kingdoms, and were preserved in exilic and postexilic times on account of Israel's nostalgia for the house of David and her messianic hope centered in that house. Psalms 2, 45, and 132 are examples of royal psalms.

5. *The Individual Lament,* the heart of the psalter, resembles, in form, the community lament. In content it consists of a crying out by an individual to God in time of need: sickness, physical or spiritual oppression, fear of imminent death. Whatever the occasion—the general nature of such poems suggests they were "spiritualized" forms of a basic type—the misfortune is attributed directly to God, who is,

therefore, called upon for deliverance. The plaintive theme of individual laments is posed in the characteristic "Why?" directed to God.

The element of "a certainty of a hearing," found in individual laments as in community laments, led in the former to a separate subtype of poem: the *Song of Trust,* an expression of faith in the trustworthiness of God in the midst of difficulties.

Individual laments and songs of trust originated in the custom of individuals of going to a sanctuary in time of need to call upon God for help. The response to a lament or song of trust was an oracle of assurance pronounced by an official of the sanctuary. The number of individual laments in the psalter makes it difficult to select examples. The most typical individual lament is probably Psalm 88; the best-known song of trust is certainly Psalm 23. Psalm 27 combines the two, its first six verses being a song of trust, and the balance an individual lament. The concluding verse of Psalm 27 may be an oracle of assurance.

6. *The Individual Thanksgiving* is characterized, at the beginning and end, by a cry to God, as in the laments, and an expression of gratitude, "Let me thank . . ." or "I will thank. . . ." The body of such poems consists of a recital of the reasons why the individual wishes to give thanks to God. It may include elements similar to the descriptions of misfortunes found in laments. The motive for their inclusion in poems of thanksgiving, however, is to show the wonderful goodness and power of God by which the individual has been rescued from his misfortunes. Sometimes these poems explicitly declare the intention of the individual to offer a sacrifice of thanksgiving.

The situation in life out of which this type of song originated was the thankoffering of individuals provided for in the cultic regulations of the Old Testament. Psalms 18 and

116 are examples of individual thanksgivings, as is Jonah 2:1-9 (verse numbers according to the English text).

7. Minor types of songs, so designated because their numbers indicate they were not central in the tradition of Israel's sacred songs, include: pronouncements of blessing or curse (no complete examples survive); pilgrimage songs (cf. Psalms 120-134); victory songs (cf. Judges 5); community thanksgivings (cf. Psalms 124 and 129); sacred legends (cf. Psalms 78, 105, 106, and Deuteronomy 32); and "torah," or instruction, songs (cf. remnants in Psalm 50:14-15, 22-23).

These, according to Gunkel, were the fundamental types of Israel's sacred songs. He argued that one could learn more about them from type classification and their histories and occasions than by raising questions of authorship and date of specific songs.

8. Two areas of Israel's life, prophecy and wisdom, although not themselves sources of poetic types, had significant influence on her poetry. In Psalms 50 and 81 the prophetic element is evident; in Psalms 49, 73, and 91 the mode of thought and the piety of wisdom literature predominate. The influence of these two areas of Israel's life is apparent in many other passages of her poetry.

Finally, in accord with his principle that the classification of forms is not a mechanical procedure but one involving aesthetic sensitivity, Gunkel argued that in the history of Israel's poetry various types exerted influence upon one another so that no static categories continued through the years. His introduction to the psalter concludes, therefore, with a discussion of the way forms came to be mixed, changing their character, so that in some cases several types became combined in one poem. Gunkel did not believe that the majority of the poems now embodied in the Old Testament, particularly those in the psalter, have the forms in which they were originally cast in the ancient cult. It was his belief that we have now a collection of poetry composed by poets of later epochs in Israel's history, in which the themes of the ancient cult have been "spiritualized" and the older forms modified and sophisticated. Gunkel nevertheless insisted that the foundation of Israel's sacred song lay in those ancient types and their settings in life, and that the songs cannot be understood apart from their origins.

CONCENTRATION ON THE SETTING OF THE SONGS: SITZ IM LEBEN

Influential studies of Israel's poetry in the last thirty years have assumed Gunkel's method even where there has been disagreement as to detail. In particular, Gunkel's proposition that the extant literature of the civilization of which Israel was a part be taken into account has been executed, and conclusions have been drawn that go far beyond anything Gunkel postulated. That the cult was the ultimate source of the patterns of the psalms has been substantiated, and it has been demonstrated that we have the psalms substantially in the form in which they were used in Israel's cultic worship. Thus, the focus of study has shifted to the setting, the *Sitz im Leben*, in which Israel's songs were sung. This has provoked a search for the living traditions underlying Old Testament literature, a search designated "traditio-historical criticism," ranking equally with form criticism in significance for contemporary Old Testament studies. There have been numerous attempts to reconstruct Israel's cult on the basis of evidence provided by the Bible itself and of the knowledge gleaned from the literature of Israel's neighbors. To give some indication of the reconstructions offered, without attempting a thorough survey, the pertinent work of three scholars will be briefly summarized.

1. *Mowinckel: An Enthronement Festival.* The Norwegian

scholar Sigmund Mowinckel figures most prominently, next
to Gunkel, in contemporary study of Israel's poetry. Gunkel's
spade work, articles, and shorter books preceded the publication of Mowinckel's work, but the latter did appear before Gunkel's commentary on the psalms and his (post-
humous) introduction to it.[12] The two scholars did, in fact,
conduct a running discussion with one another. Contemporary study of the psalms is, to a large extent, discussion with,
extension of, and objection to, the work of Gunkel, on the
one hand, and that of Mowinckel, on the other.

Mowinckel differed strongly with Gunkel's view that although the forms of Israel's poetry originated in the needs
and expression of a corporate, worshiping community, the
songs as we have them are free of that association and are
therefore more "spiritual" in outlook. Gunkel was, he argued,
hampered, despite the great contributions for which he was
responsible, by too modern a view of things. In substance,
according to Mowinckel, Gunkel succumbed to the assumption that personal, inner religion is more sophisticated and
more genuine than formal, communal worship. Gunkel had
not pursued his own method and results to their proper logical conclusion, inhibited by the presuppositions of those
who had preceded him.[13]

For Mowinckel the *Sitz im Leben,* the actual setting of
worship, was the indispensable key to an understanding of
formal, cultic songs such as those preserved in the Old Testament. He set out, therefore, to elucidate the occasions in
which the psalms were used. His singular contribution to
our understanding of the psalter is a reconstruction of the
festival at which, according to his hypothesis, the majority
of the surviving songs of Israel were sung. Mowinckel argued
that there was celebrated annually in ancient Israel a great
New Year festival, which fell near the fall equinox when
rain ended the summer drought, promising another fruitful

agricultural year, and that in that festival the enthronement
of Yahweh as king over the universe was commemorated in
the temple of Jerusalem. The argument for the likelihood
of such a festival, and the reconstruction of it, were based
on three categories of evidence: the presence in the psalter
and other poetry of the Old Testament of enthronement
songs and royal psalms; hints in postbiblical Hebrew literature that later celebration of the first day of the year did
preserve vestiges of such a festival; and authentication that
in ancient Babylon there was a similar annual celebration,
of which literature recovered from Mesopotamia provides
specific description.[14]

The Babylonian New Year festival was, in essence, an
annual cultic re-enactment of mythical events believed responsible for the very existence of the cosmos.[15] Indeed,
those who emphasize the mythological content of the Bible,
placing more stress upon it than Mowinckel does, argue that
myths are precisely a verbal elucidation of cultic action.[16]

The Babylonian myth of creation proclaims the victory of
the god Marduk, whose defeat of the lesser gods of chaos,
death, and darkness established order in the universe and
made Marduk sovereign over all things natural and super-
natural. The New Year festival was a re-enactment of that
victory, perceived in nature as inhibiting the chaotic threat
of late winter floods by the advent of redemptive spring.[17]
At the center of this cultic action stood the human king, who
dramatically assumed the role of chief of the gods. He was
subjected to humiliation imitative of the threat to Marduk
of the forces of chaos, and he then acted out the god's
arousal, his combat with the powers of disorder and death,
and his victory. The ceremony culminated in a sacred marriage in which the king's union with a young virgin ensured
fertility, life, and prosperity for land and people in the ensuing year.[18]

Mowinckel emphasized that the pattern perceived in Mesopotamian sources had been radically revised in Israel, because the pattern had been received only at secondhand, mediated through the Canaanite culture of Palestine, and because of the unique historical orientation of Israel's own faith. Nevertheless, he insisted the essential structure was there, accounting for a majority of the psalms in the Old Testament, and manifesting itself powerfully in the history of Israel's religion.[19]

2. *Weiser: A Covenant Festival.* A significant consequence of Old Testament studies, subsequent to the publication of Mowinckel's *Psalmenstudien,* has been the location of that which was formative and distinctive of Israel in her premonarchical history. Earlier theories that Israel's religion developed from primitive origins to the "ethical monotheism" of the prophets of the ninth through the fifth centuries have given way to the contemporary scholarly opinion that the faith and institutions of Israel were formed in the era of the old tribal league. It is now the consensus that "Israel" is fundamentally to be defined in terms of the covenant community of the judges, and that the monarchy represented no more than an interlude in the history of the community and its self-understanding. That consensus embraces scholars whose interpretations of the details of Israel's ultimate origins and subsequent history otherwise diverge widely.[20]

In this context Artur Weiser's exegesis of Israel's poetry was advanced.[21] Weiser, like Mowinckel and most other modern commentators, accepts the types discerned and classified by Gunkel, but is critical of Gunkel for too exclusive reliance upon form criticism. Like Mowinckel, Weiser considers that the poetry of the Old Testament must be understood in terms of the cultic life of the people by whom it was produced and in terms of the tradition by which the cult was informed. Like Mowinckel, Weiser associates the majority of the poems with a specific cultic occasion that took place annually in the fall of the year. *Unlike* Mowinckel, however, Weiser argues that the cultic occasion was independent of motifs absorbed by Israel from the surrounding culture. Rather, he says, it was dependent on the tradition of the tribal league that preceded the monarchy. Although he acknowledges that evidence for detailed reconstruction is lacking, Weiser postulates a festival of covenant renewal uniquely Israelite and utterly different from anything that took place elsewhere in the ancient Near East. This festival continued, in Weiser's view, at the center of Israel's life as a worshiping community from earliest times and through the period of the monarchy. Elements of Canaanite culture were absorbed, here and there, in the course of time, but it was the ancient tradition maintained in the covenant festival that accounted for the very existence of Israel and that was basic to her sacral literature. Weiser ascribes to that tradition, and not to later authors or historical circumstances, the real origin of the transcription of Israel's story in the Pentateuch.[22] Similarly, while the adaptation of Israel to the agricultural life of Palestine may be discerned in the psalms, most psalms had their origin in the covenant renewal festival.

Thus, though Weiser makes use of Gunkel's analysis of types,[23] the elements of the covenant festival are central in his discussion of the poetry of the Old Testament. Fundamental in the festival was its summons of Israel to renew her covenant relationship with Yahweh, her God, forged in the events and experiences of the Mosaic age. The festival's *hieros logos,* its "words of institution," was, according to Weiser, the account of covenant renewal now recorded in Joshua, Chapter 24. Its traditions are preserved in the Book of Exodus, and the focus from the time of the tribal league to the destruction of Solomon's temple (587 B.C.) was the ark. Elements of the covenant festival figuring prominently in Israel's poetry are: hymnic celebrations of Yahweh's theophany on Mount Sinai; closely related proclamations of the divine name; recital of the saving actions of Yahweh through which his character had been revealed and Israel incidentally created and sustained as a people; proclamation of Yahweh's covenant demand for righteousness; allusions to Israel's communal self-purification and its expulsion of everything not consequent with Yahweh's sovereignty over her; and solemn affirmations of Yahweh's supremacy over all nations with appropriate derisions of the deities of those nations. Expressed in various types of poetry, and in mixtures of types, these elements, not merely classification as to type, propel us, Weiser argues, directly into the substantial content of Old Testament poetry.

Weiser admits some influence on the nature of the festival by the monarchy, but regards developments after David as merely expansion of the basic motifs derived from the premonarchical cult. For example, divine creativity and divine kingship, admittedly acquired from non-Israelite sources, were, in Weiser's view, subservient to the basic, formative motifs of the covenant festival.[24]

3. *Kraus: A More Complex Cultic Picture.* Hans-Joachim Kraus is responsible for important recent work on Israel's worship and its roots in tradition, and for one of the most significant and thorough modern commentaries on the psalms.[25] Kraus's work, important in its own right, serves also to gather up the positions of a number of German scholars, including Alt, Noth, and von Rad, on questions crucial for the interpretation of Israel's poetry. His criticism of Mowinckel and Weiser is that they neglect the complexity of Israel's tradition and cultic life, sacrificing historical differentiation for an all-embracing "lump" theory. He places great emphasis upon the long and varied history behind the

literature that arose from Israel's life as a worshiping community.[26]

Kraus isolates three formative elements in the cultic tradition of Israel, all of which contributed to the autumnal festival so important in the reconstruction of Mowinckel and Weiser: the "tent festival," the theme of which was a remembrance of the events of the exodus from Egypt and the wilderness wanderings of Israel; a festival of covenant renewal antedating the monarchical era; and the traditions of Jerusalem by which Canaanite mythology and conceptions of kingship emerged in the reigns of David and Solomon.[27] Unlike Mowinckel and Weiser, he refuses to associate the cultic tradition, and the songs produced by it, with a single element. Unlike Weiser, he gives due weight to the impact in the psalter (and elsewhere) of the covenant with David and his dynasty, refusing to subsume everything under the Mosaic covenant as reflected in the covenant renewal festival. Unlike Mowinckel, he assigns basic significance in the Jerusalem cultus to the designation of the Davidic dynasty as a sign of Yahweh's presence among his people and the choice of Jerusalem as the sanctuary in which that presence was manifested. Divine kingship, Kraus argues, played no role in Israel's cult until after the fall of the state, when, as in II Isaiah, it could be dissociated from the kingdom and ascribed eschatologically to Yahweh alone.[28] Thus, following Gunkel and others, Kraus concludes that the enthronement songs, central to Mowinckel's reconstruction, are in fact postexilic and eschatological, reflecting in no way an appropriation of the cultic drama borrowed from Babylon.[29]

Kraus is in no doubt that elements of ancient Near Eastern myth and ritual were extensively appropriated by Israel, and employed in the psalms and other poetry. Indeed, the very concept of renewal is, he says, integral to myth and ritual. Nevertheless, to begin with the myths and cults of the culture around Israel is to elude accurate understanding of her worship and songs. Israel was unique. Central always was her location of Yahweh's action and revelation in historic events, whether emphasis at one time or another went to the Mosaic or the Davidic covenants. Mowinckel's concept of the historicization of myth is dismissed as putting the cart before the horse. History was, in fact, mythicized, and the cultic ritual essentially consisted of a re-presentation of the formative acts of Yahweh in past history, so as to inject successive worshiping communities into them. This was the drama of the cult, though ancient Near Eastern mythical elements were employed in the dramatization. Those elements were, however, subservient to what was central and unique about Israel, and Kraus considers that to make those elements the basis of discussion is to preclude valid results.

Thus, as do Mowinckel and Weiser, Kraus assumes that the songs of the Old Testament come to us directly from a cultic setting.[30] He would not agree with Gunkel that the psalms were the work of individual poets employing cultic patterns. He prefers, however, a middle course between the theories of Mowinckel and Weiser with respect to the specific occasion central to Israel's cult.[31] His view of the essence of Israel's faith is more akin to Weiser's than to Mowinckel's, focusing upon the covenant festival, but he supposes greater complexity and variety of development, acknowledging that Israel was profoundly influenced by the culture of which she became a part after the establishment of the Davidic kingdom.

THE PRESENT APPROACH

Our purpose in the survey just concluded has not been to review in detail all contemporary work on Israel's worship

and poetry.[32] Rather, it has been to establish a context for
the approach to that poetry which will be followed in this
book. Brief as it has been, the foregoing does set forth the
various reconstructions and the central issues which Old
Testament scholars have discussed with reference to Israel's
sacred songs. The question now is this: What approach,
without reducing the discussion to its lowest common de-
nominator, will accommodate the valid insights of recent
scholarships?

The types (classes, genres, forms) delineated and described by Gunkel are the inevitable point of departure.
Gunkel's successors all accept, with certain modifications,
his pioneering work. The introductions to the works of Mowinckel, Weiser, and Kraus make this abundantly clear.[33]
However modified in detail, however arranged in relation to
one another, Gunkel's types are fundamental to all contemporary discussions of the Old Testament.

There are cases, however, in which considerations of the
occasion and purpose of the poetry take precedence over
those of forms. In these cases the content and the occasion
for the content come to the fore in such a way that discussion of the characteristics of the poetic form as form is obviously not the primary consideration. Gunkel held that this
situation obtained when forms were freed gradually from
the cultic setting and the various "mixed types" emerged.
Indeed, he granted that this was true in four significant areas
—royal psalms, enthronement songs, songs with the prophetic
element, and wisdom psalms—even before the last phase
of Israel's history. In the royal psalms, primary consideration was to be given not to the form as such, but to their
use by (or of) the king, to the role of the king in Israel's
history. Enthronement songs, although clearly related in
form to the hymns, are set apart by their content. To the
prophetic element in the psalter, Gunkel devoted a large

section of his introduction, noting that its presence is a more important consideration than the poetic form per se. The wisdom psalms are distinguishable, he argued, not so much in terms of poetic form as in terms of content and their relation to the milieu out of which wisdom literature developed.

The conclusion drawn from this must be that form criticism, in discussion of Israel's songs, must be balanced by "traditio-historical" criticism. Thus the case may often be that a *Sitz im Leben* recoverable on other grounds than inference from the poetic form is the primary consideration. And clues to the ethos of the various kinds of poems will be found in the Old Testament as a whole, as well as in ancient non-Israelite Near Eastern culture.

This truth has been abundantly corroborated by Gunkel's successors with respect to the prophetic element in the psalms. For example, the prophetic element, it is now clear, had its origins in the faith and institutions of the tribal league that made up earliest Israel. This fact became the basis of Weiser's approach, and Kraus also heavily relied upon it. Moreover it has subsequently become a common emphasis in contemporary Old Testament studies. The premonarchical covenant community and the prophetic tradition it fostered were a profoundly formative element in Israel's life and worship. In biblical literature, especially the psalter, Israel proclaimed Yahweh as covenant suzerain, or overlord, and that proclamation precedes all other claims made for Yahweh. Accordingly, in our discussion, we shall consider first the preservation of that memory in her poetry.

The forms and motifs, however, which predominate in the psalter are not the prophetic or covenant motifs. In fact, the literary forms which stand out most clearly are those common to the culture of which Israel became a part under David and Solomon. At that point in her history, in order

to explain herself and to proclaim that Yahweh was the ultimate divine power, Israel had to employ language and
thought forms derived from, and understandable to, the culture in which she found herself. In this connection, whatever modification we might want to make in the details of
his theories, we would agree that Mowinckel surely has a
point to make—one which is ignored by Weiser and over-
minimized by Kraus. Even if Kraus is correct in the dating
of the enthronement songs in the exilic and early postexilic
periods, they represent Israel's acclamation of Yahweh as
God in terms appropriated from the cults and myths of the
"pagan" culture around her.

It will be our contention that the classic poetic forms of
the Bible and of the ancient Near East fall into two categories: the first is one in which the hymn is the basic expression, and to which other forms are derivatively related;
the second is one in which the lament is the basic expression,
and to which other forms are also related. Our two central
and longest chapters will, therefore, consider the hymnic
celebrations of Yahweh's sovereignty and the laments in
which finite man cried out to Yahweh as saviour. Attention
will be paid to the world view which engendered these two
categories of sacred song, to various aspects of that view
as expressed in the poetry of the Old Testament, and to the
ways in which Israel's distinctive and unique faith modified both the forms of expression and the content expressed.
Such an approach avoids dependence on a particular view
of how the forms are to be classified in detail and also on
detailed reconstructions of cultic occasions. The broad classifications under which the poetry will be discussed corre-
spond to major motifs on which there is broad agreement.

Finally, the wisdom tradition as it affected Israel's poetry
will be discussed. Like the element termed "prophetic" by
Gunkel, it transcends the poetic forms. It will be treated

last because of the role it played in forming the theology and piety of those responsible for the final collection of the psalms and the ultimate form of the psalter (and, indeed, all of the literature constituting the canonical Old Testament).

Our purpose, then, is to elucidate Old Testament poetry on its own terms, against its own background, according to the motifs by which it is informed. This is the first step. When due respect has been paid to the material itself, we shall proceed to interpret the material as it may have relevance and significance today. The study of Israel's sacred songs is a study of the adaptation of a cultural idiom to a unique content, and of the modification of that idiom as a consequence of the content embodied in it. It may be that therein lies the chief clue to the relevance of the songs to our own situation and time.

1 God as Overlord: The Mosaic Covenant

We begin with Psalm 81 which leads us directly into a motif not represented frequently in the songs of the psalter, but chronologically previous, so far as Israel is concerned, to other, more pervasive themes in her poetry and basic to an understanding of the nature of Israel in the formative period of her history. The psalm opens:

> Make joyful cries over Yahweh[1] our strength;
>> Give a cheer for the God of Jacob!
> Sing a song, and play the tambourine,
>> The sweet-sounding lyre together with the harp.
> Blow the trumpet on the New Moon,
>> On Full Moon, the day of our pilgrimage festival.
> Verily, it is a duty laid down for Israel,
>> A custom fixed by the God of Jacob.
> He decreed it a day of obligation among Joseph's progeny,
>> When he set out against the land of Egypt.
>
> (Psalm 81:1-5a, Heb. 2-6a.)

There is no doubt of the concrete connection of this psalm with a cultic occasion. The call to render praise to Israel's God specifically mentions those musical instruments associated with worship, notably the trumpet, actually a ram's horn, so often mentioned elsewhere in connection with Israelite cultic occasions. The occasion here described seems to have begun at a new moon and continued through two weeks to the full moon. It is clear that the festival involved is one at which those taking part repair to a designated sanctuary, a "pilgrimage" (*chag*, the Hebrew cognate of the Arabic *haj*). The psalm is emphatic about the obligatory nature of this act of remembrance of the time in which Yahweh was Israel's champion against the might of Egypt.

We proceed to the main section of the poem after a line of transition making clear that what is to follow is regarded as nothing other than a pronouncement by the divine voice itself:

> I hear [something] unlike any language with which I am
> acquainted   (Psalm 81:5b, Heb. 6b.)

Thus, what follows is, through the agency of an inspired spokesman, said by none other than Yahweh himself:

> I lifted the burden from his shoulder;
>> His hands let the carrying-basket go.
>>> In distress *you* [too] have cried, and I have delivered
>> *you*.
> I am [now] speaking with *you* from the thundercloud;
>> I am putting *you* to the test (as) at the waters of Meri-
>> bah.   (Psalm 81:6-7, Heb. 7-8.)

The effect of these lines is blurred by most English translations in which the sequence of the Hebrew tenses is not made clear and the change from the third- to the second-person pronoun is either obscured or ignored for the sake of consistency. The Hebrew, translated as it stands, makes perfect sense when we understand that it was spoken in a concrete cultic setting. Yahweh first recalls the deliverance of Israel from Egypt, the "his" referring to Joseph, mentioned previously as the personification of the generation of Israel that had undergone slavery in Egypt. What is said in the third line of the first colon, however (note the parallelism[2]), updates Yahweh's saving activity: *You* have cried,

and I have delivered *you*. The Exodus, in other words, is
understood as the classic pattern of the saving and gracious
power known by Israel also in subsequent events.

The emphasis of the psalm shifts from Yahweh's act of
deliverance from Egypt to the situation at the sacred mountain in the wilderness where the demand involved in being
Yahweh's people was enunciated (for the "thundercloud"
allusion, cf. Exodus 19:16-19), and where Israel failed the
test of hardship (for Meribah, cf. Exodus 17:1-7 and Numbers 20:10-13). The point, however, is that the present audi-
tors, even as they are witnesses of Yahweh's previous saving
activity, are also placed in a situation in which his demand
is made upon them, in which his being their God involves
their being put to the test. In this vivid cultic situation, they
stand in the same relation to Yahweh as their fathers had.
Against this background the speech of Yahweh, which constitutes the remainder of the poem, is to be understood:

Hear, my people, while I bear witness against you:
    O Israel, if you would only heed me!
There shall be among you no strange god,
    Nor shall you bow down to a foreign god.
I am Yahweh your God
    Who brought you out of the land of Egypt:
        Open wide your mouth, that I may fill it.
Nevertheless, my people have not heeded my voice,
    Nor has Israel's will been one with mine.
Thus have I let them continue in their own willful stubborn-
ness;
    They proceed according to their own counsels.
O that my people would heed me!
    That Israel would proceed in my ways!
In a moment would I subdue their foes,
    And turn my hand against their oppressors.
Those who hate Yahweh would flatter them,

And their good fortune [Israel's] would be unending.[3]
I would feed them with the choicest wheat,
With honey from the rock would satisfy them.
(Psalm 81:8-16, Heb. 9-17.)

The meaning of the poem is plain. Israel is being called to account by her God speaking through a designated spokesman in a cultic situation where she stands, in fact, in his very presence. The events of the past in which Yahweh had made Israel his people continue to be operative. The demand of Sinai is a present demand, made clear and brought up to date as Israel once again stands before Yahweh in a festival of recollection. The very witness borne against them by their God is that by which Israel discovers what gives meaning to the present. Good and evil, prosperity and distress, are not meaninglessly dealt out by a fickle fate; they are related to Yahweh, whose character is known, who saves, and who establishes an order in which life has significance because within it man is responsible.

Psalm 81 includes none of the allusions or motifs to be found in the poetry to be discussed in ensuing chapters. There is no mention of Yahweh's kingship or, for that matter, of a human king. Reference to the cosmic mythology of the culture surrounding Israel is entirely absent. The distress and deliverance spoken of involve no demonic powers, but rather are events and forces in history. This poem reflects a milieu different from that which gave rise to the majority of the psalms. We find ourselves in a setting quite different from that of the royal Temple in Jerusalem, the world of David and Solomon and the cult of the monarchy. We find ourselves, in fact, in the setting of the books of Exodus and Deuteronomy, of Moses and of the covenant of which he was the mediator. The elements of this poem may be understood only in terms of the faith and the institutions of the Israel of premonarchical times.[4]

THE ORIGINAL COVENANT COMMUNITY

Current Old Testament scholarship lays heavy stress on the two centuries preceding David (roughly 1200 to 1000 B.C.) as those in which Israel came to self-consciousness as a people and in which she achieved a distinctive and unique character. This was the period of the events and experiences witnessed to in the first twenty-three chapters of Exodus, which provided the *raison d'être* for the existence in Palestine, particularly in the central highlands of Palestine, of a confederation of twelve tribes dissociated from the city-kingdom polity characteristic of the area and of the prevailing culture. To the established society of the time, this association of independent tribes was part of an amorphous lot of groups known as *Habiru*. These groups existed politically, economically, and culturally on the fringes of the established order. The relation of the *Habiru* to established society resembled that of the barbarians to the Roman empire or later of the gypsies to European societies. The particular confederation of *Habiru* known as Israel, however, was self-conscious about its "outsideness" being no stigma. For them it was, indeed, the direct result of having been singled out as the people of the God Yahweh.

Whatever the correct reconstruction of how this came about in the history underlying the traditions of the first two books of the Bible, and however many tribes and clans may subsequently have adopted the Israelite traditions as the rationale of their own *Habiru* status over against the established order, this confederation traced its existence to events in which, though entirely outside the power structure, a people had been miraculously released from bondage in Egypt by what they were convinced was the intervention of the God Yahweh. That intervention had made them

Yahweh's people, and Yahweh Israel's God. It was in terms of that great event that he was to be identified (whatever may have been his prehistory). Israel had found a status by which its existence was justified in spite of its alienation from the established social and political and religious order of the time and place. It was also to that great event that the various clans and tribes of which the confederation was comprised related their separate prehistories in order to perceive what they had ultimately meant.[5]

Every society or nation possesses traditions and institutions, a *mythos*, in terms of which its existence is explained and maintained. Every grouping of men has to have some way of articulating the order by which it lives, the structure within which life is carried on. For early Israel the central reality from which her institutions were derived and by which order was given to her existence, her *mythos*, was the covenant between herself and Yahweh. This covenant had, she believed, been the direct result of the great exodus from Egypt. From bondage she had been delivered directly into the presence of Yahweh at the sacred mountain in the wilderness where the bond between God and people had been given form and structure in the covenant mediated through Moses. Israel was, by definition, the people united to Yahweh in the bond of the covenant, and that union was no mere event of the past, but also the determinative reality within which life was carried on in successive generations.

The Covenant Formularies

Concepts such as "covenant," however deeply they may be rooted in actual experience and however directly they may result from divine action perceived by faith, must find expression in terms available to men in human language and thought forms. One important result of recent discovery and study of the civilization of which Israel was a part is the uncovering of the origin of the form used by Israel to describe her meaning as the people of Yahweh. Rather than detracting from the uniqueness of Israel's polity and theology, what has been discovered emphasizes the elements that made Israel's point of view unique, as well as determinative of much that is characteristic of the Western culture heavily influenced by biblical tradition.

It has become apparent that the covenant statements found in the Old Testament (and through Judaism into the documents of the early Christian Church) not only conform to a consistent and discernible pattern, but that that pattern originated in the treaties concluded between sovereign and subject states in the ancient Near East over a considerable period of time. The type of treaty is one in which a vassal subscribes to the obligations laid upon him by the king exercising hegemony over his territory. The documents in question, therefore, are not parity agreements between equals, but suzerainty treaties between those who are the actual wielders of power and their subjects. The most numerous and most complete examples of such treaties are those recovered from the archives of the ancient Hittite empire at Boghazkoi in Turkey. Some fifteen such treaties, dating roughly from 1400 to 1200 B.C. (exactly the period to which the origins of the Israelite confederation are traced) have been found. The existence of other such treaties in other places, and over a wide span of time, makes it clear that in them we are dealing with a well-developed and widely used form.[6]

While our interest here does not require extensive analysis of these treaties, a brief description of the form will make their relation to the covenant formularies of the Old Testament clear, and will shed light on what the form of the covenant itself implies. With minor variations the basic pattern of the suzerainty treaties is:[7]

1. *Preamble*. The grantor of the treaty identifies himself by name and title, usually also citing the names of his father and significant forebears.

2. *Historical introduction*. A recital of the relations between the overlord and the vassal up to the time of the granting of the treaty. It may be explicit about the exact territorial boundaries of the vassal, but its obvious purpose is that of justifying, by reciting the history leading up to it, the claim of the overlord on those with whom the treaty is being made.

3. *Statement of the bases of the future relationship between overlord and vassal*. Closely connected with the historical introduction, this section of the treaties is concerned to make it absolutely clear that the loyalty of the vassal is to be given without qualification or reservation to the overlord. No compromise of the sovereign claim of the grantor of the treaty is to be allowed. He alone is overlord, and the vassal is to eschew the claims of any other.

4. *The treaty regulations*. A list of the conditions to which the vassal subscribes. They vary, of course, from treaty to treaty, but the same presuppositions underlie the specific stipulations in all the treaties. What it comes down to is that the vassal is prohibited from establishing relations with any power other than the overlord, and is to order every aspect of the life of his kingdom in such a way as to make it clear that he himself holds no independent sovereignty.

5. *The invocation of the gods as witnesses*. Witnesses are, of course, required to almost all documents embodying agreements between two parties. In the suzerainty treaties it is the gods of both sovereign and vassal who are called upon to witness the agreement to which the vassal is giving his solemn consent. The lists of the divine witnesses in the treaties are often very lengthy, as if all conceivable powers should be included. They often include mountains, rivers,

wells, the great sea, heaven and earth, wind and clouds—probably understood as deities.[8]

6. *Blessings and curses.* Finally, the treaties specify the blessings attendant upon the vassal's faithful obedience and the curses consequent upon his breaking of the treaty. It is not by accident that this section follows upon the invocation of divine witnesses, for punishment of disloyalty is not reserved to the overlord alone. Indeed, in later examples of such treaties the list of witnesses is combined with the enumeration of blessings and curses, various gods being specifically designated as the agents through which various kinds of disasters will be visited upon the vassal as punishment for disloyalty.[9]

That this pattern underlies covenant formularies in the Old Testament becomes evident when a classical covenant statement found in the "Book of the Covenant," Exodus, chapters 20-23, is described in terms of the pattern just outlined:

1. *Preamble.* "I am Yahweh your God."

2. *Historical introduction.* "Who brought you out of the land of Egypt, out of the house of bondage." These words recapitulate succinctly what the previous chapters of the Book of Exodus have recounted.

3. *The bases of the future relations between Yahweh, the overlord, and his people.* This function in the pattern is served by the ten apodictic statements of the Decalogue. Only Yahweh is to be recognized as Israel's divine overlord, and in basic relationships among members of the covenant community no one is to act toward another in any way implying rights of domination. In other words, the inner life of Israel is to be ordered in such a way as to make it clear that rights over its members, suzerainty, belong to Yahweh alone.

4. *Regulations.* The Book of the Covenant proper (Ex-

odus 20:23-23:19) contains the detailed stipulations to which Israel, the subject, is to give obedience.

5. *Invocation of witnesses.* This element in the pattern is not found in Exodus, chapters 20-23, and this is undoubtedly due to the difficulty brought about by using the treaty pattern to state the covenant structure of Israel's existence under a divine overlord who explicitly forbade any recognition of other deities. That this element was not forgotten as a part of the pattern is, however, evident in a number of passages in the Old Testament. Joshua, chapter 24 describes an occasion on which Israel renews her covenant allegiance to Yahweh and, at the point at which the listing of witnesses should come, the people themselves are invoked as witnesses and a stone is designated as witness (Joshua 24:22, 27). Deuteronomy as a whole conforms to the typical pattern of covenant formularies, and contains a number of allusions to witnesses reminiscent of those in suzerainty treaties (4:26; 30:19; 31:28). Some of these allusions, interestingly enough, mention blessings and curses. Passages in the prophetic books in which Israel is being accused of breaking the covenant demands invoke witnesses of the very type mentioned in Hittite treaties (Isaiah 1:2; Jeremiah 2:12; Micah 6:2).

6. *Blessings and curses.* Exodus, chapters 20-23, concludes with a section, 23:20-33, stressing Yahweh's constant observation of Israel's obedience or disobedience of the covenant regulations. Blessing is explicitly mentioned as the consequence of faithfulness in obeying (23:25), and the curse which will follow from Israel's breaking of the covenant is implied (23:21, 33). The importance of this element in the covenant tradition is seen even more clearly in Deuteronomy 27:11-26 where, when the provisions of the covenant have been laid down in chapters 12-26, it is provided that curses are to be solemnly pronounced by the Levites. Deuteronomy, chapter 28, then goes on to describe the blessing

consequent upon observance of the law, both cursing and
blessing having been mentioned in 27:11-13 as parts of a
solemn occasion.

We have taken Exodus, chapters 20-23, as an example of
how sections of the Old Testament in which the covenant
tradition is prominent conform to the pattern of ancient
Near Eastern suzerainty treaties, but it is only an example.
Joshua, chapter 24, has already been mentioned, and is noteworthy because of the expansion of the historical introduction. I Samuel, chapter 12, and a number of other passages
could also be mentioned.[10]

If these elements, common to Hittite and other suzerainty
treaties and Old Testament covenant formularies, make it
unavoidably clear that Israel used the treaty pattern to express the relationship obtaining between herself and Yahweh,
the evidence is reinforced by two further considerations.
(1) Ancient Near Eastern treaties of the type we have been
considering were always deposited in the sanctuaries of the
gods of the parties involved. They were, so to speak, left in
the custody of the divine witnesses to them, the idea undoubtedly being that those whose task it was to enforce, or
to aid in the enforcement of, the treaties by blessing and
curse should have copies for reference.[11] In this connection,
the traditions in the Old Testament providing for deposit of
the tablets on which the Mosaic law was written at the
sanctuary at Shechem fit squarely into the picture sketched
above (cf. Deuteronomy 27:1-8; Joshua 8:30-35). (2) The
treaties, however, were not thought of as documents re-
posing in archives, and this brings us to the second, further
consideration. Since the treaties put into words the structure
within which the vassal lived under his overlord, they were
to be read regularly and solemnly in the hearing of the
vassals. Thus, the provisions of Deuteronomy 31:9-13 for
the reading of the Mosaic law every seven years (the Feast

of Booths would place the reading at the time of the autumnal New Year festival) fits appropriately into the pattern
already clearly discernible.

The Theology of the Covenant Formularies

While the form utilized to enunciate the meaning of Israel's existence as a gathered confederation of tribes is not
unique, the purpose for which the form was used is unique.
Elsewhere the suzerainty treaty pattern was used to define
and to order relationships between various peoples within
a larger cultural setting that defined the meaning of existence. What was utilized to express the nature of things, the
basic issues and realities in terms of which life found its
ultimate meaning, was not, for Israel's neighbors, the treaty
pattern. It was rather the cosmic myth, in which the visible
order of things was accounted for in terms of what had
transpired and continued to transpire in the supramundane
world of the gods.[12] Indeed, when treaties were made between various participants in the mundane order, it was to
the supramundane order, that larger framework given expression in the cosmic myth, that appeal was made. The
invocation of the divine witnesses in the treaties is clear
evidence of this.

Israel used the treaty pattern, rather than the cosmic
myth, to get at the basic issues and realities, to give verbal
expression to the ultimate nature of existence as she knew
it. For her, the fundamental facts about Yahweh, the god
who counted, as well as about the life of man could be expressed only in the form afforded by the suzerainty treaties.
Here lies the origin of that uniqueness of Israel and of the
biblical tradition by which our own culture has been so
heavily informed, even when that culture deems itself secular. Indeed it may be argued that secularism itself is a phenomenon occurring in history as a consequence of the bib-

lical view of reality, and that shallow indictments of it by
Christians or Jews betray a misapprehension of the very
bases of biblical faith. The fact, made abundantly clear by
recovery of the pattern she used to enunciate her faith, is
that premonarchical Israel rejected the cosmic mythology
which, in one form or another, literally or figuratively conceived, is the basis of all other religion. Instead Israel discerned that only a political form could convey the meaning
of Yahweh's sovereignty and of his people's relationship
to him. The consequences of that revolutionary transposition
of ultimately significant events from the supramundane realm
to the realm in which man actually lives are still working
themselves out in human history. What was fundamentally
true of the divine involved his relationship to men as the
overlord whose treaty (covenant) was the basis of their
lives rather than myths or speculations about a supramundane world to which man was a stranger.

This concept rescued men's decisions and actions from
meaninglessness. Law was not a necessary evil according
to this understanding, but gave voice to that demand in
which God had addressed men as significant, responsible
creatures. What man did in the realms of economics and
politics and all interaction with his fellows was invested with
meaning by God's direct approach to him in the here and
now. Human existence was not rendered tragic by the location of what was ultimately significant in some inaccessible
realm, and blessing lay not in the vain hope of entrance
somehow into the realm of the gods. Human existence found
its meaning in obedience to the sovereign, or in disobedience, within the empirical events of life itself. Blessing and
curse were related to a structure defined in understandable
words in the covenant. Thus law and grace are not ultimately
opposed to one another in their biblical origins in premonarchical Israel's covenant understanding of her existence under Yahweh.[13]

The Covenant Formularies and Historical Narrative

The story that counted when it came to getting at the nature and meaning of life was, then, the introduction to the covenant, the recital of those events in which the divine overlord had created the situation in which the covenant demands made sense. This meant that the writing of history became important to Israel in a sense that it was not to others. What is unique is not so much the fact that Israel wrote history, although her achievements in doing so are both distinctive and chronologically prior to anything else of their kind. What is unique is the kind of history composed in Israel and the use to which it was put. Royal chronicles and military histories, and tales of heroes and family origins, were produced elsewhere. But it was only in Israel that the recorded drama in which man himself is a participant provided the rationale for, and the aetiology of, what life essentially is. It is only in Israel that remembered history, and not otherworldly tales, became the basis for theology and worship. This, rather than Israel's modifications of elements of pagan myths in particular biblical passages, is the point at which discussion of the question of mythology and the biblical point of view should begin. Israel's scriptures are dominated by narrative, by narrative describing the very human, real life of an historical community. Israel's answer to the question of the nature and character of God and of the ultimate issues of existence could only be given in such narrative.[14]

In the covenant between herself and Yahweh Israel found meaning for her *Habiru* existence outside the culture of her time and place. Insofar as her constituent elements were tribal entities, tracing their identity in terms of ancestry and communal history, they were outsiders to the prevailing cultural pattern in which identity was found in one's relation to the physical cosmos through the myth and cult and sanctuary and kingship of a geographical place centering in a city-kingdom. For Israel, however, this alienation was no embarrassment driving her to seek a place in the established order. On the contrary, for Israel this was the way things had been established by her God. The covenant was precisely the means by which her tribal identity, not her identity in relation to the physical cosmos, was given meaning. It was the means by which what she really *was*, though the culture round about might consider her a *Habiru* "nobody," was justified. The justification lay in Yahweh's claim as overlord, manifested normatively in his intervention against Egyptian tyranny, subsequently in his guiding of Israel to the status she enjoyed in Palestine, and reiterated in his continued defense of her against her enemies. Tribal loyalty had always to be subservient to that by which tribal identity was guaranteed. Though it was the event by which the tribal *Habiru* existence had been given dignity and meaning, Yahweh's redemption of his people and his gracious covenant demand upon them were ultimately significant. Israel's *mythos* was rooted in something, indeed in Someone, transcending both heredity and geographical location.

THE COVENANT IN ISRAEL'S POETRY

The outline of covenant formularies in the Old Testament, when they are examined in the light of the suzerainty treaties of the ancient Near East, argues for the existence of some occasion on which the laws of the covenant, together with the historical narrative by which they were justified, were read in the hearing of the community for which Yahweh was overlord. Not only can the provisions of Deuteronomy 31:9-13 be cited as direct evidence of such an occasion, but the treaty form itself, even if explicit indications were lacking, would imply it. The periodic rereading of a

treaty was always stipulated, and it is inconceivable that
some kind of central sacral observance of the gathered elements of the tribal confederation was not one in which the
covenant figured. Such an observance must be understood as
much more than the formal reading of a set of legal stipulations. Although we do not have, and shall probably never
obtain, knowledge of the exact nature of such a cultic occasion, our discussion of the meaning of the covenant for
Israel makes it clear that a covenant festival of some kind
would have been, for premonarchical Israel, the equivalent
of the new year festival on which her neighbors celebrated
the creation of the cosmos.[15] Israel's festival would have
celebrated the creation of the order within which life for her
found its meaning, the order of human history and responsibility. In it Israel was in each new generation re-created as
Yahweh once again proclaimed who he was and how Israel
had come to stand in the relationship to him that she did,
as he laid upon her anew the demand that gave life its significance. It stands to reason that such an occasion, when-
ever and wherever and however often it took place, was a
sacral one, accompanied by fitting solemnity and ceremony.

Furthermore, it may well have been more than a cere-
monial observance. We must remember that Israel existed
for at least two centuries as a covenant league of tribes before the coming of kingship in the time of Saul and David.
During so long a period complicated historical changes take
place. The makeup of Israel, of the twelve constituent tribes,
must have changed during so long a period. Some groups
would have declined and eventually disappeared, and others
would have been admitted to the league, making the covenant with Yahweh their own *mythos* even though their an-
cestors had not taken part in the events originally constituting it.[16] There must have been times at which the festival of
covenant renewal would have represented for some a first

acceptance of Yahweh as overlord. Indeed a recent and highly plausible theory about how premonarchical Israel conquered Canaanite holdings in Palestine maintains that Israel grew in size as well as in territory as various groups turned on the oppressive rule of the Canaanite city-kingdoms, the historical bases of the traditions in the Book of Joshua reflecting violent revolution as much as invasion from outside the area.[17] Thus would the covenant festival have, in more than one way, been much more than a recalling of the past. It would have been the continual re-presentation of the saving actions of Yahweh by which Israel was made a people, supremely in the Exodus from Egypt, but also in succeeding events and generations. It would have been an ever new restatement of Yahweh's overlord claim on his people.

The Covenant Formularies and the Prophets

It is within this context that we have to understand one important factor in the origins of prophecy in Israel. Moses had, when the covenant first came into existence, been Yahweh's spokesman. If the covenant is seen as the structure within which Israel lived under Yahweh, then the words by which the covenant was reduced to understandable language were of supreme importance. They gave form to what the covenant was and implied. Indeed, our present knowledge of the treaty form on which the covenant was based makes the terminology of the covenant clear. We speak of the "ten commandments" but, literally translated, the Hebrew calls them merely the "ten words." These are the basic articulation of the structure of the covenant relationship, what, in our outline of the treaty form above, was termed the statement of the bases of the relationship between overlord and vassal. They are not the result of the establishment of precedents in human courts of law, nor are they the result of

speculative deduction. They are, as Israel saw it, the direct
pronouncement of Yahweh himself, his verbalization of the
limits beyond which his people cannot go and still remain
his people. It is for this reason that the covenant tradition
laid such stress on Yahweh's calling of a spokesman into
whose mouth Yahweh's own words were put (Exodus 3:13-
15; 4:10-12; etc.). It is to this that we must look to understand the role and importance of Moses in the covenant tradition.

In the successive generations of the life of the covenant
community someone had to take Moses' place in the recital
of the words both expressive of the structure within which
that community lived and effective in calling it to ever renewed existence under Yahweh. At the very least, someone
had to recite the regulations and, even if this consisted
merely in reading them in the form in which they had come
down from the past, the nature of what was being done
would have made this a very important function. There is,
however, reason to believe that the recital of the "words," as
well as of the historical introduction, was no static, fixed
thing. If this were the case, it would be difficult to account
for the variety of "codes" incorporated into the completed
Old Testament during the course of its formation through
the years.[18] If such were the case it would also be hard to
explain a passage such as Joshua, chapter 24, a description of
covenant renewal, in which the historical introduction to
the covenant is brought up to date in terms of the point at
which covenant renewal is taking place (cf. Joshua 24:8-13).
It would seem certain that the task of reciting the covenant
was much more than that of reading an ancient document.
The word of Yahweh was a living thing, verbalizing the
reality and the demand present in each successive generation, active in the creation of new history. The office performed in succession to Moses in the covenant community

was, therefore, at least in certain crucial times, more than
a formal one bestowed by inheritance or election. From time
to time there arose, in the tradition of Moses, those in whose
mouths Yahweh put once again his words.

It is against this background that a passage such as Deuteronomy 18:15-22 must be understood. In it Moses assures
Israel that Yahweh will raise up for his people a prophet
like himself. Imbedded as it is in a book so firmly rooted, in
form as well as content, in the ancient covenant tradition,
this passage, whatever may be the date from which its written form comes to us, is surely not a mere reflection of the
presence in Israel of later prophets. Nor, in spite of the
meaning it came to have in Israel's postexilic eschatological
speculation, does it seem to refer to some one figure to arise
in the distant future. It is to be taken at face value, and is
intended to date back to Moses the assurance of Yahweh
that he will continue to address words to Israel in the new
situations produced by ongoing history, words in which the
meaning and demand of new times will be revealed to his
people so that the covenant basis of life may continue as a
living thing. Such words were the means by which the covenant was, in a more than commemorative sense, renewed in
later generations.

It may even be that the passage mentioned above in connection with the presence of blessings and curses in the covenant pattern, Exodus 23:23-33, alludes to the office of covenant spokesman in the "angel" Yahweh promises to send before Israel. The basic meaning of the Hebrew word is simply
"messenger," and it is elsewhere used of prophetic figures.
Indeed, in Malachi 3:1, the word is used in the phrase "messenger of the covenant." Furthermore Moses' promise of a
prophetic successor in Deuteronomy 18:15-22 quite clearly
refers to the context of the passage in Exodus, chapter 23,
specifically to Exodus 20:18-21. All this leads to the con-

clusion that, in connection with the indubitable centrality of the covenant to Israel's life in its most ancient period and the ceremony in which that centrality found expression, there existed an office the function of which was to fill the role in subsequent generations that Moses had filled at the beginning. This office had a long history, and underlies the function of judges, prophets, and others in various periods of Israel's history.[19] Though it was greatly affected with the rise of the monarchy by the radical changes that then came for Israel, what that office was and what it expressed were never forgotten. It was revived at the time of the Deuteronomic reformation by King Josiah as the basis of his own role in attempting to revitalize an Israel that had in his time lived for more than a half century as a part of the Assyrian empire. It plays a particularly important role in Jeremiah and the prophetic tradition of which he was the fountainhead.[20]

The office just discussed is the final step toward an understanding of the literary form of Psalm 81. The standards of the covenant provided a means by which Israel's actions had inevitably to be judged. In disobedience as well as obedience Israel acted significantly in terms of the covenant faith. The judgment of Yahweh invested all that she did with meaning, and this in her rebellion and stubbornness as well as in her faithfulness. The promise was that Yahweh would not remain silent, would send a word by which Israel's actions would be given meaning, would continue to raise up successors to Moses not only to proclaim his will but to admonish and to accuse. It is in these terms that the form, occurring but little in the psalter and typified by Psalm 81, is to be understood. Israel could never act in violation of the covenant in such a way as to remove herself from Yahweh's suzerainty. When she was faithless Yahweh gave meaning even to her disobedience by calling her to account through a word placed in the mouth of his chosen spokesman. Thus, when we find passages in the psalter as well as the prophetic books in which Yahweh accuses his people of misunderstanding and rebellion, passages which seem to conform in general to a fairly fixed pattern, we find ourselves squarely in the ethos of the faith and institutions of the premonarchical tribal confederation. Bearing in mind what has now been said of the nature of the covenant and of the function of the spokesman of the covenant, consider a passage such as Jeremiah 2:4-13:

Hear the word of Yahweh, O house of Jacob, yea all the clans
of the house of Israel! So has Yahweh spoken:
Did your fathers ever find evil in me?—
    For they put themselves far away from my side.
Indeed, they followed what was without substance,
    And, losing their only substance, ceased invoking Yah-
      weh—
The one who brought us up from the land of Egypt,
    Who led us through the wilderness,
Through a land arid and full of pits,
    Through a land of drought, under death's dominion,
Through a land neither traversed by men
    Nor inhabited by anything human.
And I brought you to a lush land,
    That you might enjoy its fruit and its beauty.
But upon entering it you defiled my land,
    Turned my covenant gift into something perverse.
The priests!
    They did not invoke Yahweh;
        The custodians of the law forgot me;
            The shepherds [of my people] rebelled against me.
The prophets! They prophesied by Baal,
    After what profits nothing did they chase.
It is for this that I once again call you to account under the
covenant—

This is Yahweh's pronouncement—
This present generation do I call to account:
For cross to the shores of Cyprus and look,
    Or send to the Kedarite Arabs for the least shred of evi-
    dence,
        See if there is anything like it.
Has any nation sold out its gods,
    Even when they are false gods?
But my people have sold out their glory
    In exchange for less than that.
Be appalled, O heavens, at this—
    Be horrified, and dry up completely!
                        This is Yahweh's pronouncement.

The elements of a definite pattern are present here: a summons to Israel; a recital of Yahweh's gracious deeds; an accusation against Israel for violating the covenant; a call to
the heavens as witnesses of the covenant. In this passage a
prophetic voice is calling Israel to account, speaking for
Yahweh who himself is directly contending with his people.
The form used is one apparently indigenous to the covenant
community, a covenant controversy. In Hebrew it is designated by the word *ribh*. It is a form underlying much of the
poetic pronouncement of Israel's prophets.[21]
Another example is found in Micah 6:1-8:

Hear what Yahweh is saying:
Arise, take your part in the covenant controversy with the
mountains as witnesses,
    Let the hills hear your voice!
Hear, O mountains, Yahweh's covenant controversy,
    Give ear, foundations of the earth!
For Yahweh charges his people with violation of the cove-
nant,
    Against Israel does he state his case.   (Micah 6:1-2.)

Having issued the summons to Israel as the accused, as well
as to the witnesses to the original provisions of the covenant,
the prophet now speaks directly for Yahweh. The recital of
what he has done for Israel alludes concretely to things recorded in the narrative in Exodus and Numbers.

> My people, how have I treated you,
>   How have I wearied you? Answer me!
> Indeed, I brought you out of the land of Egypt,
>   Even from slavery did I set you free.
> Why, I sent Moses to guide you,
>   As well as Aaron and Miriam.
> My people, just remember what was plotted
>   By Balak, king of Moab,
> And how he found his come-uppance
>   In Balaam the son of Beor.
> Remember what happened between Shittim and Gilgal
>   As tangible evidence of Yahweh's righteous deeds.
>   (Micah 6:3-5.)

Apparently the next lines are spoken sarcastically by the
prophet as he imitates the plea being entered by Israel. What
he is saying is that Israel, in her self-righteous profession of
being willing to do anything Yahweh shall ask of her, completely misses the point of what it means to be the covenant
people of Yahweh. She has come to think of him in the terms
in which other gods are thought of by their devotees.

> How shall I come into Yahweh's presence,
>   Bowing down before the exalted God?
> Shall I enter his presence with burnt-offerings,
>   With yearling calves?
> Will Yahweh look with favor on thousands of rams,
>   On ten thousands of rivers of oil?
> Shall I sacrifice my first-born for my rebellion,
>   The fruit of my own body for my sinful life?
>   (Micah 6:6-7.)

It is in this setting that the final, classic lines of the poem fall. They hinge on technical covenant terms, and the climax involves a word that never occurs elsewhere in Hebrew; thus its interpretation is difficult. The following, very free, translation tries to capture the way in which these lines contrast covenant obligation with religious observance, thus underlining the unique character of Israel's faith.

> He has revealed to you, O man, what is good,
>   And what does Yahweh require of you
> But to do what he has established as right,
>   To love being loyal to the covenant,
>   And obediently to go along with what your God ordains. (Micah 6:8.)[22]

Here again a pattern is discernible. The word *ribh*, the designation of litigation for violation of the covenant, is emphasized; the witnesses to the covenant are summoned to hear the charge of the overlord against his vassals; Yahweh's saving acts are recited; and, by sarcastic implication, Israel is accused of relegating Yahweh to a merely religious role, ignoring the claims implicit in the political form of the covenant. The setting is probably one in which Israel has refused to read the events of the late eighth and early seventh centuries, when Assyrian expansion began to affect her radically, in the light of the covenant faith and what it professed about Yahweh's sovereignty over historical events. This passage from the Book of Micah, like the one previously quoted from the Book of Jeremiah, is evidence that Israel's prophets were utilizing an established form.[23] It was the form underlying Psalm 81, and it must go back to the sacral occasion on which Israel's life was given meaning as a spokesman, in the tradition of Moses, called her to account as a responsible subject of the God whose suzerainty over her was exercised

in the events and decisions in which men find themselves involved in their life in history.

If we protest against a religion of law, grimly concerned
only with right and wrong and with accusation of men for
their shortcomings, we miss the point. Uncomfortable as it
must have been to have to undergo accusation at a high
point of worship, the kind of sarcastic accusation set forth in
the passage from Micah or of total faithlessness made in the
passage from Jeremiah, Israel experienced here a demand in
which a God whose character and whose ways were not
arbitrary and fickle imparted dignity to human life. The accusation and the demand imparted meaning to man's actions
and decisions. In the form being discussed here we are taken
back to the worship and institutions of Israel before Saul and
David, and we understand something of what it meant to be
rescued from the meaninglessness of life under the gods of
the cosmic myths for whom man was merely a menial slave.

Psalm 50 is also to be explained in terms of this form. In
this poem the introit reflects motifs to be discussed in the
next chapter, which were appropriated by Israel from the
heritage of Jerusalem. Verses 1-3 embody hymnic elements,
and specify Jerusalem as the seat of Yahweh's suzerainty.[24]
A reading of the psalm in the light of the foregoing discussion will, however, make it clear that its roots are to be located in the premonarchical covenant community. The elements of the form we have been discussing are all there.
Noteworthy is the summons of verse 5: "Let my covenant
subjects assemble before me." The Hebrew word *chasidim*,
rendered "saints" in the older English versions, "faithful
ones" in the Revised Standard Version, has to be understood
in terms of the covenant tradition. It comes from the same
word as *chesed*, which underlay the second of the three key
words in the last colon of the passage quoted above from
Micah. Variously rendered as "kindness" or "lovingkindness"

or "mercy," *chesed* is, in most cases, rendered by "steadfast love" in the Revised Standard Version. It denotes loyalty to a covenant, loyalty that is not legalistic but devoted.[25] A *chasid*, of which *chasidim* in Psalm 50 is the plural, is one related to *chesed,* one bound in a covenant relationship. The "saintliness" of a *chasid* derives from the covenant in which Yahweh has taken the initiative, not from the *chasid's* own achievement or virtue. It is for this reason that the word has here been rendered "covenant subject." It is against this background that Psalm 50 faults Israel for her attention to the details of worship, even implying that what we would call moral endeavor can lead only to self-righteousness, and exhorts Israel to concentrate on "thanksgiving," the latter denoting grateful remembrance and recital of Yahweh's saving deeds.

THE LATER HISTORY OF THE COVENANT MOTIF

Although, as we shall see, the motifs traced in this chapter were not without effect on other poetic forms, they do not figure prominently in the anthology of Israel's sacred song that is our present psalter. Only two psalms, 50 and 81, are to be classified primarily in terms of the forms and motifs connected with the Mosaic covenant. The reason for this is that the Old Testament as a collection of writings, and this is particularly true of the psalter, comes to us from eras other than that of the ancient covenant confederation of tribes. The setting in terms of which the forms underlying the majority of the psalms are to be understood is the worship of the Temple at Jerusalem during the period of the kingdom. It was in that period, beginning with David and lasting through the approximately four centuries from 1000 to 587 B.C., that Israel appropriated the forms and motifs of the culture of which she was a part both to praise Yahweh and to invoke his help in times of distress.

Both by using the form of the suzerainty treaty to give expression to her *mythos,* and in the explicit rejection of other gods or of taking on the ways of the peoples round about her, premonarchical Israel defined herself in opposition to, rather than in terms of, the culture within which she lived. Not only was she a confederation of *Habiru* groups, outcastes from the point of view of the society centering in the Canaanite city-kingdoms, but she proclaimed that status to be the order established by the God whose power was such that even mighty Egypt could not withstand it. Of the validity of her claim as to the nature of the order established by this God, she was convinced by her success not only in maintaining her identity in the Palestine of 1200 to 1000 B.C., but in her gains (whether by conquest or revolution[26]) in the face of opposition from the established order. Yahweh continued during that period to justify his suzerainty by leading the hosts of Israel in "holy war" against all attempts to overthrow the order within which Israel existed and to absorb Israel into the prevailing social and cultural order.[27]

Israel's own existence and history provided the apologia for Yahweh as a God and for the kind of order for which he was responsible among the people he had designated as his own. There was no need to explain Yahweh's power or suzerainty in the kind of mythological terms commonly used in the ancient Near East. Israel's own history affirmed them. Indeed, to recount in any way how he might have been involved in the pretemporal events that produced the cosmos would have been to compromise his distinctiveness. Whereas her neighbors looked upon the physical universe as the dominion of the gods, and located their worship in a city and temple in which the heavenly made contact with the mundane, Israel located Yahweh's presence and activity in a people and its history. So she could sing:

When Israel came forth from Egypt,
  The house of Jacob from a society that spoke unintelligibly,
Judah became his [Yahweh's] sanctuary,
  Israel the locus of his dominion.   (Psalm 114:1-2.)

Nor was there need for Israel to have a king or the kind of centralized government common in the culture surrounding her. Yahweh himself had directly intervened to provide the structure within which Israel existed as a people, had made himself Israel's covenanted overlord. To have had a king would have been to challenge Yahweh's suzerainty. Thus did pre-monarchical Israel define both her God and herself in opposition to other peoples and to the culture of her world. And through two centuries of history the facts justified such a definition.

In the middle of the eleventh century, however, the situation began to change. The Philistines, part of the sea peoples emerging from the upheaval in the Aegean area mirrored in the Homeric epics, established themselves in the southwest corner of Palestine, and set out to bring the whole land under their control. The state of affairs with which Israel was now confronted was radically different from the one that had prevailed from the beginning of her life in Canaan. For two centuries Egyptian weakness and the remoteness of the center of the Hittite empire had left Palestine in the control of numerous local kings, with whom Israel could deal one by one as necessity arose. She was now, however, up against an organized, centralized power purposefully extending its hegemony over her territory. The narrative of I Samuel, though a compilation of various sources and traditions, reveals what inexorably began to happen. The central sanctuary of the tribal confederation, at that point at Shiloh, was destroyed by the Philistines, and the ark, apparently the portable repository of the covenant regulations revered as the token of Yahweh's presence with his people, was removed to a spot at which the Philistines could be sure that Israel did not rally around it (I Samuel, chapters 1-6).

Saul, who apparently arose originally in the charismatic manner of Israel's ancient leaders,[28] was driven more and more to violate Israelite traditions in order adequately to deal with the Philistine power. The tension between the older traditions and the needs of the time finds expression in the increasing conflict between Saul and the traditional leaders of the tribal confederation typified in Samuel, as well as in the progressively apparent deterioration of Saul himself. The outcome of this tragic story is the defeat and death of Saul at the battle of Mount Gilboa (I Samuel, chapter 31). The situation at the point at which I Samuel ends is one of utter defeat for Israel. In effect, the order within which she had lived was a thing of the past. The historical introduction to the covenant had run its course, and was no longer a sufficient justification for the historical circumstances. History, long cited as the justification of Israel's claims, had now given the lie to those claims.

It is against this background that the rise of David must be seen. David was of the tribe of Judah, a member tribe of the original confederation, but apparently always independent and the possessor of distinctive traditions of its own.[29] Whatever his motives may have been, David apparently broke his earlier association with Saul at some point during the war with the Philistines, while continuing to cultivate the traditional leaders of the confederation, such as Samuel. He also gained the approval of the Philistines, and was allowed by them to remain a sort of brigand in his home territory of Judah. Thus, at the defeat of Saul, David found himself with a base of operations recognized by the Philistine

controllers of Palestine. Smiled on by luck, he skillfully
played every opportunity for all it was worth. At Hebron his
native tribe of Judah made him their king, and subsequently
the elders of the now scattered tribes of the confederation
recognized him as their leader.[30] Furthermore, he managed
in the course of time—his conquests are merely summarized
here and there in II Samuel—to bring not only the former
Israelite holdings under his control, but to extend his rule
over Edom, Ammon, Moab, and Aramean territories beyond
the Jordan. The Philistines, probably because he played the
part of a vassal to them until it was too late for effective action, failed to curb David's successes. He must also have acquired many of the Canaanite city-kingdoms which had continued to exist as pockets in the midst of the Israelites.[31]

Most important, perhaps, was David's capture of Jerusalem, up to his time an independent Canaanite city-kingdom,
and his use of it as his headquarters. Jerusalem was not only
an almost impregnable military stronghold and a site previously not associated with any of the Israelite tribes that
could be unquestionably regarded as David's own possession,
but it was also an ancient seat of the culture so long
eschewed by Israel. Everything points to the conclusion that
David took over not only the city but the institutions that
were the heritage of the city. To it, however, he brought the
ark, making Jerusalem also the central shrine of the Israelite
tribal confederation and, thus, really bringing the confederation back to life after its death at the hands of the Philistines. He apparently managed to bind the cultic officers of
Jerusalem and those of the tribal confederation together in
loyalty to himself, the former represented in II Samuel by
Zadok, and the latter by Abiathar. The revolts of both Absalom and Sheba indicate even in David's time, however,
tensions between the new state of things and the self-understanding of older Israel.[32] The designation and then acces-

sion of Solomon as David's successor represented a victory
for the Canaanite elements in David's court, and Solomon
carried to its conclusion the "culturization" of Israel begun
under David. Under Solomon a temple and palace arose in
Jerusalem, a harem of daughters of foreign kings appeared,
and all the accoutrements of an ancient Near Eastern kingdom came. Precisely these developments lay behind the
separation of Israel into a separate kingdom at the death of
Solomon.

Between the time of Saul and the time of Solomon the
empirical, historical entity that called itself Israel ceased to
exist, and was then brought back into existence in a form different from, but not discontinuous with, what it had been
before. The crucial change was that, *de facto*, "Israel" had
ceased to designate a confederation of tribes defining itself
and the nature of reality in opposition to the prevailing culture, and had itself not only become a part of that culture,
but a central factor in one of the centers of power in that
culture. Henceforth any unchanged use of the institutions of
the old confederation might be expressive of what once had
been, but not of the order now prevailing. The course of
events had resulted in the Israelites' no longer being *Habiru,*
but members of the society over against which the term
Habiru found its only meaning. Israel was now part of the
cosmos, not a parasite on it unneedful of accounting for it,
and the question had become: Is Yahweh really only the
overlord of a now extinct political order, himself in fact a
parasite on the cosmic order, or is he a cosmic god? Is he the
creator of order in the cosmos? If the former were the case,
if his meaning lay in the now past order by which Israel still
gained a part of her significance, then he might rate a sub-
ordinate place of honor in the pantheon, receding more and
more in importance. If the latter were the case, if he was the

creator of order in the cosmos, then he had to be acclaimed in other than the traditional terms.

Such was the crisis by which Israel was faced as the movement of things proceeded from what had been at Saul's death to what was when Solomon dedicated the Jerusalem Temple. It was, in kind, the same crisis faced by the Christian Church as the movement of things proceeded from the original eschatological proclamation of the Palestinian community to the controversies resolved at the Council of Chalcedon. The crisis could not be resolved by denying its existence and pretending that the past order was still an option. Of that the tragically stormy history of the northern kingdom of Israel, and its final disappearance, are evidence. The crisis began to be dealt with as, in the Jerusalem Temple, Canaanite hymns in which other deities had once been praised began to be used to acclaim Yahweh as sovereign over the cosmos, and as a writer such as the Yahwist related Israel's total past and her ancient institutions to the new setting. It began to be dealt with too as laments over the vicissitudes of human finitude, formerly addressed to other deities, began to be addressed to Yahweh. Such is the explanation of the comparatively sparse representation in the psalter, as well as in Israel's other poetry, of forms originating in the period before David, and such is the explanation of why forms mediated to Israel through the Canaanite culture predominate in the songs of the Old Testament.

Yet it was *Yahweh* who was thus acclaimed as ruler of the cosmos and as deliverer from the distresses of finitude. In the final analysis he was different from the other gods, not a new manifestation of someone else now bearing a new name. What had been said of him in the historical introduction to the treaty pattern that gave expression to the meaning of things for older Israel, and all that was implied about his nature and character in the treaty pattern itself, were part of the record. So long as it was *Yahweh* whom hymn and lament addressed as cosmic god, divinity assumed a meaning that it had not previously had. This was so not because of men's deductions about what the word "divine" implied, but simply because of the given story brought to mind by the mention of Yahweh's name. It is for this reason that we shall see as we examine the forms and motifs of Israel's song a definite transformation of those forms and motifs as they are used to assert Yahweh's divinity. Indeed it is from just such a study as this, in which the effect of the uniqueness of Israel's point of view on popular forms of religion is discerned, that a picture of the nature of Old Testament faith can be drawn.

For now we are concerned to observe that it was the covenant motif, minimally represented in its full form in the psalter and often the basis of ultimately destructive reaction within Israel's life and history, that always forcefully held before the worshiping community that it was *Yahweh* in whose praise, and to whose mercy, the songs whose forms came from pagan culture were being sung.

2 God as Cosmic King: Hymnic Praise, Temple, and King

An understanding of the world view of the culture that permeated the region Israel entered throws much light, we have seen, upon many statements and allusions that occur in Israel's songs. This culture was common to Egypt, Mesopotamia, and the Palestinian-Syrian district, the latter being the area with which Israel was closely connected. The literature coming down to us from these three centers, however, is sufficiently diverse as to make sweeping generalizations dangerous. On the other hand, it can be said that the civilization of the ancient Near East had certain broad common characteristics and that David made the hitherto *Habiru* people of the God Yahweh a very definite part of this common civilization.[1]

What this civilization, which extended from the valley of the Nile eastward around the arable lands abutting on the Arabian desert to the plain of the Tigris and Euphrates rivers, held in common was the belief that in the forces and phenomenon of the physical universe were located the basic issues of existence. Of course, life was deeply affected by what we would call political and social factors: the rise and fall of dynasties, the campaigns and invasions of armies, the movements of people from one area to another. All these had indeed their effect on the peaceful regularity of men's lives.

However, events and changes such as these had gone on

from time immemorial. They could take place, as that world
looked at it, only because there was a setting within which
the ups and downs of human life could go on. The ultimate
issues were not those arising from military campaigns or
social upheavals, but were located in those prior conditions
that made life possible at all. If the sun should retire some
evening, never again to rise with its light and warmth, what
was recorded in the annals of political strife would recede
to total unimportance. If winter should come and not leave,
or, worse still in the Palestinian area, if summer should come
with its drying heat and wind never to yield to the rains and
fecundity of fall, military exploits would be not only unim-
portant but impossible. Life itself depended on the rhythm
of nature in which water and rain conquered drought, but
not so overwhelmingly as to drown what they had come to
save. Man, like the plants and animals by which he was fed
and served, was at the mercy of forces neither subject to his
control nor in any way obligated to heed his desires. In a
word, life was always, in all the observable processes by
which it came into being and was sustained, in a struggle
with death. Here was located the real issue, and it was no
mere abstraction. It involved the forces of the natural universe present in the round of nature, the fertility or sterility
of the soil and the flocks, the rain and the drought, the stability and the shakiness of the cosmos itself.

Such was the background against which the ancient Near
Eastern peoples pictured life and the issues arising from it.
They dealt with this setting, as some have put it, not as an
object but as a "thou"—or a collection of "thous." [2] The
natural forces with which man had to deal were conceived
as living beings. The rhythm and the struggles of nature
were due not, as with us, to objectively measurable and
recordable data governed by abstract principles and laws.

They resulted from the interplay and tensions present in the relationships between the various personalities manifested in the phenomena of nature. Thus through the setting in which he lived, man was the observer of, and to some extent a participant in, the great cosmic drama, and that drama was the locus of the real issues of life.

Accordingly, the ascendancy of one people over another was not recorded in historical writings of the kind to which we are accustomed, but was pictured mythically as a struggle in the divine world in which the god of the ascendant people rose to authority in the pantheon. That significant social struggles took place, for example, in the ancient city of Ugarit located on the Syrian coast due east of Cyprus on the site of modern Ras Shamra is certain. But the history of these struggles can never be written, for they were only indirectly commemorated in the Ugaritic myths, which have been recovered from temple libraries. To understand the culture, therefore, into which Israel emerged in the time of David, we must examine the cosmology of ancient Near Eastern civilization and the ways in which man related himself to it.

THE COSMIC MYTH AND THE WORLD OF MAN

The four characteristics common to every center of culture in the ancient Near East were: the mythical narrative by which the world's origin and continued existence were accounted for; the significance of the central, sacred place at which contact between the divine and the human worlds was made; society, with the king at its head, through which the divine order was reflected in the world of men; and the cultic drama through which man expressly and actively related himself to what happened in the realm of the gods.

The Mythical Narrative

Wherever man stands on the earth, he seems to find himself within a large enclosure. Under his feet lies the earth stretching out to the horizon. Above, shaped like a dome, is the sky covering the earth and sloping down to meet it. Beneath the earth and above the dome of the sky would seem to lie a boundless, all engulfing body of water. It is always encountered in a salty form if one moves far enough toward the horizon; it makes its appearance in the waters of the wells and springs by which the earth itself is pierced in many places to give it access to the great sea beneath. Evidence for its existence above the dome of the sky is found in the rain which falls when the heavens open to let it down. This was ancient Near Eastern man's view of the setting of his life. The picture varied, of course, from place to place. The role played by the Nile in Egypt's narrow valley bounded by desert made the view in that area somewhat different, for example, from that held in Mesopotamia where an alluvial plain bordered the Tigris and the Euphrates rivers. The dry climate and harsh geographical features of the Palestinian area, which was without large rivers, made for still different emphases in the view there. In broad perspective, however, the picture of the universe which we have sketched was held throughout the ancient world in which the Bible originated.[3]

The drama of life in that world tended to focus on the waters by which the earth was surrounded above, beneath, and on all sides. On the one hand, water was very definitely an enemy, capable of wiping out life entirely as it welled up in the streams and rivers on the earth's surface or as it poured down from the heavens above. On the other hand, water was necessary for the survival of man and animals and plants, and its absence could reduce the earth to an arid, sterile desert.

The former danger, that of destructive flood, seems to have occupied the minds of men in Mesopotamia where the Tigris and Euphrates rampaged regularly in the late winter and early spring. The latter, the danger of drought, seems to have been the chief worry in the area of Syria and Palestine where the fall rains were preceded by a long, dry summer during which the Arabian desert seemed inexorably to encroach on the inhabited areas at its edge. These differences probably explain why the year was thought of in Mesopotamia as beginning in the spring, while in the Palestinian area it was thought to begin in the fall; that is, a new cycle of life in nature began when the threat most characteristic of the area was past.

At any rate, the actions and decisions of man seemed to be dwarfed into insignificance by the issues posed to his very existence by the forces of nature, particularly by the waters around him which could, through inundation or withdrawal, reduce order to chaos and life to death. This was an elemental cosmic drama which touched man's very survival. But how was man to understand this drama? How was he to picture it in his mind in order to understand it?

Myth provided the solution, for in myth the forces and tensions of life could be personified, made namable, addressable, and open to praise and petition. Myth also provided assurance that there was one divine power whose victory and whose authority kept his colleagues in order (for divinity implied neither stability nor morality), and made the continuance of life in man's world possible. Because the extant Egyptian cosmogonic myths have a character uniquely their own, probably due to the distinctive world view engendered by the setting of the Nile valley, the discussion here will draw largely on material from Mesopotamia and Ugarit, the

materials by which the biblical writers seem chiefly to have
been informed.[4] In particular, we shall concentrate on the
information provided by the Babylonian epic of creation, the
Enuma elish, and the myth of Aliyan Baal.[5]

In this general mythic view the explanation of everything
observed by man rested with the society of the gods: with
what had happened in that society before the mundane, human sphere came into existence, as well as with what continued to happen above and beyond the visible world. All
that happened in the cosmos reflected the actions, decisions,
and struggles of divine beings, each of whom personified
some element in earth or sky. There is frequent mention in
both the Babylonian and Ugaritic mythological literature of
the "divine assembly," the formal convocation of the gods at
which decisions affecting the destiny of the cosmos and life
within it were taken. It has been persuasively argued that
this assembly gives evidence for the most ancient view having been that the cosmos was originally governed by a sort
of town meeting of the deities, and that this reflects the way
in which the earliest polity of the human community in the
Near East was not monarchical but a form of "primitive
democracy." [6] The important point is, however, that the primary issues of human existence could be accounted for only
by reciting what happened in the divine community, for
man was aware only of the cosmic consequences of those
decisions and actions. And, despite the idyllic relations between the gods originally, a titanic struggle had taken place
among them, and out of it had come the reign of one hero
god over the cosmos and (in the Babylonian version) over
man and the world in which he lived.[7]

Common to the myths in question is the turning of the
progenitor and original leader of the gods against the other
members of the pantheon. Either as a result of the subdual
of the leader after he had turned on the other gods (Baby-

lon), or for reasons that are not entirely clear but with the blessing of the original divine leader (Ugarit), the god who personifies the great sea of water becomes the chief antagonist of the others, threatening to reduce things to utter chaos by wiping out the rest of the divine beings. It is interesting that in the Ugaritic myth the watery chaos is not the only threat to the forces of order, but there arises as well one known simply as "Death," who uses his powers to remove the champion of life and fertility so that things dry out and die from a *lack* of water. This undoubtedly reflects the climate of the area of Syria and Palestine in which the rainless summer conjures up all sorts of fears for the continuance of crops and life. As a result of the threat to the divine society produced by the god (in Babylonia actually the goddess) of waters, a vigorous young champion emerges who, after trials and bloody battles, is victorious. In the Ugaritic myth, "Death" has to be fought and vanquished as well. The result of the victory is that the victor, Marduk in Babylon and Aliyan Baal in Ugarit, assumes undisputed sovereignty over the assembly of the gods, with implicit assurance that the forces behind the cosmos will never again be threatened with chaos. Neither flood nor drought will finally prevail, although the round of seasons each year once again reflects the great struggle of which the myth speaks.

It must be understood that only as a result of what is described in the myth could life go on at any present moment in the cosmos. Indeed, the Babylonian epic is quite specific about how the cosmos, with the men who inhabit it, was a direct consequence of the battle described in the myth. That epic describes how Marduk, when Tiamat, the goddess of watery chaos, had been killed, split her in two so that the earth as seen by man stood in a great gash down the middle of her corpse. The water above the skies and below the earth were but her remains, now made to function in such a way as to serve an ordered cosmos under Marduk's dominion. The Babylonian epic also recounts how Marduk slew one Kingu, who had incited Tiamat to pursue her destructive course, and formed man from his blood so that the status of slavery which was the just reward of those gods who had sided with Tiamat might devolve upon a lesser being, leaving the gods to enjoy the ease befitting their dignity. The Ugaritic myth is less detailed, and the condition of the tablets upon which it is written is such that we cannot be certain either about its conclusion or its internal order. It would, however, seem to imply that the processes by which life in the cosmos is made possible were enabled to go on in a dependable and orderly fashion as a result of what it has described as transpiring in the realm of the gods.

The myth, then, was not merely a story of something that had occurred in the past. It was the explanation of things present, the expression of the truth underlying the reality of existence in the cosmos. That is what distinguishes a myth from legends or sagas.[8] We must not conclude a description of what the myth said or a discussion of its contents with no reference to the society by which it was created and in which it served its function. The myth provided the rationale for the institutions of the society out of which it came, for the social order itself.

The Temple

The basic social and political unit in the civilization of the ancient Near East was the city-kingdom. This was true from the period of Sumerian culture in Mesopotamia (2800-2400 B.C.) well into the Christian era. Status in the Roman empire, for example, was gained by one as far from its center as Saul of Tarsus by becoming a citizen of the *city* of Rome. St. Augustine entitled his great work *The City of God* not the *Kingdom* of God. The city was the basic unit of society, and, even if one city came to dominate a large area through imperial hegemony, that *city* was the center of things, other city subcenters being related to it as "daughters."

As one moved toward the center of the city, chaos was progressively conquered by order. This is clearly reflected in Hebrew terminology. There is, farthest out from the center of things, the "desert" or "wilderness." None of our translations of the term is exactly accurate, for its basic connotation has to do with society's order. It has to do with the area far enough out from the city, whether it be what we would call a desert or not (it usually was desert in the Palestinian area), for the instruments of order not to have reached it— plows as well as police. Then, as one moved inward, came the "fields," the cultivated land upon which the ordering and organizing hands of society had had their effect. Again no translation of the Hebrew original is exactly accurate, for the term finds its meaning in terms of a polity and an economy and a world view different from ours. Finally one came to the city itself, from whose houses, for the most part, the hands that brought order to the "fields" went out. At the center of the city, on its highest point, stood the complex of buildings from which the whole order emanated. These were the buildings at which the gods were worshiped and in which the king lived and ruled. One word served to denote what we would differentiate as the temple and the royal palace, and the reasons for this can lead us further into an understanding of the point of view of the culture out of which Israel's songs came.[9]

The temple in the center of a city-kingdom was the earthly counterpart of the palace in the heavens in which the god who had conquered the forces of chaos, and so earned the right to exercise sovereignty over all the gods, presided over the divine assembly and from which he ruled the cosmos. The temple was the place at which the heavenly realm of the gods impinged upon the world in which man lived. It was built on a sacred site whose character had been made manifest to some man chosen as the recipient of a revelation by the god seeking an earthly place from which his rule might reach out to bring order into the area in which men lived. It is in such terms that we are able to understand what lies behind the story in Genesis 28:10-17, which recounts the dream of Jacob beholding the heavenly messengers ascending and descending upon a stairway whose base was placed at Bethel. The story, whatever may now be its place in the total narrative of which it is a part, was originally the *hieros logos* of the sanctuary at Bethel, the legend by which the existence of the temple there was justified. The story explicitly makes the point that the sacred site is a spot at which the god concerned (whoever it was before Israel identified him with Yahweh) reaches down from the heavenly realm to work his way on earth. This is said not only in the imagery of the heavenly messengers coming and going on the stairway from earth to heaven, but in the exclamation of Jacob with which the account comes to an end: "This is none other than the house of God, and this is the gate of heaven." [10]

It is in this sense that we understand what the city at the heart of the kingdom, with a sacred site and temple at its own heart, meant. The order that flowed from the center of the city into the "fields" by which it was surrounded, that ever was threatened by, as it itself challenged, the "wilderness" or "desert" beyond, was no secular political or economic phenomenon. It was the realization in the mundane world of that victory by which Marduk or Aliyan Baal assured life and order in the cosmos. In the Jerusalem of the Davidic period and in the Assyrian city of Nineveh during the period of Israel's decline the rule emanating from the city extended far out to other cities so that the deities responsible for their temples had to acknowledge the supremacy of the god of the conquering armies. Insofar as a god was associated with the city that controlled other cities, insofar as he was the god of the city that gave to the world its orderly government, he was in fact the hero of the myth, and the city in which his temple was located was called "the navel of the universe." Thus both the Babylonian epic of which Marduk is the hero and the Ugaritic myth in which Aliyan Baal rises to supremacy in the cosmos give an important place to the description of how a "house" is built for the conquering god. In the way in which these myths are the explanations of what is actually there in the cosmos, these accounts of building are not meant only to refer to imaginary palaces high in the heavens or far off on Mount Zaphon (the Syrian equivalent of Olympus). They are the aetiologies of the "houses" standing in Babylon or Ugarit in which the earthly throne room of the divine sovereign is located. Babylon or Ugarit is not just a political capital but is the sacred center from which the myth is extended in the actuality to the world inhabited by mortals.[11]

The King

It is in this sense too that we understand the meaning of the king who lived in that other building at the center of the city-kingdom, that building known in the languages of the ancient Near East by the same word used to designate the temple. The king was the person from whom order extended to the "fields" and conquered territories of the central city, and he was no merely human figure whose office could be accounted for in terms of secular politics and power. He was the earthly vicegerent of the god who had established and who maintained order in the cosmos. It is for this reason that the Babylonian monarchs traced their ancestry back in a king-list which in its Sumerian prototype began, "When kingship was lowered from heaven. . . ."[12]

And thus the Egyptian pharaoh was considered himself to be one of the gods. In the king's "kingdom," the word denoting the effects in society of the presence of a king as much as the geographical area touched by it, the order won and maintained by the god whom the myth described as responsible for life in the cosmos was something in which that god was still as much at work as he had been in what the myth recounted. Conquest and victory by an earthly king were not simply military and political accomplishments; they were extensions of the struggle and victory of which the myth spoke. And, conversely, defeat of an earthly king had cosmic connotations. It had something to do with who presided over the heavenly assembly of gods in which the destinies of the world were determined. That is why Marduk could replace Ashur in the *Enuma elish* when Babylon conquered Ashur's people, the Assyrians, just as Ashur had once replaced another. The king and his accomplishments and failures were accounted for not in terms of pedestrian political causes and effects, but in terms of the drama and the order of which the myth was the expression. Through him as well as through the sacred city, the divine realm related itself to the world of men.[13]

The Cultic Drama

If the meaning of the city-kingdom and of its king was that the myth is no mere story but an expression of the truth about the cosmos, then it is easy to appreciate that the myth was more than a document to be read as we modern men might read a book. That the Ugaritic myth of Baal was read aloud in the hearing of an audience, presumably at a sacral cultic occasion, is clear from the rubrics for the reader found in some tablets on which it is written.[14] The Babylonian epic of creation, as we know from a description of what happened on New Year's Day in ancient Babylon, was read in the hearing of the people, and the events described in it were ritually re-enacted, the king himself taking the part of Marduk in the battle with the forces of chaos. Each spring, at the overflowing of the Tigris and Euphrates rivers, in which the threat of subdual of order by the watery chaos of which Tiamat was the personification, once again passed without total destruction, the *Enuma elish* was solemnly read. This took place as part of a cultic celebration in which the king assumed the identity of Marduk and vanquished the foes of order. The myths of Egypt were likewise dramatized cultically,[15] and so must those of Ugarit have been.[16] Thus did the polity and economy and worship of ancient Near Eastern society serve as means by which society related itself to the cosmos where the real issues were located, having been created by what took place in the assembly of the gods. The myth gave expression to the reality which undergirds life.

ISRAEL ENTERS THE COSMOS

It was into this culture that Israel intruded when David made Jerusalem the central shrine of the old tribal confederation. Both in terms of the elements of which the Davidic empire was made up and in terms of the traditions of the city itself, Israel found herself intimately associated with that culture in opposition to which she had for so long defined herself. There is every reason to believe, although the evidence is such that only conjecture is possible, that the pre-Israelite, Jebusite city-kingdom of Jerusalem had a long history of its own, and possessed its own form of the mythic and cultic view of reality.[17] Jerusalem is mentioned in extrabiblical documents as well as in biblical passages referring to times long before David's in such a way as to suggest it held an important place in the area long before it became the

center of the empire put together by David.[18] It is inconceivable that such a city would not have participated in the
pattern prevalent in the culture surrounding it, and it is
probable that the form of the myth found in the literature
from Ugarit characterizes the nature of the belief and practice of pre-Davidic Jerusalem. Evidence is abundant that the
appellative used to designate the god, who in Jebusite Jerusalem played the role of Marduk in Babylon or Aliyan Baal
in Ugarit, was *Elyon* ("Most High") or *El Elyon* ("God
Most High"), and that *Zedek* ("Righteousness") or *Shalem*
("Peace") are likely candidates for his more personal, first
name, or that these two words are the names of divinities
closely associated with him. It can also be persuasively argued that *Melek* ("King") was a divinity of importance in
the Jerusalem tradition.[19] Jerusalem seems to have established a contact between Israel and one form of the cosmic
myth of the prevailing culture of the Near East. A concordance would show that the terms mentioned occur frequently
in the psalms. The following takes on new significance in the
light of what we have now elucidated:

> For Yahweh [as] *Elyon* is to be feared,
> [As] *Melek,* great over all the earth.
> (Psalm 47:2, Heb. 47:3.)

Furthermore, there is every indication that David, having
taken Jerusalem by a clever ruse that did not result in much
destruction or bloodshed,[20] sold himself to the Jebusite in-
habitants of the city as the valid inheritor of the kingship
that must have existed there before his arrival.[21] Once David
established himself in Jerusalem, Zadok (note the connection
of the name with Zedek mentioned above) appears in his
retinue alongside Abiathar, whose connections seem to go
back to the Israel of the tribal confederation. Zadok seems
to represent the pre-Davidic priesthood of Jerusalem, and his

presence with Abiathar in the royal entourage suggests how David fused Israelite traditions and institutions with those of the city he made his capital.[22] Moreover, from the Jebusite Arunah, David bought a threshing floor, such a place apparently being a sacred site,[23] as a fitting place on which to locate the ark, the portable shrine of the Israelite's God Yahweh, the presence of which in the later Temple of Solomon was the link between the older Israel and the Davidic empire.

With the coming of David, Yahweh had become the God of the reigning king in a city-kingdom. From the point of view of those who were the heirs of mythic tradition this meant that Yahweh had now manifested himself as the conquering leader of the divine assembly. It meant that Yahweh was the one who had defeated the powers of chaos and death, and who was responsible for life and order in the cosmos. This became even more emphatic at David's death with the victory of Solomon (the name itself is related to *Shalem*) in the struggle over succession to the throne, a victory for the Canaanite elements in David's court as against those whose roots lay in the Israel of old. Solomon proceeded to build a temple comparable to those of other city-kingdoms of the time and area, as well as a palace for himself. Yahweh had become the God whose sovereignty over the cosmos was accounted for in the myth, and, through the king he designated as his vicegerent, Yahweh ruled the world from the temple-palace complex on the sacred height of Jerusalem.

To some Israelites these developments compromised the old faith, Israel's original covenant *mythos* having been subverted, and Yahweh himself obliterated. To such Israelites what had begun to happen in the days of Samuel and Saul constituted, as some of the narratives now preserved in I Samuel suggest, rebellion and apostasy. The same restiveness was evident even in the time of David.[24] It was on this

account that "Israel" broke away from the Davidic kingdom
and from Jerusalem at the death of Solomon. The fact re-
mained, nevertheless, that conditions were now such that
Yahweh either was the chief God of the cosmos, or a minor
deity who had led Israel to the Davidic period and to a life
over which another god with the proper qualifications must
now preside. The northern kingdom was the place where the
older traditions were most vividly kept alive in Israel's memory, but it was also a place of continual upheaval because it
was not willing, or could not find a way, to acclaim Yahweh
as sovereign over the setting in which Israel now found herself. It proved difficult to get the *mythos* really to speak out
of and to the setting, for her setting, once Israel had in fact
ceased to be a *Habiru* community, was the cosmos as conceived in the culture of the ancient Near East.

THE HYMNS OF PRAISE

The connection between the old and the new, a painful
and complicated process, was made and maintained in Jerusalem. The forms of expression and the institutions common
to the prevalent culture were first used there to proclaim that
Yahweh was God in all the ways that counted. It is in this
context that we may understand the presence among Israel's
songs of that category designated as hymns. It is in the same
context that we may understand those types of songs which
speak specifically of Yahweh's kingship over the cosmos, as
well as those in which the sacred city and the king are central. A strictly formal analysis of the songs distinguishes a
number of types, but the motifs underlying them go back to
a theme common to the culture out of which they came. That
theme is the proclamation of God's, Yahweh's, sovereignty
over the forces of the cosmos. Connected with it are celebra-

tions of the places and persons through which it is both symbolized and carried out in human society.

The Hymn Proclaims God's "Godness"

Psalm 29 is probably the purest example of a hymn in the Old Testament. To read it in a translation which attempts to convey some of the overtones of the terms it employs is to see how closely it parallels the mythical cosmology we have been discussing:

> Affirm with regard to Yahweh, O you divine beings,
>   Affirm with regard to Yahweh glory and strength,
> Affirm with regard to Yahweh his glorious reputation,
>   Fall prostrate before Yahweh at his holy epiphany.
>   (Psalm 29:1-2.)[25]

This introduction to the hymn contains a series of verbs in the imperative plural, calling for praise of God, and it is clear that the imperatives are addressed not to a human congregation, but to the assembly of gods itself. The gods are to "affirm"—the verb is difficult to translate, "ascribe" being too intellectual—the "glory of his name." The latter phrase can be rendered "his glorious reputation" in order to convey something of its connotations. In connection with such a call to the gods as is found in this psalm, we recollect the beginning of a passage near the end of the Babylonian epic of creation wherein Marduk is praised at great length by the pantheon as the bearer of fifty names in which his fame is recounted in terms of every good function imaginable:

> As for us, by however many names we pronounce, he is our god!
>   Let us then proclaim his fifty names:
>   He whose ways are glorious, whose deeds are likewise.
>   . . . (VI, 121-123: Pritchard, *Ancient Near Eastern Texts*, 69)

In this passage from the *Enuma elish* it is the assembly of gods that speaks.

Tablet IV of the Ugaritic myth of Baal is one of the last in the sequence of the myth. In it the goddess Anat announces to the divine assembly ("sons of God" as in the psalm) that Baal has been victorious over "Death" and that—this is significant in view of what is to follow in Psalm 29—rain is to come with life for the earth. Anat goes on to signify her intention to come before Baal in his palace with sacrifices appropriate to such a sovereign and, although the end of the column in question is lost (IV AB i), it is reasonable to conjecture that the purpose of her announcement of Baal's victory to the gods was to exhort them to join with her in his praise.

Thus the reference to the "divine beings" ("sons of gods") in Psalm 29 as well as in the passages from the *Enuma elish* and the Baal myth make clear that the imperatives characteristic of introductions to hymns of praise originated in a call to the assembly of all the gods to make affirmation of the right to praise and worship earned by a victorious deity in his subdual of the forces of chaos and death. Insofar as the imperatives are addressed to the human congregation in a temple on this earth, and there is no question that they are so addressed as well as to the gods, they demonstrate that what happened on earth was but a reflection of activity in the realm of the gods. The hymn originated, therefore, in the cosmic myth and what it described. The "names" of the god refer to his powers manifested in the victory he had won, to the reputation he had gained in the titanic struggles described in the myth. Thus the passage from the *Enuma elish* proceeds from its introductory invocation to a lengthy listing of the concrete ways in which the divine powers of Marduk are manifested, and Anat's proclamation to the gods in the Baal myth includes a listing of the blessings that are to re-

sult from the supreme reign of Baal after his victory over
"Death." So too, Psalm 29, with its introductory call to the
gods to acknowledge Yahweh's supremacy, goes on to describe how his power is manifest. Here, as always, this description forms the body or main section of the hymn:

> The sound of Yahweh [is] over the waters,
> > The glorious God has sounded [his] thunder,
> > > Yahweh [prevails] over the Great Waters.
> The sound of Yahweh [explodes] with power,
> > The sound of Yahweh [explodes] in theophany.
> The sound of Yahweh breaks [even] cedar trees,
> > Why, it has shattered the cedars of Lebanon.[26]
> It has made Lebanon dance like a calf,
> > Sirion like a young wild ox.[27]
> The sound of Yahweh is making the wilderness writhe,
> > Making the wilderness of Kadesh writhe.
> The sound of Yahweh is inducing labor in hinds,
> > It has caused the premature birth of kids.
>
> (Psalm 29:3-9a.)[28]

The body of the hymn clearly describes a thunderstorm,
seeing it as the manifestation (note how the end of the introduction referred to an epiphany or theophany) of the
power wielded by Yahweh. Two aspects of the divine sovereignty central to the Ugaritic Baal myth are alluded to:
while the first verse indicates that a thunderstorm sweeping
into the Syrian-Palestinian area is that to which the song has
concrete reference, there is a *double-entendre*, in that the
passage of the storm over the waters of the Mediterranean
moving toward the land brings to mind the defeat suffered
by watery chaos at the hands of the hero of the gods, and so
the verse ends by alluding to Yahweh's victory over the
"Great Waters." [29] The body of the song goes on to describe
not only how the storm unleashes its fury as it moves from
the sea into the Lebanon mountains, mocking even the pro-

verbial strength of the cedars of that range, but how it in-
vades the arid wilderness as it turns southward through the
area to the east of the Jordan River and finally peters out in
the neighborhood of Kadesh in the desert south of Palestine.
Just as the opening verses alluded to Yahweh's victory over
the chaotic waters, the latter verses seem to allude to the in-
ability of the lifelessly dry desert or wilderness to escape the
waters poured down by the thunderstorm. This brings to
mind the battle Baal fought with "Death" who sought to
dispose of the bringer of rain and fertility after Baal had
been victorious over watery chaos.[30] The impression is reinforced by Psalm 29's reference to a theophany in the form of
a thunderstorm which is reminiscent of celebrations of Baal
as the master of thunderstorms in the literature from Ugarit
(II AB vii, 27-41):

> The windows inside his palace
>   Baal, with rain from the clouds, opened.
> Baal gave forth with his holy sound,
>   Baal went on making utterance with his lips.
> His holy sound made the earth quake,
>   . . . the mountains shook . . .
> The eyes of Baal note where his hand should strike,
>   Yea, his right hand makes the cedars tremble.[31]

It is impossible to miss that the poem acclaiming Baal makes
use of imagery also found in Psalm 29. In both, the theophany involves rain, thunder, and lightning, and a number
of words are common to the two.

If the body of Psalm 29 claims for Yahweh what the myth
discovered at Ugarit claims for Aliyan Baal, its conclusion
begins with words pointing even more emphatically to such
a transferal of power:

> And in his temple it all is saying, "Glory!"
>   (Psalm 29:9b.)

The parallelism characteristic of Hebrew and other Semitic poetry is violated by the last line of verse 9. One half of a colon stands alone without a counterpart. It is for this reason that one scholar offers what, in the light of all that the song suggests, seems to be a reasonable conjecture as to what the original complete colon might have contained:

> [The assembly of the gods *does* acclaim him,]
>   And in his [heavenly] palace they unanimously say, "Glory!" [32]

Not only would such a verse be expected from what we know of the Canaanite myth of Baal, whose power was manifest in the thunderstorm, but it is supported by the reference to the divine beings in the introduction to the hymn. Thus does the conclusion say that the assembly of gods called upon at the beginning, representing as they do all the forces operative in the cosmos, has obeyed the command to affirm the sovereign power manifested by Yahweh at his appearance in the storm. So it is that what took place in the realm of the gods makes it possible for the human community to face life in the cosmos with assurance and confidence:

> Yahweh, the primeval flood has to admit, is enthroned!
>   For Yahweh is enthroned, king forever!
> Yahweh, might for his people is ordaining,
>   Yahweh is blessing his people with peace.
> (Psalm 29:10-11.)

The repetitive emphasis on Yahweh's own name in the final two verses of Psalm 29 is significant. The content and allusions of the song up to that point would lead an impartial authority on the literature and culture of the Syrian-Palestinian area to conclude that this psalm was a hymn to Baal whose accomplishments were described in the myths uncovered at Ugarit. That is why the final words of the hymn insist that it is Yahweh, Yahweh, Yahweh, Yahweh who is responsible for the cosmic order ascribed to Baal by others.[33] By substituting Yahweh's name for Baal's (or his equivalent in the tradition of pre-Davidic Jerusalem), and possibly by appending a conclusion in which it is emphasized that the hymn is addressed to Yahweh, Israel has adapted a Canaanite hymn to her own purposes. Comparison of this psalm with the Ugaritic Baal myth confirms that conclusion. Psalm 29 provides us with an example of how the entrance of Israel into the civilization over against which she had originally defined herself and her God prompted her to assert that what was elsewhere claimed for Marduk or Baal or others, namely sovereignty over the cosmos, was henceforth to be attributed to Yahweh. Though some fought this as apostasy and betrayal of Yahweh's true character, Israel came to maintain that the God of the exodus and the covenant was more than his original *Habiru* devotees had ever thought. He was the ruler of the cosmos.[34]

The Hymn Acclaims God's Victory

The *form* of the hymn with its summons to a group to laud the victory of the supreme god over the chaotic powers of the cosmos undoubtedly goes back to the content of the cosmic myth. The basis of the summons to praise, what makes it possible in the human community which is included in the summons, is the obedience to it in the first place of the members of the assembly of the gods above the heavens. It is because Yahweh has compelled the cosmic powers, by his victory over his cosmic antagonists, to acknowledge his orderly rule in the universe that men can live in peace and utter their praises. Thus the results of victory in the cosmic battle described in the myth are stressed again and again in Old Testament hymns.

There are, for example, many allusions to Yahweh's sub-

dual of that same watery chaos fought by Marduk as the
goddess Tiamat and by Baal as the god Yam. It is control of
the primeval antagonists that alone makes life possible.[35]

> At the word of Yahweh the heavens were formed,
>   At a mere whisper from him the host inhabiting them.
> [He's] the one who gathered as into a bottle the sea's waters,
>   [Who] placed in storehouses the waters of chaos.
>
>   (Psalm 33:6-7.)

The relation of these verses to the cosmic myth becomes apparent when we note that the word for "sea" in the third line
is precisely the word *Yam,* the name of Baal's adversary in
the first part of the Ugaritic myth, and that the last word in
the lines cited is *tehomoth,* the plural form of the Hebrew
cognate of the name Tiamat, Marduk's adversary in the
Babylonian epic.

The same imagery occurs elsewhere, associating the ups
and downs of international life with the chaotic impulses of
the elements from which the cosmos was formed:

> [Thou art] the one who calms the roaring of the seas,
>   The roaring of their waves,
>   The peoples' agitation.   (Psalm 65:7, Heb. 8.)

Here again the word for sea is the name of Baal's adversary.
Psalm 104, a hymn in which the body is extended into a considerable catalogue of the manifestations of Yahweh's control over the universe, contains a similar allusion, the word-
ing of which recalls very vividly the nature of the universe
presupposed in the Babylonian epic:

> [Thou art] the one who set the earth on its foundations,
>   Not to be unsteady at any future time.
> Watery chaos like a garment thou didst place over it,
>   Above the mountains the waters are in place.
>
>   (Psalm 104:5-6.)

The assurance here is that the waters (again the Hebrew cognate of Tiamat is used) will never burst through the heavens to wipe out life, just as the waters underneath will not disturb the stability of the earth on which man lives.

The biblical hymns also frequently allude to Yahweh's responsibility for life-giving rain and fertility, implying that, as the Ugaritic myth claimed Baal had, he has defeated the powers that seek rather to stop the rain from falling than to annihilate by inundation. Such is the background of these lines:

> Thou hast paid heed to the earth by watering it,
>> Hast made it abundantly fertile.
>>> The channels of Yahweh are [always] filled with water.
> Thou hast provided grain for them,
>> Yea, in this manner dost thou provide it:
> Drenching its furrows,
>> Leveling its clods,
> Softening it with showers,
>> Blessing its growth.
> Thou dost crown the year with thy good things,
>> Thy chariot's tracks drop down fatness.
>>>> (Psalm 65:9-11, Heb. 10-12.)

In poetic imagery in which the words trip over one another the fertility brought by the rain is pictured, its effects as the progress of Yahweh's chariot traverses the sky (probably in the movement of a rainstorm) being anticipated by the assertion that what falls in the raindrops by which the young grain is watered is "fatness," abundance of crops. The figure of the clouds as a chariot in which the supreme god rides is a familiar one, often used of Baal and of Hadad, his Syrian counterpart with whom he is at times identified as Baal Hadad. It is not, therefore, surprising that the hymns of the Old Testament apply it to Yahweh, that they acclaim his

victorious sway over the unruly powers as the storm moves
above the earth:

> Sing to God, praise his name in song!
>> Make your songs a highway for the one who rides the
>> clouds
>>> By [shouting] Yahweh, his name!
>>>> Yea, engage in exultation before him.
>>>>> (Psalm 68:4, Heb. 5.)

The basis of the claims made for Yahweh's control over
the watery chaos and for his sovereign freedom to send the
rains by which the fertility of the earth is ensured is that he
is no less than the God by whom the divine assembly is kept
in order, under whom the various other gods perform their
appointed functions. So, finally, the hymns of the Old Testament explicitly acclaim him as the chief of the gods, the
supreme divinity.

> For a great God is Yahweh
>> And King supreme over all the gods:
> In whose hand are the depths of the earth,
>> And the peaks of the mountains are his too,
> To whom belongs the sea—*he* reduced it to order,
>> And the dry land—his hands shaped it.
>>> (Psalm 95:3-5.)

Both "God" in the first line of this passage and "King" in the
second line were originally proper names. The former, El,
was head of the pantheon of the Ugaritic myths, the latter,
Melek, probably a deity in the traditions of pre-Davidic
Jerusalem. The connotation of lines such as these in their
original setting would have been that Yahweh had taken
over the functions of El or Melek as the chief of all the cos-

mic powers. The same point is asserted in a different form
of hymn, Psalm 103. This song is an "I hymn," the singer being identified as an individual. For Gunkel it represented the
adaptation of the hymn form to expressions of individual
piety, and was therefore late in date.[36] Although an "I" style
is not necessarily an indication of lateness in view of what
we now know of Near Eastern hymns,[37] the general content
of this psalm as well as the way in which it utilizes the hymn
form for personal thanksgiving does suggest a postexilic origin.[38] This makes its use of ancient imagery the more remarkable, showing how pervasive the cosmic mythology had become:

> Yahweh! In the heavens has he established his throne,
>   His kingship has dominion over everything.
> Bless Yahweh, you heavenly messengers of his,
>   You mighty ones who carry out his command. . . .
> Bless Yahweh, all you hosts of his,
>   You servants of his who carry out his will.
>   (Psalm 103:19-21.)

Here, though in less explicit mythological form, the imagery
of an assembly of gods, over whom Yahweh has gained dominion and through whom his orderly government of the
cosmos is carried out, continues to be used at a relatively
late date. Similar imagery is found in many places.

> Who is like Yahweh our God,
>   The one who is enthroned on high,
> The one who looks down from afar
>   Upon the heavens as well as the earth?
>   (Psalm 113:5-6.)

> For I know that Yahweh is great,
>   Our Lord is greater than any god.
>   (Psalm 135:5.)

> Give thanks to Yahweh, for he's good,
>> For limitless is his *chesed*.
> Give thanks to the God of gods,
>> For limitless is his *chesed*.
> Give thanks to the Lord of lords,
>> For limitless is his *chesed*.
>> > > (Psalm 136:1-3.)

Here, in a hymn celebrating Yahweh's *chesed*, a covenant term discussed in the previous chapter, and celebrating Yahweh's historical actions, the imagery of supremacy in the divine assembly is still used to assert Yahweh's rule over all.

It would be wrong to leave the impression that the hymn, the celebration of Yahweh's "godness" in terms of the mythology of the ancient Near East, is confined to the psalter. Its motifs are found elsewhere in the Old Testament as well. The "Song of Moses," in which the escape of Israel from the Egyptian forces at the Sea of Reeds is celebrated, employs hymnic language and allusions:

> At a blast from thy nostrils the waters were dammed up,
>> The floods were contained behind a barrier,
>>> Watery chaos congealed in the depths of the sea. . . .
> Who among the gods compares with thee, O Yahweh?
>> Who compares with thee in holy majesty?
>> > > (Exodus 15:8-9, 11.)

This song must come from a time later than that of Moses, when Israel had learned to use the idiom of her culture to acclaim the supremacy of the God who had brought David to Jerusalem. All the terms are there. They are there too in bits of a hymn interspersed among the prophetic materials collected in the book of Amos:

> [He's] the one who shapes mountains and calls the wind into being,
>> Who lets man see what he is about [in the following ways]:

[He's] the one who makes dawn and darkness,
  Who treads on the earth's high places [in clouds?],
    —Yahweh, God of hosts, is his name!
[He's] the one who made the Pleiades and Orion,
  Who turns deathly darkness into morning,
    Then darkens the day [so it's] night.
[He's] the one who speaks with authority to the waters of
the sea,
  And pours them over the earth's surface
    —Yahweh is his name!   (Amos 4:13; 5:8-9.)[39]

Here again, the imagery of the myth is the basis of the acclamation of Yahweh as supreme ruler of the cosmos, and the emphasis on its being *Yahweh* who does so is reminiscent of Psalm 29.

Enthronement Hymns

Closely associated with what are commonly designated as pure hymns is that special category of psalms called songs of Yahweh's enthronement. This is so whether they be dated in the period of the monarchy or in the exilic period in connection with the powerful assertions of Yahweh's absolute sovereignty over all things found in Second Isaiah. Surely, however, if a hymn such as Psalm 29 is to be dated as early as it commonly is, there is no reason why the enthronement songs could not also have originated prior to the fall of Jerusalem.[40] It is not necessary to postulate an enthronement festival in Jerusalem modeled closely on the lines of the Babylonian New Year ritual in order to support an early date for the enthronement songs in the psalter. There is no indication, to cite a very important point, that the cosmic myth in the form it takes in the area closest to Israel, that is, in the Baal myth from Ugarit, has to do with an annual death-resurrection cycle or necessarily implies an annual enthronement festival.[41] Whatever the date and setting of the en-

thronement songs, and the literature on the subject clearly
reflects disagreement, the songs do emphasize a particular
motif. Psalm 93 is a classic example:

> Yahweh is King! [Mowinckel: has become king]
>   Splendor is his vestment;
>   Yahweh has put on his vestments,
>   Has girded himself with power.
> So firmly is the world established that it cannot be shaken;
>   Established more firmly is thy throne;
>   Forever art thou [God supreme]!
> The floods have raised, O Yahweh,
>   The floods have raised their voice,
>   The floods are raising up their roar.
> Than the sound of the Great Waters,
>   Than the mightiness of the sea's breakers,
>   Is Yahweh mighty in [his] exalted place.
> Thy decrees are unshakably determinative,
>   [So that] thy house is without equal,
>   O Yahweh, as long as time shall last.

What is said here is rooted in the view of reality characteristic of the cosmic myth, particularly in that aspect of the myth
which speaks of a battle between the god of order and watery chaos. The other complementary motif, the celebration
of the supreme deity as the one who cannot be restrained
from bringing the rain that is the basis of fertility on the
earth finds expression in another of the enthronement songs:

> Yahweh is king! [or, has become king]
> Let the earth rejoice,
>   Let every human habitation celebrate!
> Clouds and divine darkness surround him,
>   Righteousness and justice are the basis of his rule.
> Fire precedes his coming,
>   Thoroughly envelopes his adversaries.

> His lightning makes the world shine,
>> The earth looks on and writhes.
> The mountains as wax do melt,
>> At the presence of the Lord of all the earth.
>>>>>> (Psalm 97:1-5.)

Even this brief discussion of that form of song designated as the hymn (of which we take the songs of Yahweh's enthronement to be only a special group) makes it clear that Israel came to claim supremacy for Yahweh in terms available to her in the *mythos* of the culture of which she found herself a part when David had lifted her to life again after the disaster of the Philistine war.[42] Those terms were not the terms of the covenant *mythos* of the old tribal confederation. The issues of existence were located in what transpired in the assembly of the gods. But if Yahweh was indeed the one who posed the issues and gave life its meaning, those terms had to be faced. Otherwise, he was not Lord of the situation in which Israel had come to find herself.

THE SACRED CITY AS THE LOCUS OF GOD'S RULE ON EARTH

We have pointed out that the cosmic myth was no mere story recounted in the abstract, but the *raison d'être* of the institutions of society, and that the role of the city from which dominion was exercised over a larger or smaller territory was crucial. In Israel, once the terms of the cosmic myth came to be utilized to proclaim the ascendancy of Yahweh over the assembly of the gods and so over the cosmos, Jerusalem was the crucial city. The importance of Jerusalem in the Bible's imagery both of God's rule in the world and of hope for the future, imagery found as early as Genesis, chapter 14, and running into the Revelation of St. John, is concretely rooted in the world view assumed by Israel when

David and Solomon made her a part of ancient Near Eastern civilization. The city, both in its functions as political
capital and in its role as the site of the sanctuary of a kingdom, was more than figuratively the trysting place where
divine and human society encrouched upon one another, as
is seen in Psalm 48:

> Great is Yahweh, one worthy of the highest praise,
>> In our sacred city.
> His holy mountain, exaltedly beautiful,
>> Is the joy of the whole earth.
> Mount Zion is the genuine Zaphon,
>> The city of the great King.
> Yahweh has, in her strongholds,[43]
>> Made himself known as the source of security.
>>> (Psalm 48:1-3, Heb. 2-4.)

From what we now know of the Ugaritic literature it is
clear that these verses derive from Canaanite culture and
mythology. Two words in particular merit attention. *Zaphon*
is the Hebrew word used to denote the compass direction
"north." Hebrew characteristically contains few abstractions,
and makes use of concrete words to denote the various direc-
tions. "West," for example, is indicated by the word for "sea,"
since the Mediterranean is in fact what lies to the west of
Palestine. "South" is indicated simply by the word *Negeb,*
the name of the region south of Palestine proper. Thus, it is
not surprising that the Ugaritic myths locate the home of
Aliyan Baal on Mount Zaphon, later known as Mount Cassius, in the northern part of Syria. Zaphon was the Olympus
of the western Semitic area, and the Hebrew word for the
compass direction "north" had, therefore, a concrete point
of reference. The overtones of this and a number of other
biblical passages could not be understood without reference
to this mythology.[44]

Psalm 48, therefore, proclaims that Mount Zion in Jerusalem *is* Zaphon, the place the myth describes as located on
a distant mountain. The Hebrew word by which Zaphon is
preceded in the psalm further emphasizes this. It is a word
that can denote "side," or "innermost parts." It is for this
reason that, by extension, the Revised Standard Version
translates it "far." To indicate that the psalm claims Jerusalem's sacred height as the closest approximation to the
home of the gods in man's society, we have rendered the
line: "Mount Zion is the genuine Zaphon." That such a claim
is being made is stressed again in the colon which declares
that Jerusalem is the "city of the great King," clearly locating Yahweh's function as King of the cosmos (or, as we have
seen, possibly his identification with the deity Melek) in the
imperial sway over the surrounding area held from Jerusalem by the Davidic dynasty. Yahweh, exercising his dominion from the sacred city, reduces the chaotic elements of
human society to order, even as he had already reduced the
cosmic powers:

> For behold, the kings assembled solemnly,
>   They came along together.
> They *too* saw, thus were they astonished,
>   They were terrified, fled in alarm.
> Trembling laid hold of them there,
>   Writhing, as of a woman in labor.
> As an east wind does it shatter them
>   Like ships of Tarshish.
>   (Psalm 48.4-7, Heb. 5-8.)[45]

As the "too" indicates, the "they" referring to the kings
of the nations cited in the second colon is emphatic. The
lines that follow make clear that the point of this emphasis
is to include those kings with Jerusalem's own people, and
to indicate that both have witnessed evidence of the mean-

ing of Jerusalem in the cosmic constitution. The reference
is clearly to some cultic enactment of the way in which Yahweh's cosmic sovereignty is related to Jerusalem's role in the
world:

> Just as we had heard, so now have we seen
>> In the city of Yahweh of hosts.[46]
> In our sacred city does Yahweh
>> Make it continually a reality.
> We have cultically portrayed thy *chesed*, O Yahweh,
>> In the precincts of thy temple.
> Like thy reputation, O Yahweh, so does cultic praise of thee
>> Keep the ends of the earth in order.
>
>> (Psalm 48:8-10a, Heb. 9-11a.)

The translation of the last two lines takes some liberties
with vocabulary and syntax. But context and cultural setting make clear the intent of what must be recognized as a
difficult text. We need not subscribe to any particular theory
of the cultic practice of Israel, or of the occasion on which
a psalm such as this was used, in order to appreciate that
Psalm 48 arose from a cultic setting rooted in the view of
reality common to the world in which Israel sang it. The
meaning of the cultic re-enactment of Yahweh's sovereignty
over the world, to which the "kings assembled solemnly" are
witnesses along with Israel, is that through it, as well as
through the political and military power that brought the
kings in obeisance to Jerusalem, the victory of the ruler of
the cosmos is made effective so as to "keep the ends of the
earth in order." Thus were the sacred and the secular one
in that ancient world, both sacrament and political sovereignty expressing one reality. Thus had Yahweh's *chesed*,
his covenant commitment, been translated into terms the
culture could accommodate. Thus could a procession through
the sacred city express the stability of the cosmos itself:

Victory fills up thy [Yahweh's] right hand,
  So let Mount Zion rejoice.
Let the daughters of Jerusalem [the subject cities] revel
  In thy just actions.
March around Zion, process around her;
  Count her towers!
Give your full attention to her ramparts,
  Pass between her citadels!
In such manner shall you recount in each generation
  That *this* One is God!
Our God is eternal;
  He shall lead us [to victory] over Death.
                              (Psalm 48:10b-14, Heb. 11b-15.)

These verses return to the theme central to the hymn proper
with reference to the sacred city. They emphasize, as Old
Testament hymns often do, that *"this* One," known in Israel's past, is the sum of all that has ever been claimed for
any other god. Indeed it is Yahweh who guarantees the
demise of that final adversary of Baal, Death.[47]

Psalm 48 in its praise of Yahweh emphasizes the enemy
Death, who seeks to stop the fertile flow of rain; Psalm 46
concentrates on watery chaos that is the other threat to
existence:

Yahweh for us is both a refuge and a strong [warrior],[48]
  As a help in adversities has he proved to be without equal.
Therefore would we not fear if the earth should sway
around,
  Or the mountains stagger into the heart of the seas.
Let the waters of the sea roar and foam,
  Let the mountains quake at its surging.
Yahweh of hosts is with us,
  Our source of security is the God of Jacob.
                              (Psalm 46:1-3, Heb. 2-4.)[49]

The song continues to relate the cosmic order of which the myth speaks to what we today call the political order of which Jerusalem was the focus (cf. Psalm 46:6-11, Hebrews 7-12). Once again, this was no merely secular affair, but the visible manifestation of a cosmic event, as is seen in two remarkable lines:

> [The] River: its streams make joyous the sacred city,
> The most sacred of the sanctuaries of Elyon.
> (Psalm 46:4, Heb. 5.)

The claim here is explicit: Jerusalem is the place where orderly contact between the great subterranean sea and the earth is made so that watery chaos is made to serve life and order. *Nahar*, "river," is one name of the god of watery chaos in Ugaritic mythology. The concrete reference is certainly to the spring of Gihon, the source of Jerusalem's water supply, but what is being said has to do also with the fundamental forces of the cosmos. The focus of Yahweh's control of them is located in Jerusalem as center of worship and as center of society's order.[50] Thus that city is the most sacred sanctuary, for in it the God who is highest of all (Elyon) has chosen to make his divine, life-giving power available to the human community.

Psalm 87 elaborates the theme of Jerusalem's centrality in the scheme of things, making explicit claim that its order is that in which the origin and existence of all the nations find their meaning:

> Of Zion it is said:
> "This one and that one originated there."
> For none other than Elyon stands behind her.
> Yahweh makes note, as he keeps track of the peoples,
> "This one originated there. . . ."
> (Psalm 87:5-6.)

No wonder she meant so much to Israel whose status had so
radically changed when Jerusalem became the "city of
David":

> How lovely is thy dwelling place,
>   O Yahweh of hosts!
> I long, indeed I faint, in my very being
>   For the courts of Yahweh.
>   (Psalm 84:1-2, Heb. 2-3.)

As do other songs, or allusions within songs, Psalm 84 suggests that pilgrimages were made to the city where cosmic
order made its contact with the world in which men live:

> How happy those men who locate their strength in thee,
>   Who have resolved to set out on pilgrimage.[51]
> Passing through Baka Valley [some arid place],
>   They transform it into a source of water;
>   Yea, the early rains clothe it in pools.
> As they move on, their ranks swell
>   Until the supreme God is seen in Zion.
>   (Psalm 84:5-7, Heb. 6-8.)

As an inspection of the commentaries will show, these
verses are very difficult to translate, and any attempt to do
so must be tentative. Their main point, however, is clear.
They picture the ultimate happiness, or blessing, as arising
from that with which man makes contact in Zion. In these
verses the resolution to make the pilgrimage leads to the pilgrimage itself, which apparently grows in size as others join
it. Moreover, the central verse seems to claim that even some
desert, arid part of the earth shares in the triumphant sovereignty of Yahweh, not only as it is watered by the early rain,
but as the passing of pilgrims through it bring it into a relation to Zion as the site of Yahweh's rule over the world.[52]

It is in connection with the role played by Jerusalem in

Israel's life as a part of the culture she entered when David became king that those psalms obviously created for liturgical purposes of various kinds are significant. Psalm 15, for example, is no abstract lesson in morality, but very likely a liturgical exchange between priest and pilgrim at the entrance to the sacred place:

PILGRIM: Yahweh! Who can be granted a place in thy tent?
         Who can keep tryst [with thee] on thy holy hill?
PRIEST: The one who conducts himself with integrity,
             And who does what is right,
             And whose thoughts are worthy.
SOMEONE VOUCHING FOR THE PILGRIM (?):
         He's not slandered with his tongue,
             Hasn't wronged his friend,
             And hasn't reproached his neighbor.
         Despised by him is the excommunicate,
             But the fearer of Yahweh he honors.
         Having given his word to a friend, he reneges not,
             His money he's not increased with usury,
                 Nor has he taken a bribe to impugn the innocent.
PRIEST: The one who does these things shall never be threatened by chaos.

Behind such a ritual exchange are texts recovered from ancient Egypt and Mesopotamia in which the purity required of him who enters a sacred area is described.[53] Psalm 15 is but one example of a number of Israel's songs the origins of which are associated with the sacred site at which contact was established between the human and the divine spheres.[54]

Psalm 24 begins with hymnic praise of Yahweh:

            Yahweh's is the earth and what fills it,
            The world and its inhabitants.

> For he laid its foundation over the seas,
> And on top of the rivers established it.
>   (Psalm 24:1-2.)

The last two lines use two names given the god of watery chaos in the Ugaritic myth, *Yam* ("sea") and *Nahar* ("river").

The psalm proceeds to another "form," a liturgy of entrance similar to that in Psalm 15:[55]

PETITIONERS: Who shall go up onto Yahweh's hill,
                 Or who shall stand in his holy place?
PRIEST: The one whose hands are clean, and whose heart is pure,
                 Who has not falsely taken a solemn oath,
                   And has not given his word deceitfully:
                 He will be offered blessing from Yahweh,
                   And vindication from his divine Saviour.
ADVOCATE (?): *This* generation are his disciples,
                 Seeking to stand where Jacob stood!
                       (Psalm 24:3-6.)

The dialogue is familiar to us from Psalm 15. The last verse, however, makes it clear that there is a company that would enter the sanctuary, who would be the heirs of Jacob as they engage in the cultic activity by which they are included in the divine action of which tradition speaks.[56] It is in this light that the final section of the psalm finds its meaning, for in the concluding verses we see what action it is by a present generation that includes them in the story of Yahweh's enthronement on Zion and in the heavenly palace of which Jerusalem's Temple is but the earthly counterpart.

> Lift up, O gates, your heads,
> And be lifted up, you everlasting doors
> That the glorious King may enter!
> Who is this glorious King?

> Yahweh, strong and mighty,
>> Yahweh mighty in battle!
> Lift up, O gates, your heads,
>> And be lifted up, you everlasting doors
>> That the glorious King may enter!
> Who really is this glorious King?
>> Yahweh of hosts!
>> He is this glorious King!
>>> (Psalm 24:7-10.)

Not only are the great portals of the Temple enjoined to open wide, but the real ruler of the cosmos, not just the company spoken of in the entrance liturgy, is proclaimed to be the one who is to enter through them. That act by which a present generation is enabled to stand as in Yahweh's active, victorious presence as did Jacob of old is one in which Yahweh himself enters his Temple. The language in which the entrance is spoken of provides a clue to what is involved. It was in connection with the ark, the sacred portable sanctuary of the tribal league, that Yahweh most characteristically functioned as a leader in war, as one mighty in battle, and that he was most often spoken of as "Yahweh of hosts." Thus it becomes clear that the background of Psalm 24 is some kind of re-enactment of the bringing of the ark to Jerusalem by David, of its deposit in the most holy place of the Temple by Solomon. Various interpretations of such a cultic occasion have been given.[57] The important point is that both the historical fact of the bringing of the ark to the Jerusalem Temple and the important role it played in the cult there (cf. below on Psalm 132) provided a connection between the Davidic era and the era by which it had been preceded. The ark had been the symbol around which the tribes had rallied, the sign of Yahweh's guidance of them through the vicissitudes that made them a people and gave them a land. When it rested in Jerusalem, that city had become the

league's center. Its presence there validated the claim of the
Davidic monarchy to be the successor of the older Israel.

From another point of view, the coming of the ark to Zion,
and the conquest of David's and Israel's enemies that was a
part of the coming, were the basis of the claim that Yahweh
was indeed chief of the gods. In other words, the presence
of the ark in Jerusalem was assurance to *Israel* that Zion was
Yahweh's valid sanctuary, while to David's formerly *Canaanite* subjects it was the sign that Yahweh was the ruling God.
It is for these reasons that the account of the fortunes of the
ark in I Samuel 4:1-7:2, the conclusion of which is now
found in II Samuel, chapters 6-7, has been called the *hieros
logos* of Davidic Jerusalem.[58]

THE KING AS EARTHLY VICEGERENT
OF THE SOVEREIGN GOD

It was not for reasons of mere political preference that the
older Israel eschewed any attempt to introduce kingship
into her life.[59] To do so, as she saw it, would be to abandon
the covenant *mythos* for the cosmic *mythos* over against
which she defined the meaning of things under Yahweh.
Yet when David had finally led her to victory against the
Philistines, had brought the ark to Jerusalem so that Israel
once more had a place at which to rally as Israel, Yahweh's
people did have a king. Moreover, they had in a real sense
been rescued from death as a people and brought to life
again in the course of events that had also led her to a king.
This precipitated a tension that accounts for revolts even in
David's time, for the separation of north from south after
Solomon's death, for the tumultuous history of the northern
kingdom when it claimed to be Israel without possessing the
outward symbols of that claim, and for the final claim of

Judah alone to be the true Israel. It also resulted in songs in which Israel, as did her neighbors, conceives her king as the one through whose conquest and orderly rule of all disorderly elements the order dramatized in the cosmic myth is realized in the human realm. This is demonstrated in Psalm 2, both the form and content of which seem to argue for its origin in an actual cultic occasion at which the king's vicegerency under Yahweh was affirmed:

[A chorus?]
Why have the nations got themselves so stirred up?
    Why, peoples are contriving a vain plot!
They stand only on their own, these earthly kings,
    And rulers take counsel only among themselves
        Against Yahweh and against his anointed one, [saying]:
"Let us tear off the bonds they've [Israel] put upon us,
    And let us fling their cords from us!"
[A single, "prophetic" spokesman?]
The one enthroned in the heavens is laughing,
    The true Lord is mocking them.
Now he is making a pronouncement concerning them,
    In his wrath and in his fury is terrifying them:
"But *I*, I have consecrated *my* king
    On Zion, my holy hill."
[The king himself speaks?]
Let me recount the details of Yahweh's decree:
He said to me, "You are my son,
    I today have begotten you.
Just say the word
    That I may ordain nations as your heritage,
        That I may make the ends of the earth your possession.
You shall shepherd them with a rod of iron!
    Like a piece of pottery shall you shatter them!"
[The chorus again?]
So now, O kings, act wisely;

Be warned, O *earthly* rulers.
Serve Yahweh with fear,
  With trembling kiss his feet!
Lest he be angry and you perish without warning,
  For his wrath can be kindled at any moment.
How happy are those who take refuge in him!

For fuller discussion of this psalm reference should be
made to the various commentaries.[60] It contains a number
of problems, many of which probably exist (or are believed
to exist) because its transmitters and expositors have not
understood its original setting. For our purposes it is sufficient to note how thoroughly it is rooted in what we have already discussed. The nations and their kings are the earthly
counterparts of the forces of disorder in the cosmos. The
bands by which their threat is controlled are those laid on
them by Israel. It is a mockery for the nations to resist, for
what has been done is the result of the cosmic supremacy
of Yahweh. In explicit terms Yahweh relates his ordering of
the universe to the action of the king he has anointed. The
king is called his son, and the extension of Yahweh's rule
throughout the world is at the king's disposal—"Just say the
word!" The clear meaning of the psalm is located in the conceptions of kingship held in the ancient Near East. Though
later interpreted as referring to a heaven-sent eschatological
Messiah (the word is the same as that for "anointed one" in
the psalm), the poem is evidence of the extent to which
David and his successors were thought of, in some circles at
least, in the terms of the culture into which David brought
Israel.

In terms relating Davidic monarchy more specifically to
the pre-Israelite traditions of Jerusalem, Psalm 110 acclaims
David and his successors as the earthly vicegerents of the
ruler of the cosmos:

An oracle of Yahweh concerning my lord:
"Be seated at my right hand
  Until I make your enemies
  The stool for your feet."
Yahweh is stretching out your mighty scepter;
  From Zion exercise dominion over your enemies. . . .
Yahweh has sworn, and will not change his mind:
  "You are a priest forever
  After the order of Melchizedek."

(Psalm 110:1-2, 4.)

This song is notable for its designation of the Davidic king as the successor of Melchizedek, apparently either the pre-Israelite king in Jerusalem or the founder of the pre-Israelite dynasty there (cf. Genesis 14:18). It is notable also for the emphasis it lays on the house of David as the permanent representative on earth of Yahweh as ruler of the cosmos. It is through David and his successors, reigning from Jerusalem, that the divine order extends into human society.

Despite the fact that it arises from originally non-Israelite circles and is even contrary to the point of view of pre-Davidic Israel, what finds expression in Psalm 110 (and in Psalm 2) is central to biblical theology. There is a most vivid expression of that confidence in a covenant of promise between Yahweh and David by which so much of the literature of the Old Testament is informed. There is a resemblance to II Samuel, chapter 7, with its account of how Yahweh blessed the Davidic dynasty through the word of the prophet Nathan. The great epic of the Yahwist, the formative stratum of the Old Testament narrative, has as its primary motif the same theme of promise and fulfillment implied in Psalms 2 and 110. It is precisely because Yahweh, in the events following the Philistine advance into Palestine by which Israel was raised from disaster and made part of ancient Near Eastern culture under David, had proved himself ruler of the cosmos that Israel's original *mythos* could be espoused as the source of meaning for all of life.[61] St. Paul's appeal beyond the covenant of Moses to the covenant of promise with Abraham was not only early Christian polemic, although it certainly was that; it was an accurate rendering of the theology of the Yahwist. And that theology was possible precisely because the Israelites were satisfied that Yahweh was capable of the action celebrated in songs such as Psalms 2 and 110.[62] Certainly the *mythos* underlying such songs was different from that of premonarchical Israel and the *mythos* of the Mosaic covenant. But once the old order was gone and Israel was forced to confront the cosmic order, of which the Mesopotamian and Egyptian and Canaanite myths spoke, either Yahweh's day had passed or he became God also in terms foreign to earlier Israel. That he was God indeed in the cosmic order, though it brought tensions, was what the Israelites proclaimed who sang of their king and of Yahweh his Father in Psalms 2 and 110.

What is expressed in the "royal psalms" is, furthermore, central to the hope so fundamental to biblical theology. The promise and fulfillment expressed by monarchical Israel's joy in the Davidic dynasty were the source of the ultimate biblical hope. That hope finds its most characteristic expression in *messianic* terms. "Messianic" is an adjective originating in the term applied to the Davidic king in Psalm 2 and elsewhere: "Messiah" or "Anointed One." Belief that the final outcome of history and of the cosmos would be good beyond imagination was rooted in that experience originally vouchsafed to Israel in the concrete, noneschatological Messiah who was her king. Through David she had been raised from disastrous oblivion to a position of consequence in the world. Through David and his successors and the order they established Israel was assured that good and not evil, Yahweh and not chaos, prevailed in the cosmos. So David came to be held as a symbol of the ultimate and final state of things—even in the trying and terrible times of the exilic and postexilic agonies. And when Christians express their faith in Jesus of Nazareth by acclaiming him "Christ" (the Greek equivalent of "Messiah"), they also appropriate pagan motifs found in Psalms 2 and 110.[63]

The songs of the Old Testament include many in which the king figures prominently. His weddings as well as his wars are their subjects.[64] We must be content to mention only one more, important for its connection of kingship with Israel's premonarchical traditions. Psalm 132 clearly associates Yahweh's election of David's dynasty as his anointed ones with David's finding of a home for the ark:

> Remember, O Yahweh, in David's favor
>   All that he went through:
> Namely how he took an oath to Yahweh,
>   Made a vow to the Mighty One of Jacob.
> [David said], "I swear not to enter my family's tent,
>   I swear not to get into my own bed,
> I swear not to allow sleep for my eyes,
>   Slumber for my eyelids,
> Until I find a place for Yahweh,
>   A sanctuary for the Mighty One of Jacob."
>   (Psalm 132:1-5.)

This account of David's vow concerning a sanctuary for Yahweh is followed by two verses in which reference is made to the ark as it languished on the borders of the territory of the Philistines until David and his men rescued it. The "it" in these verses refers to the ark.[65]

> Lo, we heard of it at Ephrathah,
>   We found it in the fields of Jaar.
> [We said,] "Let us bring it to his sanctuary,
>   Let us fall prostrate at his footstool."
>   (Psalm 132:6-7.)

The song is not only a narration of past events but, as in
Psalm 24, the accompaniment of ritual action is indicated
by these verses of supplication to Yahweh:

> Be situated now, O Yahweh, at thy resting place,
> > Thou and thy mighty ark.
> Let thy priests be robed in righteousness,
> > Let thy covenant subjects shout loudly;
> For the sake of David thy servant,
> > Never take from us thine anointed one.
>
> > > > (Psalm 132:8-10.)

As in Psalm 2, there follows a section, probably spoken
by a prophetic figure in response to the preceding petition,
in which Yahweh speaks in an oracle of his election of the
Davidic dynasty:

> Yahweh has taken an oath,
> > From faithfulness he never turns back:
> "[Kings] from the fruit of your body
> > Will I place on the throne after you.
> If your sons will observe my covenant
> > And my testimonies which I shall teach them,
> Their sons also forever
> > Shall sit on the throne after you.
>
> > > > (Psalm 132:11-12.)

The psalm then goes on to present an oracle in which
Yahweh proclaims his choice of Jerusalem as his dwelling
place on earth. The significance of Psalm 132, whatever may
have been the specific nature of the occasion on which it
was used liturgically,[66] is that it relates all that the Davidic
line meant in the life of monarchical Israel to what Israel
had been earlier. It associates the claim of the Davidic dynasty to primacy in Israel with David's rescue of Yahweh's
ark from the humiliation and oblivion that resulted from the
Philistine war. It was through David that Yahweh reasserted
himself as a divine power. It was through David, and his son

Solomon, that, within the ark which symbolized his presence, Yahweh had gained a "place." This corresponds with an element in both the Babylonian and the Ugaritic versions of the cosmic myth: when a god demonstrated his ascendancy in the cosmos, a house befitting his position had to be provided.[67] That Yahweh reigned over the cosmos from a house of which the sanctuary in Jerusalem was the earthly counterpart was inseparably connected with David.

David, therefore, and that David present in each generation in the heir of the original anointed one, was the earthly vicegerent of the heavenly king, none other than the Yahweh of the ancient Israelite covenant federation. Thus history had not only brought a radically different polity to Israel, but there was also a continuity between kingdom and covenant federation, between the era of David and the era of Moses. Some of the successors of David blurred that continuity by smothering the older *mythos* under Canaanite culture; other reactionary elements in Israel tended to blur the same continuity by implying that significant history ended with Samuel. How to be affirmative about new cultural situations without sacrificing revelations and standards of the past, or how to preserve the past without denying significance to the present is no new dilemma. For Israel the solution was the house of David.

Psalm 132 also relates the Davidic era to the Mosaic by setting a condition upon Yahweh's designation of the dynasty of David as his vicegerent: a descendant of David will occupy the throne forever *if*—

> *If* your sons will observe my covenant
> And keep my testimonies which I shall teach them. . . .
> (Psalm 132:12.)

Verse 9 of Psalm 132 calls those who celebrate the monarchy, and all that it and its sanctuary mean, *chasidim*, "covenant subjects." The psalm thus stresses the ambiguity of what happened under David. On the one hand, Yahweh *as cosmic ruler designated the Davidic dynasty as his kingly vicegerents*. On the other hand, however, *it is the Yahweh of the Mosaic covenant who has done this*. Kingship in Israel, though we cannot discuss it without thoroughgoing reference to the culture in which it was rooted, was also bound up with a cosmic sovereign the nature of whose character and demands was a product of what Israel had learned and become in the premonarchical period. The heirs of David were to "keep my testimonies which I *shall* teach them." That seems to refer to future events in which it will be necessary for successors to Moses to speak words by which the covenant will be updated, and by whom even kings will be called to account. Kingship in Israel was rooted in ancient Near Eastern culture, but what shot up from the roots was ever formed by the nature of the God who had instituted it. When Yahweh sent a prophetic spokesman, king as well as commoner had to listen. And even the story of David, the founder of the dynasty, was not in Israel the apotheosis characteristic of stories of monarchs elsewhere. The remarkable narrative in II Samuel, chapters 9-20, is sufficient evidence of that. Israel's king, the Yahwistic faith would not let him forget, was a man like other men.[68] Thus did forms and motifs, taken over by Israel from the culture into which she came in David's time, come to be affected by the content they were compelled to carry when Yahweh appeared as ruler of the cosmos.

ISRAEL'S MODIFICATION OF HYMNIC MOTIFS

When Israel in fact found herself a participant in the order to which the mythological religion of the ancient Near East addressed itself, she used the language and forms of that religion to proclaim that Yahweh was the supreme God.

Yet the assertion that *Yahweh* was supreme God involved a *mythos* quite different from the one that provided the new language and forms. If the character of that earlier *mythos* was not to be forgotten, Yahweh simply becoming another name for the head of a mythical pantheon, the motifs and literary forms of the cosmic myth had inevitably to be affected by the use to which they were put in Israel. If the Yahweh of the Exodus and the Mosaic covenant was indeed the God responsible for the existence of the Davidic covenant, then his unique sovereignty would prevail even in the terms of another culture. The idiom through which ancient Near Eastern culture spoke of the meaning of things was altered, as Israel used it to claim for Yahweh sovereignty over the cosmos. We suggest three ways in which Israel's songs give evidence of how this took place.

1. *Yahweh and the divine assembly.* Many passages in the Old Testament presuppose the theology prevalent in the ancient Near East. We have seen that the hymns often assert Yahweh's sovereignty by asserting his supremacy among the gods. An assembly of divine beings in the heavens, responsible for the forces and phenomena of the universe and held in control by Yahweh as ruler, is presupposed elsewhere. It is found in the account by the prophet Micaiah of how he arrived at his prophecy (I Kings, chapter 22; cf. verses 19-23). It is found in the prophetic inaugural visions of Isaiah, chapters 6 and 40. It figures in the narrative introduction to the Book of Job (cf. 1:6 and 2:1). It is what explains the plural pronoun in the opening chapters of Genesis: "Let *us* make man in *our* image" (1:26); "The man has become like *one of us*" (3:22).[69] A song of ancient Israel in which this theology is assumed, but significantly modified, is Psalm 82:

Yahweh[70] has taken his place in the divine assembly,
  In the midst of the gods does he pronounce judgment:

"How long will you continue to rule unrighteously,
   Maintaining the fortunes of the wicked?
Do what is just for the invalid and the orphan,
   Protect the rights of the downtrodden and the poor.
Rescue the invalid and the needy,
   From the power of the wicked provide relief.
For both alike lack knowledge and understanding,
   Wandering aimlessly in darkness,
      So that the very foundations of the earth are insecure.
I gave you your status as gods,
   Made each of you a son of the Most High.
But now I sentence you to human mortality,
   And to fall like any prince."   (Psalm 82:1-7.)

What is described is a dramatic scene of cosmic significance. Yahweh is pronouncing a sentence by which the divine members of the heavenly assembly are stripped of their
divinity. It is evident that the mythological situation, as in
those found in non-Israelite literature, accounts for what has
happened in human society by postulating a significant related occurrence in the divine society.[71] This song celebrates
the successful conquests of David by which, according to
the point of view of that world, Yahweh had achieved ascendancy over the gods of the conquered places. Two remarkable points are also made.

One, the *reason* for the downfall of the other gods is that
they have not made it clear in the societies over which they
bore rule that justice and righteousness are fundamental to
the cosmos. Yahweh, who made that clear when Israel came
out of Egypt, is still acting to make it clear. The arbitrariness
by which the activity of the gods has been characterized
(manifest in the reading of any pagan myth) has resulted in
purposeless existence for man, and so in no righteous standards for his behavior. Thus it is the God of the Mosaic cove-

nant who is still at work in David, bringing to the cosmos the kind of order he brought of old to *Habiru* Israel.

Two, precisely that mythology by which Yahweh could be acclaimed as ruler of the whole cosmos and not just the God of a people on its fringes provides the terms in which the very reality of the claim of the other gods to divinity is challenged. There is something here that outruns a merely logical argument for monotheism. Indeed that term should be left out of the discussion, for it was not that Israel reasoned her way to the theory that there could be only one God; it was that she continued, even when her songs employed the terms of the culture of which she became a part, to insist that she was acquainted in Yahweh with the God whose "godness" really mattered, whose "godness" was the criterion by which the term "god" found its meaning.[72] What was characteristic of Israel's acclamation was not some logically impeccable theology, for she used whatever terms were available to her, but a *dynamic* through which the world was lifted from darkness and insecurity as Yahweh made things right. Psalm 82 in response to the divine pronouncement of sentence on the gods concludes:

> Arise, O Yahweh, rule the earth,
> Yea *thou* art taking possession of all the nations!
> (Psalm 82:8.)[73]

This verse summarizes the double point we have sought to make all along. On the one hand, it was the thorough appropriation of the motifs of the *cosmic myth* that made it possible for Israel to acclaim Yahweh as universal sovereign whose reign touched everything. On the other hand, it was the retention of the basic motif of the *covenant mythos* that afforded a knowledge of Yahweh and his nature. There was tension between the two, but this song demonstrates that the

tension could be creative and that it must be assessed posi-
tively if Old Testament faith is to be understood.

2. *The cosmic ruler's demand on his people.* Discussing the
hymns in which Yahweh is, in terms borrowed from ancient
Near Eastern culture, acclaimed as ruler of the cosmos, some
verses of Psalm 95 have been cited. A reading of that song
in its entirety will permit further appreciation of the ways
the forms of that culture were modified by covenant motifs:

> Come! Let us sing to Yahweh,
>> Let us make a joyful noise to the rock of our salvation!
> Let us come into his presence with thanksgiving,
>> With songs of praise let us make a joyful noise to him!
> For a great God is Yahweh,
>> And King supreme over all the gods:
> In whose hand are the depths of the earth,
>> And the peaks of the mountains are his too;
> To whom belongs the sea—*he* reduced it to order,
>> And the dry land—*his* hands shaped it.
> Come! Let us worship and fall down,
>> Let us kneel before Yahweh our maker.
> For *he* is our God,
>> And we are the people of his pasture,
>>> The sheep whom he guides.   (Psalm 95:1-7a.)

Thus far the psalm is a hymn, a song in which the divinity
of a god is proclaimed and extolled, the celebration of Yahweh's control over the watery forces of chaos by which life
is enabled to go on. Suddenly a different motif is introduced,
and we find ourselves in the world discussed in the first chapter of this book, brought to the same moment of decision
central to the covenant motif:

> *Today!* If you would heed his voice,
>> Harden not your hearts as at Meribah,
>>> As on that day at Massah in the wilderness.
> Then did your fathers try me,

> Test me, though they had seen me in action.
> Forty years did I loathe that generation,
>> Saying, "They are a people whose understanding is con-
>> fused,
>>> For *they*, they don't know my ways."
> So I took an oath in my anger
> That they should not enter the homeland I'd prepared.
>> (Psalm 95:7b-11.)

It is clear that, though he is the sovereign of the universe
to whom hymnic praise is due, Yahweh remains the covenant overlord by whom his people are called to account responsibly for the life they live as men. It is also clear that
the *mythos* of the ancient covenant community has been
projected into the center of the cosmic power structure. That
is something we cannot appreciate without some knowledge
of the role occupied by man in the ancient Near Eastern
world view. Man's purpose in the scheme of things, as the
cosmic myth had it, was to perform the menial, mundane
work unworthy of the gods. Man's life was essentially meaningless, significant activity in the cosmos being located
wholly in the realm of the gods. In the era inaugurated for
Israel by the successes of David, however, Yahweh came to
reign in the divine realm and kept the gods in order, and
man's role was radically altered. That the God of hymnic
praise is also one who honors covenant (as Psalm 95 insists)
means that human life has been invested with a dignity
totally absent under other supreme gods. The *mythos* of an
outcaste *Habiru* people has been proved, by the accession of
Yahweh to supremacy over the gods, to be the *mythos* by
which man's significance in the cosmos is assured. It is no
longer a matter of a deity of sufficient power to guarantee
the freedom and dignity of a renegade people over against
the arbitrary order of the cosmos. That deity has made himself known as the ruler of the cosmos.

Psalm 95 says that what the old Israel had clung to in opposition to the cultural and political and social order is not
the ideology of rebels but the truth about the nature of
things. To put it in the idiom of Israel's songs, Psalm 82 has
proclaimed that Yahweh, now the supreme God, has tried
the divine beings who were the significant actors in the
cosmic drama and, finding them failures by his standards,
has deposed them. Psalm 95, having made it clear that Yahweh is the cosmic ruler worthy of hymnic praise, asserts that
he has now addressed his demand to men.[74] Thus the whole
human enterprise, not just the life of Israel, takes on new
meaning.

3. *The extension of hymnic praise into narrative.* The
classic hymn form begins with an imperative verb, calling
a group (originally probably the divine assembly) to praise
the supreme God. The body of the hymn recounts what
entitles the god to such praise, alluding to the mythical
narrative in which he vanquished the adversaries of order
and life and fertility in the universe. Hymns, particularly
those in which sacred city and divinely appointed king are
celebrated, allude often to the upheavals of nations, as
manifestations of the cosmic forces of disorder, but the fundamental issues are always located in the realm of the gods.
This explains, of course, the low position given man in the
epic *Enuma elish*.

What took place in Psalm 82 and in Psalm 95 (and it is
not implied that things developed in any neat chronological
order) was that the cosmic issue had to be located more
and more in the drama in which man was an actor. So it is
that hymns quoted earlier in this chapter show a tendency,
while using all the imagery of cosmic myth, to append in
their descriptions of Yahweh's power over the universe the
actions for which men are responsible and the events in
which they have had a part. Psalm 33, for example, after

allusions to the cosmic battle, invests human deeds with significance:

> From heaven does Yahweh look down,
>> He sees every mortal man.
> From his royal seat he looks out
>> Over all the inhabitants of the earth.
> He's the one who formed the minds of them all,
>> Who discerns their every deed.
>>> (Psalm 33:13-15.)

Psalm 97, an enthronement song proclaiming Yahweh's cosmic reign, moves from imagery used of Baal in the Ugaritic myth to a description of his concern for mortals:

> Yahweh is one who loves those who hate evil,
>> One who guards the lives of his covenant subjects;
>> From the power of the wicked does he deliver them.
>>> (Psalm 97:10.)

There came into being in Israel extended hymns in which the bulk of the description of why Yahweh is entitled to honor as the supreme God is located precisely in the course of historical events in which Israel had come to know him. Psalms 135 and 136 are examples. This development and modification reaches its fulfillment in that long type of psalm classified by Gunkel as "legend." Psalms 78, 105, and 106 are so classified. They are characterized by an extended catalogue of the ways Yahweh's power and goodness are to be seen in the history lying behind his people, alluding to events narrated in the books at the beginning of the Old Testament. They should not, however, be looked upon as a special category of song. They are, so to speak, hymns that got out of hand. They are to be explained in terms of Israel's transferral of the location of the drama in which the issues of existence are located from the realm of the gods to the stage on which human history takes place. They, and the development of the hymn form in Israel of which they are the end product, exemplify something basic to the biblical point of view.[75]

That which the old tribal league had sturdily resisted came to be employed to bear witness to what the tribal league believed: Yahweh rescues men from bondage to the arbitrary cosmic powers and the human kings who are their agents. The appropriation of the cosmic myth by Israel when she entered the culture for which that myth was a cosmic explanation made it possible to affirm the faith of the tribal league more radically than could originally have been imagined. No longer were Yahweh and his work defined against the established order, for now Yahweh was responsible for cosmic order, so the hymns could properly be sung to him, and his city and his king replace their predecessors. *But* Yahweh's character and record were such that the account of that order had to be drastically revised. Psalms 82 and 95 insist that Yahweh has not only controlled the gods but deposed them, and assigned their significance and role to men. The extended hymns, such as Psalms 135, 136, 105, and 106, while they develop in the framework of his establishment of order in the physical cosmos, insist that the living drama of Yahweh's reign takes place in history where the generations of men beginning with Israel reach out to include all the nations of the earth.

Thus examining Israel's songs and their motifs, Israelite and pagan, we encounter the colossal meaning of the Bible's assertion that man bears the image of God. What it means arises not from metaphysical speculation. Its meaning is functional and dramatic. "Let us make man in our own image, after our likeness; and let them have dominion over the fish of the sea, and over the birds of the air, and over the cattle, and over all the earth" (Genesis 1:26) means, in terms of its cultural setting, nothing other than that what the cosmic myth attributed to the gods has been invested by the supreme God in man. The role attributed by ancient Near Eastern *mythos* to the gods is the role in which the genuine supreme God, Yahweh, has cast man. This is the wonder of the hymn known to us as Psalm 8:

> When I look at the heavens,
>   The product of thy fingers,
> The moon and the stars
>   Which thou hast set in place,
> How is it that thou payest such regard to man,
>   That thou takest mortal man so seriously?
> For thou didst withhold from him only thy supreme divinity,
>   With glory and honor didst crown him.
> Thou dost put him in charge of the products of thine hands,
>   Everything hast thou set under his feet.
>
> (Psalm 8:3-6, Heb. 4-7.)

This touches the source of what we reduce to a pale abstraction by speaking of monotheism, the source of freedom from superstitious bondage to natural objects and forces, the source even of the practical and theoretical atheism that flourish only on soil touched profoundly by the biblical point of view. For here the significance of man is affirmed not in terms of the tragic *hubris* that challenges uncaring or inimical Fate; here the significance of man is affirmed as the work of that supreme God whose power over other gods is such that they are destroyed for their inadequacy, and their role and function assigned to men. What we call monotheism and humanism (not contrary to biblical faith) spring from the same root.

Thus, in Genesis, chapters 1-11, the cosmic myth is incorporated into the epic produced out of Israel's long experience and reflection, and its very nature is transformed. For Israel's neighbors the myth of how the cosmos had come

into being out of the struggle among the gods *was* the whole
story. It was, for them, the account of what was ever hap-
pening as the round of the seasons went on year by year.
So they recounted it year by year, using it to explain their
ritual attempts to placate the gods of whom it spoke and
identify their life with the order it described. The issue was
the stability or instability of the cosmos, the physical universe, and to that the issues of social and political and historical existence were related secondarily. Israel took what
was the whole story for others and, the characters in it having been thoroughly vanquished (cf. Psalm 82), made it
but the preface to the *real* story. Genesis, chapters 1-11, is
saying this may be how things got started but the real issues
are not located there. What others worry about and address
their worship to year by year is settled, and the locus of
the cosmic drama has moved on. The words with which the
Yahwist closes his collection of material from the myths
are an indictment of the irrelevance of pagan religion:

And Yahweh said to himself, "Never again will I curse the
earth because of man. Yes, man's propensity for evil is there from
his youth, but I will never again destroy everything living as I
have done. As day succeeds day in the earth, seedtime and harvest, cold and heat, summer and winter, day and night shall not
cease.   (Genesis 8:21-22.)

The covenant with Noah (Genesis 9:1-17) is the Priestly
source's more elaborate statement of the same thing.[76]

Thus did Israel's epic concentrate in a more organized and
considered way than her songs on the drama that had begun to unfold from the time of her obscure origins, through
the revelatory event of the Exodus and the knowledge of
the nature of Yahweh's rule in the covenant community, to
the Davidic empire in which Yahweh had asserted his cosmic significance. In that historical drama the movement

from chaos to order, from meaninglessness to meaning, of which the myths had spoken was confirmed. And it continued to go on, the classical prophets perceived, in the upheavals bringing about the collapse of the Davidic era, as the nations of the world were brought into it. The decisions and actions of men, their responses and responsibility, were as ultimately significant as those of Apsu and Tiamat, of Yam and Mot, had once been considered to be. And, in this light, the meaning of the New Testament is that, through the faithfulness of a man unto death, the drama moved outward from Near Eastern soil ultimately through European civilization to include the world. Even the extreme secularism of modern man is related in a real way to the songs of a community holding that Yahweh had overthrown the gods and located the ultimate issues in the drama in which men were involved.[77]

3 God as Saviour: Lament and Deliverance

The sacred songs of the peoples of the ancient Near East include, as we have seen, a category of song in which the gods, whose actions and conflicts are determinative of what transpires in the cosmos, are acclaimed for their divinity and for the victories by which order is assured on earth. That class of songs is dominated by one basic motif: the celebration of the power and sovereignty of the god by whom order is maintained among the gods and, thereby, in the cosmos as a whole. In a word, the song is a cry of praise *of* the god. The second category of sacred song is, in contrast, a cry of need *to* the god. The form into which these songs are cast is that of the lament, man's invocation of the gods in his need and his distress. In the lament, and the songs related to or derived from it, expression is given to man's response to the effects upon him of those forces at work in the cosmos.

In the culture surrounding Israel the myth embodying the struggle between chaos and order was no mere description of what had happened "once upon a time," but a description of a drama ever taking place. Chaos and death did, every year, manage to reassert themselves in the spring floods or the summer drought. What was going on as man stood by, capable only of waiting and watching, was a gigantic struggle of which the human eye saw but a fraction. The whole story could be told only in the myth.

118

The basic issues for that culture, as it came to Israel, did not lie in the area in which the decisions and actions of man himself had an effect. They lay in what decisions were taken, what acts were performed, what was done—and what was left undone—among and by the divine beings who determined all that happened in the universe. The fact of man's finitude precluded his ability to cope with the forces by which his existence was affected. His illnesses, his misfortunes, the humiliations he might endure were immediately related to things in that unseen world of which the myth spoke. Thus a substantial portion of sacred poetry in the ancient Near East consisted of laments in which man cried out to the gods for succor in his need, and laments certainly are by far more numerous in Israel's psalter than the other types of songs. The reason for this, however, should not be located solely in the self-centeredness of man.

What happened when illness struck, when a person was unjustly accused of wrong or suffered social humiliation, when an invading army or insurrection threatened the order of a kingdom, had cosmic significance. The forces by which it had been brought about were not autonomous. They were, in one way or another, related to those evil and rebellious beings of whose opposition to the powers of well-being and stability the myth spoke. The reaction of the man or the community involved was not, therefore, rational diagnosis through which autonomous causes were sought. It was immediate invocation of the powers whose sovereignty— and reputation—were involved. It was immediate effort to excite the sympathy of the divine sources of succor who might be of help—if not because they were merciful, at least because what had befallen an individual or a community represented a challenge to the divine sovereignty and cosmic order by some more than human power. The reaction also involved imprecation of the evil powers, human or more than human, responsible for the misfortune. There was questioning of the forces of order about their responsibility and their stake in the larger or smaller infraction of cosmic order taking place. The laments of the ancient Near East, and so the laments of the Old Testament, have to be understood as more than petitions of individuals. Their origin is cultic and liturgical rather than individual, and they are rooted in the same sacral world view which underlies the hymns and the songs of praise related to them.[1]

THE FORM AND CONTENT OF THE LAMENT

Characteristic of the lament is an invocation the essence of which is a crying out of the name of the god involved. The most primitive and essential lament is the cry in distress, "My God!" (cf. Psalm 22:1). Often biblical laments begin simply with "Yahweh!" (cf. Psalms 3:1; 6:1; 7:1; etc.). In the Babylonian laments the invocation was often expanded into a hymnic recitation of the attributes and exploits of the god being asked for succor. In the prayer to the goddess Ishtar, for example, some forty lines of praise precede the lament proper. Biblical laments contain no such lengthy hymnic introductions, usually confining their invocations to a crying out of Yahweh's name, frequently specifically identifying him as "my God" (cf. 7:1; 88:1), and as the one in whom the lamenter "takes refuge" (cf. 7:1; 57:1; 71:1). Given the world from which these laments arose, the cry "my God" is more than an aboriginal exclamation. It is a specific designation of the god that the lamenter turns to for concrete action against the forces of evil and chaos. It is an identification of the god in whom the suppliant places his faith.

In the lament proper, voice is given, usually in a general

and stylized way, to the distress in which the suppliant finds himself. The focus shifts among three objects of attention: the lamenter himself and his suffering; the persons or beings held responsible for the low estate to which he has come; and the god being addressed who is directly or indirectly accused of not having properly cared for the suppliant.[2]

The Plight of the Suppliant

Descriptions of the unhappy condition of the lamenter can be lengthy and heart-rendering indeed. Following are lines from a lament addressed to Ishtar, a Mesopotamian goddess of war:[3]

I toss about like flood-water, which an evil wind makes violent.
My heart is flying; it keeps fluttering like a bird of heaven.
I mourn like a dove night and day.
I am beaten down, and so I weep bitterly.
With "Oh" and "Alas" my spirit is distressed. . . .
. . . Sickness, headache, loss and destruction are provided for me;
So are fixed upon me terror, disdain, and fullness of wrath,
Anger, choler, and indignation of gods and men.
I have to expect, O my Lady, judgment of confusion and violence.
Death and trouble are bringing me to an end.
Silent is my chapel; silent is my holy place;
Over my house, my gate, and my fields silence is poured out.
As for my god, his face is turned to the sanctuary of another.
My family is scattered; my roof is broken up.

(Lines 62-66, 69-78.)

This description of distress moves from spiritual and mental confusion to physical debility to a suggestion that the suppliant is as good as dead, deserted by the god to whom he customarily turns, having lost possessions and even family. Speculation about what specific circumstances prompted this lament would be fruitless. In the first place, the lament is probably stylized so as to be usable on more than one occasion by more than one person. In the second place, whatever specific distress the suppliant may lament, his point is that the forces of chaos afflicting him are an incipient threat to cosmic order itself. The whole purpose of this recital is to call attention to the "I" who laments so that Ishtar will be moved by pity, or by concern for the threat to order involved, to take appropriate action. The first-person-singular pronoun occurs no less than nineteen times in the above fourteen lines, and this is typical of laments. The point involved is not a specific illness or condition of the suppliant, but a supplication that the order promised and proclaimed in the cosmic myth be extended by *his* god to *him* in *his* need.

Many laments of the Old Testament concentrate on a similar supplication. Psalm 102, according to the rubric in the Hebrew Bible, is "A prayer to be used by a sufferer when he is languishing and would pour out his lament before Yahweh." Like the prayer to Ishtar, it focuses upon the troubles of a sufferer, liberally employing the first-person pronoun:

> For my days go up in smoke,
>   And my bones are aglow like a furnace.
> Like blighted grass my heart is dried up,
>   For I neglect eating my food.
> I am weary with loud groaning,
>   My flesh sticks to my bones.
> I look like a desert buzzard,
>   Have turned into an owl in a deserted ruin.

Lying awake, I've turned into a bird,
  All alone on the housetop.

(Psalm 102:3-7, Heb. 4-8.)

These verses seek to draw Yahweh's attention to physical suffering (fever seems to be what is implied), but biblical laments, as in the prayer to Ishtar, also insist that in the distress of a sufferer death and chaos are at work in opposition to Yahweh's creative sovereignty over the cosmos. This is apparent in Psalm 88, a relentless lament full of allusions to Ugaritic mythology:

Yahweh! My saving God!
  By day I cry out,
    At night I'm in thy presence.[4]
  My prayer comes before thee,
  Incline thine ear to my cry.

(Psalm 88:1-2, Heb. 2-3.)

This is an excellent example of the short invocation characteristic of biblical laments. Then there follows a description of the state in which the suppliant finds himself:

For loaded with troubles is my being,
  And my vitality is as good as in Sheol.
I am reckoned as one on his way to the Pit,
  I've become as a man with no strength.
In the guest house of the underworld was I like them,[5]
  Those slain who lie in the grave,
Whom thou hast no more in mind,
  For they are outside thy power.

(Psalm 88:3-5, Heb. 4-6.)

This lament is not concerned with terminal death as such, for it assumes that all die, that the shadow left due to their having existed remains in the amorphous region of Sheol (or "the Pit"), and that that region—though presumably contained so that it cannot encroach on the "land of the living"—is off bounds to Yahweh's sovereignty over the cos-

mos.[6] The point is rather that in the suffering, presumably
physical, undergone by the lamenter death is encroaching
on the area over which Yahweh is presumed to wield power.
The suppliant draws attention to his plight in striking figures
by which he seeks to show Yahweh how, in his case, the
powers of darkness have usurped authority in the cosmos.
Such laments have to do with the issues posed in the cosmic
myth, not with the death that inevitably overtakes an individual when his life has run its course, as is seen in Psalm
102:

> Broken while still in mid-course is my strength,
>   Shortened are my days.
> I say, "O my God,
>   Remove me not in the midst of my days,
>   Thou whose years transcend the generations of men!"
>   (Psalm 102:23-24, Heb. 24-25.)

The essence of such laments is manifest in the invocation
to Psalm 69, especially in light of the cosmic myth we discovered underlying the hymns:

> Save me, Yahweh![7]
>   For the waters have threatened my existence!
> I have sunk in the mire of the abyss,
>   And there is no foothold.
> I am gone in the water's depths,
>   And the currents sweep over me.
>   (Psalm 69:1-2, Heb. 2-3.)

Such laments, and others, are characterized by concen-
tration upon suffering in terms of cosmic order though they
seem to imply specific illness and physical pain. In other
laments the integrity and reputation of the suppliant is al-
leged to have been challenged in such a way as to threaten
his standing in the social order through which he participates
in the larger order of the cosmos.[8] He protests his innocence,

calling upon Yahweh to be the judge by whom he is vindicated:

> Hear, Yahweh, a righteous cause; pay heed to my cry!
>   Heed my prayer which is on lips that do not deceive!
> From thy presence shall judgment on me come,
>   Thine eyes shall discern what is right.
> Having tried my heart, having tried me by night,
>   Having tested me, thou shalt not find me guilty of evil.
>   (Psalm 17:1-3.)

The Babylonian laments might seem to indicate that such
outcries merely demonstrate why the suppliant should be
delivered from his suffering. The prayer of Ishtar, for example, asks for forgiveness in such a way as to imply that
righteousness is a condition of divine intervention:

> To thee have I prayed; forgive my debt.
> Forgive my sin, my iniquity, my shameful deeds, and my
> offence.
> Overlook my shameful deeds; accept my prayer;
> Loosen my fetters; secure my deliverance;
> Guide my steps aright; radiantly like a hero let me enter
> the streets with the living.   (Lines 80-85.)[9]

The Wickedness of the "Enemies"

The biblical laments, however, once the suppliant protests his innocence, go on to allude to accusers, and convey
the impression that they are essentially appeals for vindication from false charges of wrongdoing. Psalm 17 expresses it:

> Pity have they shut out of their hearts,
>   With their mouths have they spoken arrogantly.
> They've tracked me down, now have surrounded me,
>   Have made it their avowed purpose to cast me to the
>   ground.
> They're like a lion longing to claw something,
>   A young lion lying wait in ambush. (Psalm 17:10-12.)

Psalm 35 is even more explicit:

> Witnesses who say I've done violence appear,
>   On things I know nothing about they examine me.
> They reward my good deeds with evil,
>   They're out for my hide.
> But *I*, for *their* sickness I went into mourning,
>   Weakened myself with fasting.
> O that I'd kept my prayer to myself,
>   As both friend and brother have in my case!
> I kept at it as one who grieves for his mother,
>   Bowed down, dressed in mourning clothes.
> But when *I* stumbled, they rejoiced and assembled,
>   Assembled against me!
> Like foreigners I don't even know,
>   They slander me unmercifully.   (Psalm 35:11-15.)

There is here a clear shift in focus from the plight of the suppliant to the "enemies," those whom the sufferer holds responsible for the lamentable situation in which he finds himself. This latter emphasis appears in extrabiblical Near Eastern laments as well as in Old Testament poetry. Once again, some lines from the Babylonian prayer to Ishtar are relevant:

> How long, O my Lady, wilt thou be infuriated so that thy spirit is enraged?
> Turn thy neck which thou hast set against me; set thy face toward good favor.
> Like the water of the opening up of a canal let thy emotions be released.
> My foes like the ground let me trample;
> Subdue my haters and cause them to crouch down under me.   (Lines 94-98.)[10]

Such "foes," the subject of many lines of poetry in Old Testament laments and the object of violent imprecation, have been a source of much discussion and debate in study of the psalms. The problem is that of identification. No simple theory fits all occurrences without straining.[11] There are laments in which the "foes" of the suppliant accuse him of wrong and against whom he asks God to establish his innocence. Such "foes" are presumably human accusers of the lamenter.[12] Reference to "foes" in certain laments prompted by physical infirmities might also involve human accusers. In the later history of Israel, as the Book of Job indicates, suffering was often traced to wrongdoing, and the lament of a sufferer might be a plea both for relief from pain *and* for a confirmation of moral rectitude (cf. Psalms 28, 38, 41, 69, 71, 86, 102). The "righteousness" often mentioned in laments could mean "vindication," and persons designated as "righteous" could be understood to be "those vindicated."

Even, however, when the "enemies" of the laments are presumably human, more is involved than the status of the suppliant in the human community. Behind every experience of the men of the ancient Near Eastern world lay that drama given expression in the cosmic myth. Though self-righteousness was as much a human characteristic then as it is now, for ancient more than for modern man private crises were related to the cosmic struggle between the forces of order and the forces of chaos. The "enemies" spoken of in many of the laments, particularly those probably used in times of illness and suffering, were surely other than human. Psalm 13 describes suffering as a battleground on which powers other than Yahweh vie for supremacy in the case of a faithful Israelite:

> How long, Yahweh, wilt thou forget me? Forever?
>   How long wilt thou hide thy face from me?
> How long must I bear pain in my innermost being,
>   Sorrow in my heart continually?

How long shall my enemy raise himself against me?
Pay heed, answer me, Yahweh my God.
  Light up my eyes, lest I sleep in death,
Lest my enemy say, "I have defeated him,"
  Or my foes rejoice because I am reduced to chaos.
                          (Psalm 13:1-4, Heb. 2-5).

The "him" in danger of defeat could as well be Yahweh as
the petitioner, a likelihood enhanced by the final verb (literally "totter" or "shake") which is used with cosmic connotations in other passages (cf. Psalms 46:3; 82:5; 93:1; 96:10).
This lament represents that the illness of the suppliant is
a challenge to Yahweh's cosmic sovereignty by some demonic power, that in private suffering chaos is overwhelm-
ing order.[13]

The source of "enemy" imagery in the laments is not,
then, so much human vindictiveness as cosmic disorder.[14]
Certainly there are individual laments in which "enemy"
applies more generally and extensively in its reference than
it does in the instances of false accusation. Psalm 59, a
harrowing lament directed exclusively at "enemies" appears
to identify them with an invading army (cf. also Psalms
3:6; 27:3; 55:18; 56:1-2—verse numbers as in the English
text). In the "we" laments (where Israel as a nation speaks),
in the laments of royal psalms, and in many individual, private laments the movements of nations are seen as manifestations of attempts by the powers of darkness to challenge
the sovereignty and order of Yahweh.[15] The laments reflect
a world in which everything upsetting to man—sickness,
loss of reputation, international instability—is seen as a consequence of the unseen struggle described in the myth. Distinctions between individual and national tragedy, between
private and public disaster, are blurred.

The savage imprecation of enemies found in many psalms
must also be understood in the same larger—cosmic—con-

text. Any suffering or injustice or upheaval or evil was directly connected with the actions of divine beings. When the Moabites moved to upset the order established by the house of David, Chemosh, the god of Moab, was rising against the cosmic order established by Yahweh; when Elijah and Elisha revolted against the innovations of Ahab and Jezebel in the northern kingdom, what might to us constitute civil war to them constituted a struggle between Yahweh and Baal; when a man's neighbors falsely accused him of wrongdoing, demons were at work to overthrow the stability of Yahweh's good rule in the cosmos. There may be no more justification for the laments of Israel than there was justification for the slaughter of heretics or of American Indians, but the laments must nevertheless be read in the context of cosmic involvement.

Though violent imprecation is often found, it has validity in the world view out of which the psalms came, as is seen in Psalm 58:

> Do you, you gods, ever really decree what is right?
>   Do you direct mortal men uprightly?
> No! With wicked hearts do you ordain what is to happen on earth;
>   Your power lets violence come easily.
>
> (Psalm 58:1-2, Heb. 2-3).

This most vengeful of psalms is reminiscent of Psalm 82. Not without justification in the context of the myths of the ancient Near East, it traces wickedness and violence on earth to the gods. It then turns to the consequences of that wickedness as reflected in the human world:

> Degenerate are the wicked, delinquents from conception,
>   Speakers of lies from birth.
> Venom have they like the venom of a serpent;
>   Like a deaf adder have they plugged ears

So that they heed not the voice of magicians,
  Or the worker of cunning charms.
(Psalm 58:3-5, Heb. 4-6.)

Vague as to *who* the "wicked" are, the psalm ascribes *what* they are to causes lying beyond their own ability to decide or to set their venomous course. The conjunction of the opening verses about the power of the gods who oppose Yahweh to direct mortal men into paths of wickedness and violence with the verses about the wicked who were wicked even before their birth makes clear that cosmic order is at stake. Proximate religious remedies, scathingly referred to as magic and charms, cannot, therefore, address the situation. The sovereign of the cosmos himself must intervene if effective remedy is to be realized. Hence these vigorous imprecations:

God, break their teeth in their mouth!
  Their jaw-bones, which are like lions', break, Yahweh!
Let them vanish as water running off,
  As grass by the road let them fade away,
As the snail that turns into slime,
  Or a premature birth that never lives.
In only the time it takes a pot to feel a fire of thorns,
  Whether green or burning, may he sweep them away.
(Psalm 58:6-9, Heb. 7-10.)[16]

Such lines are scattered throughout the psalter (even in verses 19-24 of that otherwise serene hymn, Psalm 139). Psalm 58 concludes with a lively if terrible confidence in the righteousness of Yahweh:

The righteous man rejoices when he beholds such
vengeance,
  Bathes his feet in the blood of the wicked:
So that mankind can say, "Yes, being righteous bears fruit;
  Yes, there *is* a God directing things on earth."
(Psalm 58:10-11, Heb. 11-12.)

Terrible as this lament may be, it is rooted in the conviction that God is not arbitrary, that his righteousness is that by which life is given meaning, and that he—not amoral, fickle powers—is in ultimate control of events.

The Negligence of God

The third emphasis of the lament proper is upon God himself. The suppliant asks why God does not act, or he rebukes God for having permitted his faithful to endure suffering and wickedness. That is why the "How long?" is characteristic of many laments. It may be found in Babylonian laments:

> How long, O my Lady, wilt thou be angered so that thy face is turned away?
> How long, O my Lady, wilt thou be infuriated so that thy spirit is enraged.
>
> > (Prayer to Ishtar, lines 93-94; Pritchard, *Ancient Near Eastern Texts*, p. 385.)

The "How long?" motif is common also in biblical laments (cf. Psalms 6:3, 13:1,2; 74:10; Jeremiah 12:4—verse numbers as in the English text). It reflects a central emphasis of Israelite piety, sometimes characterized as "the Promethean element" in the Old Testament.[17] False reticence, feigned saintliness, are alien to Israel's approach to God. So natural to her is the reality of Yahweh that the embarrassment of reverence never hinders her from accusing him or questioning him. It is precisely a deep conviction of Yahweh's righteous, dependable rule that is the source of Israel's blatant querying of him in the face of meaningless disaster—the source even of her rebuke of him:

> My God, my God, why hast thou forsaken me,
> > And art so far from being my salvation,
> > > And from the things making me groan?

> My God, I cry by day, and thou heedest not—
> Even by night, but there is no rest for me.
>   (Psalm 22:1-2, Heb. 2-3.)

The suppliants sometimes accuse God of being responsible for disaster, implying that Yahweh has abandoned his steadfast trustworthiness for the fickleness characteristic of deities of neighboring peoples:

> For ashes instead of bread do I eat,
>   And tears do I mingle with what I drink,
> Because of thy curse and thy wrath;
>   For thou hast lifted me up and cast me off.
>   (Psalm 102:9-10, Heb. 10-11.)

As the motive behind the extensive, heart-rending descriptions of a sufferer's plight is to excite God's compassion, so the motive behind accusations of God is to shame him into action. In certain laments God is reminded that a suppliant's miserable condition has become an occasion for mocking by others:

> I would say to God my Rock,
>   "Why hast thou forgotten me?
> Why should I have to be in the role of a mourner
>   Over the oppression of the enemy?
> Causing pain as bad as that of a mortal wound,
>   My adversaries taunt me,
> Saying to me continually,
>   'Where is your God?'"
>   (Psalm 42:9-10, Heb. 10-11.)

Divinity was no abstract, no vaguely spiritual entity. A god's claim to divinity rested squarely on his record in confronting the forces of chaos, meaninglessness, and death. In accusatory outcries those who lament forthrightly remind Yahweh that in their suffering the sovereignty of Yahweh himself is defeated and mocked by hostile forces. Some laments

even imply that the suppliant is more concerned for Yahweh's reputation than Yahweh himself seems to be. In that
exhaustive lament, Psalm 88, this theme finds expression in
sardonic reproof:

> I have called on thee, Yahweh, continually.
> I have spread out my hands to thee.
> Dost thou ever work a wonder for the dead,
> Or do shades ever stand up to bear thankful witness to
> thee?
> Is thy covenant faithfulness [*chesed*] recounted in the grave,
> Thy trustworthiness in the realm of the dead?
> Is any of thy wonders known in that darkness,
> Or thy righteous deliverance in the land where all is
> forgotten?
> Yet I, *I* cried unto thee, Yahweh,
> And in the morning my prayer confronts thee.
> Why, Yahweh, hast thou cast off my very being,
> Dost thou conceal thy presence from me?
>
> (Psalm 88:9b-14, Heb. 10b-15.)

We have noted that this psalm assumes that the powers
of death are contained in an area outside Yahweh's life-
giving sovereignty. The suppliant, having defined his condition as one consigned to that area before his time (cf. Psalm
88:3-9a, Heb. 4-10a), points out to Yahweh that the presence
of death in his suffering implies an area within the cosmos
where Yahweh's victorious role is not manifest. The plain-
tiff protests that he, though Yahweh gives no evidence of
concern, remains faithful to Yahweh and to his order: "Yet
I cried unto thee." Only the lamenter's persistent cry, he
alleges, redeems the situation from meaningless chaos,
though he is not the cosmic king with power to prevail. The
complaint is also a rebuke: "What kind of an advertisement
is my situation for all that is claimed for thee, Yahweh?"
This is typical of the down-to-earth piety inherent in bibli-

cal laments, and further evidence that the laments participate in the cosmic drama recounted in the myth and celebrated in the hymns.

Petition and Vow

Petition is, of course, implied in the act of lamentation.
There is repeated cry to Yahweh to give heed to the suppliant's cry (Psalms 5:1-2; 17:1,6; 54:2; 88:2; 143:1—verse
numbers as in the English text). God is implored to look
mercifully on the condition of the petitioner (cf. Psalm
25:18). In vivid anthropomorphic language, characteristic
of the questioning and accusing of the laments, God is be-
seeched to bestir himself to action (cf. Psalms 7:6; 35:23;
59:4-5). "Help me!" or "Deliver me!" or an equivalent, is
the central petition of all laments (cf. Psalms 3:7; 6:4; 22:21;
54:1; 109:26). These and others of the manifold forms of
petition in the laments are paralleled elsewhere in the Bible
and in many Babylonian laments.[18] The petitions must, however, be read in the context of the cosmic imagery which
figures so importantly in all of Israel's song. The desperate
cry of the suppliant asks that in *this* suffering, in *this* challenge to integrity, in *this* disaster the cosmic myth celebrated
in the hymns be applied to specific circumstances of suffering.

Many laments include vows. These vows say, to use a
common idiom, that the intervention of God will induce
the suppliant to "sing a different tune":

I will give thanks to Yahweh as befits his righteousness,
  And I will sing the praises of the name of Yahweh as
  Elyon.   (Psalm 17:17, Heb. 18.)

Yahweh's deliverance will obligate the suppliant to acclaim
him as *Elyon,* "Most High" of the forces of the cosmos (cf.
also Psalms 13:6; 22:22-25; 35:9-10; 71:22-24; 142:7—verse

numbers as in the English text). Certain passages make
clear that to give thanks was a cultic action rather than a
private devotional exercise:

> With a free-will offering will I sacrifice to thee,
>   I will give thanks for thy reputation, Yahweh, for it is
>   good.   (Psalm 54:6, Heb. 8; cf. also 56:12 and 61:9.)

Such laments vow to praise God as saviour when the prayer
is answered and good fortune restored.

THE OCCASION OF THE LAMENT

Israel's songs, like those of her ancient Near Eastern neighbors, were sung in cultic settings. Neither the hymns and
those songs related to them nor the laments were prayers
privately uttered in closets. What we know of the culture out
of which they came, confirmed by many allusions in the
songs themselves, compels such a conclusion. Furthermore,
the stylized terms in which most laments are cast argue for
their being intended for use by many people on different
occasions of need rather than by one person in a specific
situation. The form, so much a part of life, must have been
the basis of many compositions by many individuals but,
as we argued in the introduction to this book, more is learned
about the nature of a formal song by studying the form
itself and the setting in which it was used than by seeking
the specific occasion on which a particular song might have
been written by a particular poet. It is our further contention that the world view of the cosmic myth is the key to
understanding the origins of the forms and motifs of Israel's
poetry rather than the special psychological and spiritual
experiences of individuals.

The setting out of which the lament form came involves
us immediately in the identity of the "I" who utters the

laments, about which there is as much difference and debate as there is about the identity of the "enemies" denounced in the laments. Traditional Jewish interpretation, adhered to by a majority of nineteenth-century critics, held the "I" of such psalms to be collective so that the laments were cries of Israel in her communal distress.[19] In the early part of this century there was a reaction, and Gunkel's position, for example, in his influential work on the psalms, is that the "I" always refers to an individual except in cases where it is explicitly identified with the community (cf. Psalm 129:1-2).[20] Gunkel reads the laments as prayers of individuals in distress, illness being the predominant occasion of the distress.[21] On the other hand, particularly among scholars who stress the participation of Israel in the cultic pattern of the ancient Near East, a partial return to the traditional identification of the communal "I" has taken place.

For those who argue that the principal occasion of Israelite psalmnody was an annual festival at which the cosmic victory of Yahweh over the powers of chaos and death was celebrated, the laments are songs composed for the king as part of the ritual humiliation and suffering he assumed as cultic king of the cosmos. Since that drama was, in the view of such interpreters, an expression of cosmic significance, the prayers of individual suppliants were modeled on the royal original, and the king's lament was one in which the petitions of the total community were gathered up.[22] As with identification of the "enemies" in the laments—closely related to identification of the "I"—a responsible approach requires attention to both sides in the discussion. In whatever way the form of laments may have been modified in the course of time, the roots lie in two settings, both cultic and both grounded in the ancient Near Eastern world view expressed in various forms of cosmic myth.

1. One occasion for laments must surely have been when

the king, or some other cultic figure, led the community in an expression of identification with the struggle depicted in the cosmic myth. Such a ritual was performed by the Babylonian king, as indicated by this excerpt from the temple program for the New Year festival:

When he (that is, the king) reaches [the presence of the god Bel], the *urigallu*-priest shall leave (the sanctuary) and take away the scepter, the circle, and the sword [from the king]. He shall bring them [before the god Bel] and place them [on] a chair. He shall leave (the sanctuary) and strike the king's cheek. He shall place the . . . behind him. He shall accompany him (that is, the king) into the presence of the god Bel. . . . he shall drag (him by) the ears and make him bow down to the ground. . . . The king shall speak the following (only) once. . . .

The king thereupon protests his innocence of disloyalty to the god in lines suggestive of elements in biblical laments where God is reminded of the suppliant's faithfulness and by implication rebuked for his own inaction. Although some of the text is missing, it seems clear that the king in ritual suffering and humiliation—a preface to his enthronement—is uttering a lament. This is confirmed by the words of the priest when the text again becomes legible:

Have no fear. . . . The god Bel [will listen to] your prayer.[23]

Despite the position taken by those who stress Israel's participation in a Babylonian-Canaanite cult pattern, there is no explicit evidence in the Old Testament that a comparable role was played by Israel's king.[24] But the penitential and expiatory rites of the Day of Atonement (cf. Leviticus 16, and the tractate *Yoma* in the Mishnah) are closely associated with New Year's day—following it by ten days—and immediately preceding the fall ingathering festival of Tabernacles. The only record of that ritual comes from the postexilic period but may be assumed to have had prece-

dents in the era of the monarchy. It is not fanciful to postulate that there was an occasion—associated with the New
Year celebration of the kingship of Yahweh—on which
humiliation of and lamentation by the king were ritually
enacted and in which the Israelite community identified
itself symbolically with the suspense of the cosmic drama
out of which Yahweh had emerged victorious, thereby
achieving the sovereignty acclaimed in his people's hymnic
praise. Such a setting may be suggested as a likely source
of the laments.

We are on tentative ground in speculating that the Israelite king represented Yahweh in the cultic ritual, but
we are on firm ground in affirming that there were occasions on which the king spoke for Israel to Yahweh.[25] On
occasions of national disaster, days of fasting and penitence
were proclaimed during which, with appropriate acts of
humiliation and supplication, the mercy of Yahweh was en-
treated by the community as a whole (cf. Judges 20:26;
I Samuel 7:6; I Kings 21:9,12; Jeremiah 36:9; Joel 1:14).[26]
Moreover, Solomon's lengthy prayer in I Kings, chapter 8,
whatever its date, reflects tradition that the king, on occasion, did pray on behalf of the people using the first-person
singular (verses 23-30), and that the community did repair
to the Temple in Jerusalem to cry out to Yahweh in times
of distress (verses 33-40, 44-53). Likewise, II Chronicles
20:1-12—again, whatever its date—clearly describes an occasion on which the king both proclaims a fast and speaks
a lament on behalf of his people.

This evidence is confirmed by examination of the royal
psalms. Echoes of laments, or allusions to them, are found
in some of these psalms. In the royal song recorded in Psalm
18 and in II Samuel 22:1-51, the "I" is obviously the king
celebrating deliverance by divine intervention:

Therefore will I bear thankful witness to thee, Yahweh,
among the nations;
And thy name will I praise in song.
He is one who makes the saving works of his king great,
And one who shows covenant loyalty to his anointed,
To David and his scions forever.
(Psalm 18:49-50, Heb. 50-51; II Sam. 22:50-51.)

The psalm associates the action of the king in restoring order
with Yahweh's function as saviour in the phrase, "saving
works." But the king also remembers circumstances in
the past when he had occasion for lament:

Death had bound me with ropes,
And the flood waters of utter nothingness were terrifying
me;
Sheol had wrapped ropes around me;
Death had set traps for me as if I were a bird.
In the straits in which I found myself I called on Yahweh;
Yes, to my God I cried for help.
(Psalm 18:4-6, Heb. 5-7; II Sam. 22:5-7.)

The king laments when disaster for his rule threatens
cosmic order, and the people identify themselves with the
king's lament. Thus Psalm 20 begins:

May Yahweh answer you in a time of disaster,
May the reputation of Jacob's God lift you above danger!
(Psalm 20:1, Heb. 2.)

The conclusion of Psalm 20 makes the point incontestably
explicit:

Yahweh, work salvation through the king,
Let him be the answer when things cause us to lament!
(Psalm 20:9, Heb. 10.)

Psalm 89, also a royal song, becomes a lament at its conclusion, bewailing Yahweh's apparent forgetfulness of the
promise to bless human society through the Davidic monarchy.

The "I" of many biblical laments, then, *could* originally
have been the king through whose voice the human community called upon God for deliverance. Thus many of the
psalms which appear superficially to be prayers of *individual
men* may actually be laments in which *man* cries, through
an anointed one, for salvation from death and chaos.[27]

2. A communal and royal setting is not, however, the
only situation in which the lament form was shaped. In no
mere derived (democratized) sense, *laments originated
from situations, also cultic, in which individuals besought
their gods in time of need.* The ancient Near Eastern "man
in the street" had a personal relationship to and could directly approach the divine powers. Evidence from Babylonia, like much material from the world of the Bible, sheds
light on Israel's culture and accents the uniqueness of Israel's faith. The prayer to Ishtar includes this relevant line:

As for my god, his face is turned to the sanctuary of another.
(Line 77, Pritchard, *Ancient Near Eastern Texts,* p. 385.)

Invoking Ishtar, the suppliant complains that his own god
has deserted him. The line suggests that, although the fundamental relation of man to the great world of the gods was
communal in character, taking place through the social
order of which he was a part and in which direct address
to the great gods could be made only by king and priests,
an individual did have his own accessible personal god.

Just as the serf rarely has intimate personal relations with the
lord of the manor, so the individual in Mesopotamia looked upon
the great gods as remote forces to whom he could appeal only in
some great crisis and then only through intermediaries. Close

and personal relations—relations such as he had to the authorities in his family: father, mother, older brother and sister—the individual had only to one deity, to his personal god. (T. Jacobsen, *The Intellectual Adventure of Ancient Man,* Frankfort, *et al.,* p. 203.)

Jacobsen substantiates this assertion by quoting a letter written in illness by a Mesopotamian to his personal god:

> Why have you neglected me [so]?
> Who is going to give you one who can take my place?
> Write to the god Marduk, who is fond of you,
> that he may break my bondage;
> then I shall see your face and kiss your feet!
>
> (*Ibid.,* p. 206.)

Appeal to the god's pity and shame, regard for his reputation, even appeal to his pride ("the god Marduk is fond of you"!), are also familiar characteristics, as we have seen, of biblical laments. Appeals in the lament form could be made by private individuals to a personal god. The existence of a "prayer to any (or every) god" would seem to confirm this. This prayer, similar to what we expect of a lament, seems to have, so to speak, left a blank space for the name of the addressee, so that it could be used by devotees of different personal gods.[28] Furthermore, the existence of such a form indicates that laments were made in time of need in a formal way at a sanctuary, and that extant laments are forms for use in that way and at such a place, and are not compositions by individuals for themselves.

Israel differed, however, from her neighbors in that Yahweh was, in the faith of the old, premonarchical confederation, the "personal god" of every Israelite, between whom and the Israelite no other god could stand. When Yahweh had become ruler of the cosmos, the chief God was every man's "my God!" But it is reasonable to assume that Yahweh as saving God of individuals, as well as of the cosmos, was approached in a formal way at the sanctuary.

Indications of the formal procedure are found in the laments themselves.[29] There is explicit evidence in some laments that they were uttered at a sanctuary:

> Hear the sound of my supplication
>> As I cry to thee for succor,
>
> As I lift up my hands
>> Toward the holy of holies in thy sanctuary.
>>> (Psalm 28:2; cf. 5:7.)

Introductory verses to Psalm 5 (1-3, Hebrews 2-4) indicate either that a sacrifice accompanied the solemn recital of the lament or, more likely, that the moment of climax in the ritual action came at the hour of the regular morning sacrifice in the sanctuary. Other hints indicate that the suppliant may have spent the night in the sanctuary in preparation for his lament, engaging in acts of mortification and penitence:

> I have thee in mind upon my bed,
>> In the night watches do I keep murmuring of thee.
>>> (Psalm 63:6, Heb. 7.)

Prayer offered as an evening sacrifice at its beginning and desperate petition at its end suggest that Psalm 141 is a lament uttered at the outset of a night watch (cf. also the conclusion of Psalm 4). The opening verse of Psalm 63 (earlier versions bring out in English the meaning of the key verb glossed over, unfortunately, in the Revised Standard Version) indicates dawn as the climactic moment of the ritual:

> Yahweh, my God! At dawn do I look for thy sign,[30]
>> Athirst for thee is my very being.
>>> (Psalm 63:1, Heb. 2.)

Similarly, the opening verses of Psalm 5:

> Yahweh! At morn wilt thou heed my voice,
> At morn shall I be ready for thee; yes, watching for thine
> answer.   (Psalm 5:3, Heb. 4.)

The Oracle of Reassurance

The word for "being ready" was often associated with preparation of a sacrifice, but could also refer to rites of purification common in other laments and perhaps elements of the overnight vigil (cf. Psalm 26:6; 51:7, Hebrews 8; and cf. the commentaries on such passages for Babylonian parallels). Furthermore, the verb for "watching" connotes a sense of waiting for divine answer (cf. Isaiah 21:6 ff.; Micah 7:7). Thus we can conjecture an occasion when a suffering individual came to the sanctuary in the evening, spent the night in prayer and rites of mortification, and at the morning sacrifice awaited reassurance from his God. The climax seems to have been an oracle of reassurance delivered by a priest or other cultic functionary. This oracle is seldom included in the texts of biblical laments because it was not part of the "liturgy" of the lamenter and for other reasons. There is reason, however, to see it as a significant element of the ritual of the lament.[31]

According to II Chronicles, chapter 20, after King Jehoshaphat made his lament over the military disaster threatening Judah (verses 1-12), a Levite named Jahaziel, inspired by "the Spirit of Yahweh," responds: "Fear not, and be not dismayed at the great multitude; for the battle is not yours but God's. . . . Fear not, and be not dismayed; tomorrow go out against them, and Yahweh will be with you" (verses 13-17). It is interesting to compare these verses with the words of the priest to the king in the Babylonian New Year ritual: "Have no fear. . . . The god Bel will listen to your prayer." Such an oracle appears to follow the lament with which Psalm 27 concludes:[32]

(The suppliant:)
Hear Yahweh! I am crying aloud;
   Do be gracious to me and answer me!
I have heard thee speaking in my heart: "Seek my presence!"
   Thy presence, Yahweh, I am seeking.
     Do not conceal thy presence from me.
Do not in anger turn thy servant away;
   Thou hast been my help.
Cast me not off, nor forsake me,
   My saving God!
When my mother and my father have forsaken me,
   Yahweh will take me in.
Teach me, Yahweh, thy way,
   Put me on a path on which I can make my way—
     On account of my enemies.
Do not deliver me into my adversaries' hands,
   For false witnesses have stood up against me
     In order to stir up violence.
O that I could have faith enough to see
   Yahweh's goodness in *this* life!
(The priest, or cultic prophet:)
Wait expectantly for Yahweh, hold on,
   That he may strengthen your heart.
     Yes, wait expectantly for Yahweh.   (Psalm 27:7-14.)

Israel's laments originated as prayers for use in concrete cultic situations. The sacred sanctuary, the sacred rites engaged in by the king speaking for the community or by the commoner crying out in his need, the oracle of reassurance pronounced by Yahweh's spokesman, were all elements of Yahweh's ordering, life-giving power. In the vicissitudes of human existence powers other than human weakness and wickedness were at work, powers of which the cosmic myth spoke, and the laments addressed themselves to those situations. The laments also addressed themselves to the God who controlled those forces, and who had provided means of tapping his power.[33]

THE DEVELOPMENT OF THE SONG OF TRUST

The main point of the cosmic myth was not that there are powers arrayed against life and well-being and order, but that there is one who has subdued those forces. When the human community, or a member of that community, cries out of a situation in which death is threatening life and chaos threatening order, the cry implies confidence, or hope, that there is someone capable of overcoming the threat. There is someone who will heed the cry. Even the chiding of God common in laments supposes that he is acting out of character when he is silent, and that the suppliant has hope that he can penetrate to the true nature of God.

There is, then, in the laments an element which Gunkel called "the certainty of a hearing." Indeed, one element by which biblical laments are distinguished from those of Babylonia is the atmosphere of trust. Could it be otherwise when consistent, righteous, demanding Yahweh is contrasted with unpredictable, arbitrary, fickle deities in *Enuma elish* or the Baal myth? Could it be otherwise when the God who deposed the fickle and unjust gods (cf. Psalms 82 and 58) is contrasted with Ishtar to whom a man in distress had to appeal over the head of his personal god? Could it be otherwise when a culture where prayers had to be composed to "any god" is contrasted with Israel, a people of a God whose righteous power had been openly seen in consistently righteous acts?

The "certainty of a hearing" may be merely implied, or it
may find more explicit expression as a lament reaches its
conclusion:

> But I, in thy covenant faithfulness have I trusted;
>   My heart shall rejoice in thy salvation.
>   (Psalm 13:5, Heb. 6.)

> For thou, thou dost bless the righteous, Yahweh;
>   As with a shield, with thy favor dost thou protect him.
>   (Psalm 5:12, Heb. 13.)

Both the "but I" of Psalm 13 and the "thou dost bless the
righteous" of Psalm 5 contrast the lamenting devotee of
Yahweh, and Yahweh's action toward him, with the "enemies" and Yahweh's action toward them. Again we recall that
the "enemies" of the laments involve antagonistic forces in
the cosmic struggle spoken of in the myth. Thus they intrude
not only into descriptions of the suppliant's distress and
imprecations, but into lines bespeaking the confidence un-
dergirding the lament:

> Yahweh has heard my supplication,
>   Yahweh will grant what I pray for.
> Shame and terror shall overtake my enemies,
>   They shall retreat in shame momentarily.
>   (Psalm 6:9-10, Heb. 10-11.)

Trust for the Israelite was no pious, romantic fantasy; it
was rooted in the cosmic victory which the hymns celebrate.

This element in laments came to be the core of some songs,
as we begin to see in Psalm 27. The first six verses of that
psalm are a song of trust, the last eight a lament. Some have
argued that Psalm 27 is two separate songs artificially put
together, but this is not necessarily a valid speculation. That
psalm can be understood as an expression of an element less
stressed and not expanded in other laments. The result of

such expansion is a series of songs, among them some of the most beautiful and beloved of the psalms:

> Yahweh's my shepherd: nothing shall I lack;
>> In green pastures does he let me relax.
> By nonturbulent waters does he lead me;
>> My being he keeps alive.
> He guides me along safe paths,
>> In accord with his reputation. . . .
> Surely goodness and his covenant faithfulness shall pursue me
>> As long as I am alive;
> And my dwelling place shall be Yahweh's house,
>> To the end of my days.
>> (Psalm 23; cf. also Psalms 4, 11, 16, 62, 131.)

The figure of a shepherd's guidance of and care for his sheep is, of course, the basis of this song.[34] The second and third lines, however, refer to cosmic "enemies," watery chaos and death, and are another demonstration that motifs of ancient Near Eastern culture pervade all of Israel's songs. The basis of confidence is Yahweh's cosmic victory. It is also his character manifested in his actions from the beginning of Israel's experience. *Chesed*, "covenant faithfulness" or "steadfast love," is present in the conclusion of Psalm 23, and figures often in these expressions of trust (cf. Psalms 13:5; 57:10; 58:17; 62:12—verse numbers as in the English text). Yahweh's character, as it were, introduced a new motif into the lament that led to a new form of poem.

THE THANKSGIVING: DELIVERANCE CELEBRATED

Laments frequently include vows, promises by the suppliant that upon the deliverance for which he pleads he will acknowledge the saving intervention of his God. The vows speak of "giving thanks," with specific mention of singing

(Psalm 17:17, Hebrew 18). They also pledge the offering of sacrifice (Psalm 54:6, Hebrew 8). That private, occasional sacrifices for specific situations were customary is clear from the regulations in the Priestly Code (Leviticus, chapters 1-7). These were personal rites either of penitence or of thanksgiving, to which the worshiper would invite those who might, because of kinship or friendship, fittingly share his distress or his rejoicing. They were outside the regular round of daily and annual communal fixed sacrifices.

In the first chapter of I Samuel, for example, Hannah laments her childlessness at the sanctuary at Shiloh, "vowing a vow" in connection with her petition (I Samuel 1:10-11). After she has borne Samuel, "Elkanah (her husband) and all his house went up to offer to Yahweh the yearly sacrifice, and to pay his vow" (I Samuel 1:21)—indicating, on the one hand, the fulfillment of duty as a member of the sacral community and, on the other, the fulfillment of personal, private obligation. The word rendered "vow" can also be translated "free-will offering," which indicates its purport. Amos' scathing denunciation of Israel's formal, self-satisfied piety includes a verse shedding light on the customs of the ritual thanksgiving:

> Yes, make your thankofferings gourmets' delights,
>   Pretentiously announce free-will offerings, send invitations!
>   (Amos 4:5.)

These lines, decrying the practice of turning worship into a social affair, indicate that a part of the sacrifice in a thankoffering was kept back for a meal in which those invited to share the joy of the offerer would join. Finally, Jeremiah 33:11 lists among the blessings to be enjoyed in the future "the voices of those who sing . . . as they bring sacrifices of thanksgiving to Yahweh's house," indicating that songs of thanksgiving were sung during the offering of sacrifices.

An understanding of the terminology of thanksgiving in the Old Testament is a necessary preliminary to an appreciation of the songs under discussion. Just as one and the same word denotes "vow" and "free-will offering," intention inseparable from concrete, outward action, so one and the same word (*todah*) denotes "thanksgiving," "thankoffering" or "thanksgiving sacrifice," and "song of thanksgiving." Three separate, if related, thoughts were for the Israelite one. No distinction is made between cultic action, poetic expression, and the attitude (or emotion) out of which both spring. "To do *todah*" involves all three (the verbal root is *yadah*). Furthermore, "to do *todah*" has also the connotation "confess," having as its object "transgressions" (Psalm 32:5; Proverbs 28:13). Its fundamental meaning is, in fact, that of the English word "confess," which can be used both in the sense of "confession of sin" and in the sense of "confession of faith." Basically it expresses a setting forth, a recounting, a recital, a making known.[35]

Thus the Old Testament conception of thanksgiving is not abstract, nor is it rooted in human attitudes or emotions. Its meaning lies in God's gracious action, in *his* deliverance of his devotee, in *his* salvation. It is a setting forth of God's action, a witness to his victory over the powers of chaos. That is the meaning of the "free-will offering" vowed by a suppliant. Indeed that is the meaning of the very existence of the suppliant once he has been delivered from the threat of death (cf. Psalm 88:3-5, Hebrews 4-6) or the waters of chaos (Psalm 69:1-2, Hebrews 2-3). He has himself become *todah* of Yahweh's sovereign, saving power. Against this background we understand passages in the laments in which the suppliant asks, in effect, "Yahweh, what kind of an advertisement am I for your 'godness' in this kind of condition?" (cf. Psalm 88:9b-14, Hebrew 10b-15).

The poems of thanksgiving are, therefore, *todah* put into

words, which explains why it was customary in Egypt and
elsewhere in the ancient Near East to inscribe prayers of
thanksgiving on stelae, where they could be visible to all.[36]
Reference to such inscriptions seems to occur in Isaiah 56:4-
5, and in the superscription to King Hezekiah's song of
thanksgiving in Isaiah 38:9 ("a writing [inscription?] of
King Hezekiah"). The man, his sacrifice, his offering, were
concrete witness to Yahweh's right to the acclamation of
the hymns. That is what the songs of thanksgiving are about.

It is not surprising that these songs sometimes contain
lines similar to those found in hymns. Classified by Gunkel
as a thanksgiving, Psalm 107 is much like a hymn. The opening and closing verses of Psalm 118, a thanksgiving, contain
plural imperatives characteristic of the hymn, as do the conclusions of Psalms 30 and 32. These imperatives, however,
are usually commands "to do *todah*," and may well be a
jubilant bidding by the person giving thanks that those invited join him in his celebration, whereas the imperatives
in hymns probably represent calls to the assembly of gods
to acclaim the sovereignty of the victor in the cosmic battle.

Despite the similarities—understandable given their common praise of Yahweh—there is a fundamental distinction
between the hymn and the thanksgiving. Compare Psalm
136, a hymn, with Psalm 118, a thanksgiving. Both begin
and end with the command (an imperative plural), "Give
thanks!" Psalm 136, however, in the recital following its introduction, speaks of Yahweh as "him who alone does great
wonders . . . him who smote the first born of Egypt" (using
the Hebrew participle), and introduces the tense of completed action only in verse 18 as the song comes to its conclusion. Psalm 118, on the other hand, has an "I" as its subject, and its verbs are finite: "I called . . . they surrounded
me . . . Yahweh helped me." Psalm 136, although it does

refer to acts of Yahweh (and slips incidentally into the style
of the thanksgiving in verses 23 and 24), is primarily concerned to proclaim *who* Yahweh *is*. Psalm 118 is concerned,
although its terms are general enough to make it usable on
more than one occasion by more than one person giving
thanks for more than one deliverance, to focus on an "I" and
on the event in which Yahweh rescued that "I" from distress.
Therein lies the fundamental distinction between the hymn
and the thanksgiving. The hymn, with reference to what is
recounted in the cosmic myth (modified in Psalm 136 to include his historical deeds involving Israel), acclaims the
God as God. The subject is God himself. The form of the
Hebrew verb denoting the one who performs the actions is
characteristically employed. The thanksgiving, although the
deliverance it celebrates is understood in terms of the cosmic
myth, proclaims how in a specific situation God *acted* as
God. Its subject is a specific "I" whose very existence is
todah of God as God, and the verb is characteristically in the
tense denoting completed, accomplished action. The hymn
is sung with reference to the cosmic struggle recounted in
the myth. The thanksgiving is sung with reference to the
particular distress described in the lament.[37]

The "I" of songs of thanksgiving must, therefore, be expressive, as is the "I" of laments, now of the king with whose
experience the community as a whole identifies, now of an
individual devotee whose lament has been heard. Precedents
for the offering of thanksgiving by kings are found in the
ancient Near East, as in the following from Babylonia, addressed to Marduk. Note how an introduction is followed
by reference to deliverance from a particular threat:

I will extol the godness, proclaim the power . . .
  [Of Marduk] the merciful, whose drawing near . . .
Whose heart [was touched], who was moved by pity.

[He heeded] my supplication, he gave me his attention,
  [He whose heart] was touched, who was moved by affection.
The Elamites, who feared not his great godness,
  Spoke presumptuously against his sublime godness.
Thy weapons [went out] against those insolent Elamites;
  [Thou didst cast down] their host, didst shatter their power.
[Their numerous places] didst thou destroy by fire (?);
  Their great . . . didst thou over run like a deluge.[38]

We have referred to the account of Jehoshaphat's difficulties with enemies in II Chronicles, chapter 20. Not only does that narrative describe the king's lament (verses 5-20) and the responses of a spokesman for Yahweh in an oracle of reassurance, but it speaks of thankful worship, singing by the Levites, and Jehoshaphat's response (verses 18-19). It describes a joyful act of thanksgiving, of which Jehoshaphat was leader, when the battle was finally won (verses 27-28). It concludes with Jehoshaphat's *todah* to Yahweh, an expression through which Yahweh's sovereignty brought order to society (verse 29). Just as the king is the voice of the community in lament, so he is here the voice of the community in thanksgiving.

Psalm 118 is an example of a thanksgiving in which the "I" was the king. Because we have had occasion to discuss their significance, certain key Hebrew terms have been transliterated rather than translated, because to translate them would be to restrict them.[39]

Do *todah* for Yahweh, for he is good,
  Surely his *chesed* stands for all time.
Will Israel please say it:
  "Surely his *chesed* stands for all time."
Will the Aaronites please say it:
  "Surely his *chesed* stands for all time."

> Will those who are converts to Yahweh please say it:
> "Surely his *chesed* stands for all time."
> >   (Psalm 118:1-4.)

The Israelites, their priests, and those worshipers of Yahweh not Israelite by birth (literally "fearers of Yahweh") are bidden to take part in the act of *todah*.[40] What is being celebrated is more than the deliverance of a private individual, and the "I" who speaks is probably the king. As is often the case in thanksgivings, the lament preceding the *todah* is quoted (cf. Psalms 30:9-10; 41:4, 8; 116:4—all verse numbers as in the English text):

> Out of distress I called, "Yah!"
> >   He answered me by setting me free, did Yah.[41]
> Yahweh is mine, I have no fear!
> >   How can mortal man do anything to me?
> Yahweh is mine, my helper!
> >   And I, I shall outlast those who hate me.
> It is better to seek refuge in Yahweh
> >   Than to trust in mortal man.
> It is better to seek refuge in Yahweh
> >   Than to trust those whose power is only human.
> >   (Psalm 118:5-9.)

Next comes the recital of the distress, and of Yahweh's intervention. As in certain laments, the accent is upon the "I," for the "I" is the primary *todah*. And the description of the distress, although general enough to make possible its use on more than one occasion, makes it likely that the singer is the king, the plottings against whose person and power by the nations are manifestations of the checked but still rebellious cosmic opponents of Yahweh (cf. Psalms 2 and 110):

> All nations surrounded me:
> >   By the name of Yahweh—I swear it!—I warded them off.
> They surrounded me, yes, they surrounded me:

By the name of Yahweh—I swear it!—I warded them off.
They surrounded me like bees,
> Blazing up as hot and quickly as a fire of thorns:
>> By the name of Yahweh—I swear it!—I warded them
>> off.
I was driven to the wall, was about to fall,
> But Yahweh intervened to help me!
My might, and the subject of my song, is Yah!
> He has acted in my behalf with salvation!

(Psalm 118:10-14.)

Thus the king has told his story, has verbalized how he is
todah. He pauses to take note of those who share in his rejoicing. Their joy has to do with cosmic well-being, is not
grounded only in human affection for him. The king speaks,
and the song of the people follows:

The noise of cheering for salvation
> Resounds in the tents of those who have been vindicated:
"Yahweh's right hand is a powerful performer,
> Yahweh's right hand is capable of the utmost,
>> Yahweh's right hand is a powerful performer!"

(Psalm 118:15-16.)[42]

Now the king proceeds, identifying himself as *todah,* and associates what has happened with the cosmic issues set forth
in the Ugaritic myth in which Baal's antagonist is "Death"
(Mot):

I am not dead! I swear it, I am alive!
> And I am living testimony of the deeds of Yah!
Yah may have put me through the most rigorous discipline,
> But he did not deliver me into the hands of Death!

(Psalm 118:17-18.)

Visualize the king standing at the entrance to the sanctuary proper. An exchange such as occurs also in Psalms 15 and
24 takes place:

(King:)
Open for me the gates of vindication,[43]
    I would enter them to do *todah* for Yah!
(Priest:)
Here is the gate to Yahweh:
    Those who are vindicated may come through it.
                      (Psalm 118:19-20.)

There follows formal proclamation of *todah*, possibly spoken as the king placed his hand on the sacrifice to be offered by the priests, in token that it was his:

    I offer thee *todah*, for thou didst answer me:
    Thou hast acted in my behalf with salvation!
                      (Psalm 118:21.)

After the *todah* the people of Yahweh who have, through the king, experienced their God's righteous vindication of his claims (cf. how the king referred to them in verse 15) celebrate the king's deliverance. The "work salvation" with which their song finishes is "Hosanna," in Hebrew as in the Greek *Kyrie eleison* also a "Hurrah" for the one whose power merits the supplication:

    The stone which the builders rejected
      Has become nothing less than the cornerstone.
    At the initiative of Yahweh has this thing happened:
      It is a miraculous thing in our eyes.
    In the very present has Yahweh acted,
      Let us celebrate, let us rejoice in this moment!
    We beseech thee, Yahweh, work salvation!
      We beseech thee, Yahweh, bring about prosperity!
                    (Psalm 118:22-25.)

The priests, as the sacrifice is about to be offered, pronounce a blessing on the king and the congregation, and then bid all approach for the climax of the rite:

Blessed be the one who approaches in the name of Yahweh!
  We bless you all from Yahweh's house!
    May the supreme God, Yahweh, cause light to shine
    upon us!
Form the procession, carrying boughs:
  Move right up to the foot of the altar!

                                        (Psalm 118:26-27.)

As the psalm draws to a close, the royal "I" continues to sing
todah and, with the words used at the beginning, bids those
who celebrate with him to join in:

    For me thou art supreme God, so I do *todah;*
      My God, I do extol thee!
    Do *todah* for Yahweh, for he is good,
      Surely his *chesed* stands for all time.

                                        (Psalm 118:28-29.)

This reconstruction, like any, is conjectural. But there is
reason to believe that it provides a paradigm of the cultic
action with which a song of thanksgiving was accompanied.
Furthermore, Psalm 118, the most complete example we
have, includes all the elements of a typical song of thanksgiving. This extensive examination of a thanksgiving in
which the "I" was probably a king and the bidden guests
the whole congregation of Israel, makes it easier to appreciate what took place when a less significant "I" in a song such
as Psalm 30 did *his todah* and bade *his* family and friends
join him. In either case the struggle recounted in the cosmic
myth had been revived in illness or humiliation or social upheaval. The suppliant had cried out to the bringer of order,
calling attention to his plight, naming his adversaries, and
prodding the saviour to act. In a particular way the saviour
had acted. In a concrete individual (of greater or less significance in the cosmic picture) order had replaced chaos,
life had conquered death. That individual *was todah*, wit-

ness to the saviour's power to bring order and to his goodness in doing so. That individual, therefore, offered *todah* in
sacrifice and in song.

ISRAEL'S MODIFICATION OF THE LAMENT MOTIF

That it was *Yahweh* to whom the Israelite could cry "my
saving God!" and be heard resulted in significant modifications of the motifs of the lament. When Yahweh came to be
addressed in the lament and the forms associated with it,
his unique character affected those forms and their motifs.
"Godness" took on a new meaning when Yahweh was the
God, and a standard prayer to "any god" could not continue
unchanged as a vehicle to address him. Laments were still
made, and thanksgivings were still sung, but the understanding of lament and thanksgiving in a cosmos in which Yahweh
was the sovereign ruler underwent significant modification.
We shall look at three areas where this was the case, in each
of which the issue is fundamental to biblical understanding
of existence.

1. *The nature of Israel's faith prompted a fundamental
change in what was being lamented, and a consequent re-
definition of the human problem.* For the general culture out
of which the lament and its motifs arose, the fundamental
human problem derived from decisions made and actions
taken by greater and less divinities (and demons) with
whom the mythical drama was peopled. Man did not participate in decisions and actions taken, and was at the mercy
of forces outside himself and beyond his control. For Israel,
on the other hand, within the faith and polity of the covenant confederation, the fundamental human problem lay in
the demand established by the righteous God Yahweh.
Man's failure to fulfill the demand through which Yahweh
invested decisions and actions with significance constituted

the problem. Thus the lament in Israel came to be employed to bewail sin rather than the perplexities and sufferings occasioned by finitude. When Yahweh was invoked and experienced as deliverer his character involved a new perspective, resulted in accusation of self rather than accusation of the situation within which that self found itself.

Penitence was characteristic also of Babylonian laments, and not unique to biblical laments. The Babylonian "prayer to any (or every) god" is distinctly penitential:

O Lord, my transgressions are many; great are my sins.

O my god, [my] transgressions are many; great are [my] sins.

O my goddess, [my] transgressions are many; great are [my] sins.

O god whom I know or do not know, [my] transgressions are many; great [are] my sins;

O goddess whom I know or do not know, [my] transgressions are many; great are [my] sins.

The transgression which I have committed, indeed I do not know;

The sin which I have done, indeed I do not know.

The forbidden thing which I have eaten, indeed I do not know;

The prohibited [place] on which I have set foot, indeed I do not know.

The lord in the anger of his heart looked at me;

The god in the rage of his heart confronted me;

When the goddess was angry with me, she made me become ill . . .

How long, O my goddess, whom I know or do not know, ere thy hostile heart will be quieted?

Man is dumb; he knows nothing;

Mankind, everyone that exists,—what does he know?

Whether he is committing sin or doing good, he does not even know . . .

Remove my transgressions [and] I will sing thy praise.
Make thy heart, like the heart of a real mother, be quieted
toward me;
Like a real mother [and] a real father may it be quieted
toward me.

(Lines 21-32, 50-53, 63-65; Pritchard, *Ancient Near
Eastern Texts,* pp. 391-392.)

The suppliant accuses himself of "transgression" and "sin,"
but penitence is not the substance of his lament. The ten-
dentious refrain, "I have transgressed, I have sinned," is only
prologue to the suppliant's pathetic protest that he does not
know how he has erred, does not know what forbidden food
may have passed his lips, what taboo place his foot may have
trodden. His illness or misfortune, he supposes, is caused by
an offended deity in retribution for some undisclosed act of
the sufferer. The gods are arbitrary and whimsical; there is
no way of knowing at what they may take umbrage. Man is
at their mercy and has no way of knowing how to please
them or how to keep from displeasing them:

Man is dumb; he knows nothing;
Mankind, everyone that exists,—what does he know?
Whether he is committing sin or doing good, he does not
even know.   (Lines 51-53.)

There is no responsible self-examination and self-accusation.
The endeavor is to make the proper gesture of sorrow for
whatever offense may have been committed. The implication, almost the explicit statement, is that whatever it was, a
purely arbitrary, formal, amoral requirement has been violated. The gods are fickle, man is an outsider to the structures
of power and meaning within which life acquires significance. Man is denied such dignity as would permit him to
feel responsible.

Such lament is never made to Yahweh, although the attitude underlying it sometimes creeps into questions asked of him. The conviction, made clear in the Mosaic covenant and its literature and songs, that Yahweh's character and purpose are not fickle, gave life a significance that encouraged the narrow self-righteousness, the violent imprecations, the almost blasphemous presumption of Israel's laments. It is the dignity with which Yahweh invested Israel's faith that produced the sometimes bumptious attitude of Israel's laments toward self, others, and God. Yahweh ordained that man assume the role occupied by other gods in the cosmic myth. Whatever may be said, therefore, about the offensiveness of many lines in Israel's songs, it cannot be said that there is found anywhere among them the low, groveling view of man given expression in the Babylonian prayer quoted. The biblical view of man, despite extensive appropriation of the idiom of the surrounding culture, is unique because of the nature and work of the God to whom the Bible, and Israel's songs within it, bear witness. Neither the confusion of Near Eastern man praying to "any god" nor the *hubris* of the Greek tragedies can characterize Israel's cry to the God whose covenant demand has redeemed human existence from meaninglessness.[44]

For the culture neighboring Israel, the problem was that man *was* man—finite, limited in knowledge and power, at the mercy of cosmic forces. For Israel meaning and purpose were conferred by Yahweh's sovereignty and stable purpose. For Israel, therefore, the problem lay in what men did or failed to do. The problem was defined in terms of sin, not finitude. Man sought not pacification of a fickle deity, but forgiveness from a responsible God. Consider the lament, Psalm 51, in which Israel expresses *her* penitence:

Be gracious to me, Yahweh, in accord with thy *chesed*,[45]
   In accord with thy boundless mercy, erase my transgressions.

Do thou thoroughly wash my guilt from me,
    And from my sin cleanse me.
For of my transgressions I am well aware,
    And of my sin am I ever conscious.
Against thee, only thee, have I sinned,
    Have done what it is clear to me is evil.
The result of this is that thou mightest be vindicated through
thy covenant requirements,
    Mightest be blameless in thy rule over things.
Behold, in iniquity was I born,
    In sin did my mother conceive me.
Behold, responsible trustworthiness is thy delight . . .
    Thou wouldest make my innermost being acquainted with
    wisdom.   (Psalm 51:1-6, Heb. 3-8.)[46]

This reflects a quite different atmosphere from that found
in the "prayer to any god." Yahweh's *chesed*, his continuing,
loving faithfulness to the covenant is the crux. *Chesed* involves the Mosaic demand and the Davidic promise by
which Yahweh gave human life discernible and hopeful
meaning. He calls, and his call is a sign of a commitment on
his part on account of which even imperfect and rebellious
(the root meaning of "transgression") response will be for-
given and cleansed. The suppliant is in no ignorance of some
offense he may have caused some arbitrary god: "Of my
transgressions I am well aware, and of my sin I am ever
conscious. . . . Against *thee* . . . have done what it is clear
to me is evil." The suppliant acknowledges his human cul-
pability—"in iniquity was I born"—but he grasps that his
transgression and sin are themselves a negative witness to a
structure within which life is by no means meaningless: "The
result of this is that thou mightest be vindicated through
thy covenant requirements." Law and grace, demand and
promise, responsibility and redemption, are concomitants of
one unified reality. That reality is the commitment of God.

It is he who has invested man's history with that significance
formerly restricted to the inscrutable and inaccessible realm
of the gods. He asks of man a corresponding commitment
by which man invests his responsibility and actions with the
significance God accorded them. It is that recognition that
invigorates the climactic lines of Psalm 51:

> My sacrifice, Yahweh, is a broken spirit,
> A broken, crushed heart, O God,
> > Wilt thou not despise.
> > > (Psalm 51:17, Heb. 19.)[47]

Out of her knowledge that the supreme God is Yahweh,
Israel learned what truly merits lament: not the finitude of
mortal man, helpless in a structure he cannot affect, but
failure to be faithful as God is faithful. There *is* cause for
lament. And that cause is, when discerned, deliverance from
the trap in which the suppliant of the "prayer to any god"
is caught. A heart broken and crushed by proximate sense-
lessness in a context of ultimate meaning is a heart bearing
witness to divine faithfulness. Israel, in Psalm 51, has professed a unique definition of the human problem. In terms
of that definition the ritual laws of later Judaism could be
construed as gracious gifts of a God whose demand in itself
afforded his people a vehicle of obedience. In terms of that
definition the emphasis of the laws on cleansing from sin and
guilt, on atonement, is explained. In terms of that definition
Jesus' proclamation of forgiveness as part of the kingdom
he announces is intelligible.[48]

2. *Israel, in accord with her faith, developed "we" laments
and thanksgivings out of the "I" form.* No neighbor of Israel,
to judge from the many laments recovered from the ancient
Near East, produced laments or thanksgivings in the first-
person plural.[49] Many laments—notably those from Babylonia—are, though couched in an "I" form, really "com-

munal" in character. "I" and "we" are not, however, auto-
matic clues to whether a lament originated in the distress of
an individual or of the people as a whole.[50] The "we" lament
does, nevertheless, represent modification of a form appropriated by Israel from her cultural milieu both in relation
to communal (royal) "I" laments and in relation to the "I"
lament addressed to a god by a private individual.

With regard to "I" laments originating in the king's role
in the cult, the development in Israel of a "we" form does
not represent merely a more democratic approach. According to the ancient Near Eastern mythic view of life, hu-
manity occupied a significant position only when the gods,
by procreation or adoption, made some man a vicegerent of
their power. Thus Israel's neighbors were almost totally un-
concerned to record history, producing instead lists by which
the claim of a reigning king was traced through the generations of his predecessors to a divine fiat, or chronicles of
the king's campaigns and conquests. Human activity was
significant only as it related to the great account of divine
activity given in the myth through the king. Ordinary history
of which everyman was part, its origins, mutations, economics, and politics, was not significant. What took place in
it in Babylonia and Ugarit can only be inferred as we read
between the lines of the myths.[51]

Israel defined herself over against this view of reality. For
her the supreme God had deposed the other divinities, had
transferred the drama in which life found its meaning to the
human sphere, had done this concretely in a people whose
continuity persisted through historical events from the generation of Abraham to the generation of Moses to the generation of David, and so on. Within that history the old covenant confederation had fallen before the Philistines, and
David had become king. Kingship had not come to Israel
from heaven in the manner catalogued in the Babylonian

king-list. Kingship in Israel had arisen out of a historical
continuity that went back through David to Moses and to
Abraham. Israel found herself still more deeply involved in
that continuity after the Davidic monarchy had fallen before
the successive assaults of the Assyrian and Babylonian empires. The "we" lament arose, it appears, after the fall of
Jerusalem (cf. Psalms 74 and 79).[52] For Israel what counted
was neither a heavenly "they" nor a royal "he." What
counted was the communal "we" *of which every Israelite
was a part*. The "we" laments include highly unedifying imprecations of political enemies (cf. Psalms 60:6-8; 137:7-9—
verse numbers as in the English text), due not so much to
vindictiveness as to the biblical location of the significant
issues in the continuity of a *people's* history. The "we" with
which Israel replaced the royal "I" is rooted in Yahweh's
character and actions, on account of which every man's part
in communal history has significance. It is another manifestation of a radically unique view of the nature of reality.

Israel was not, however, led in this to an individualistic
piety and view of reality: "individualism" in the modern
sense is not involved. The development of the lament into
a "we" form also says something pertinent about the effects
of Israel's faith on the "I" laments deriving from the distress
of private individuals. In such laments an individual in
whose particular, private disaster the forces of chaos and
death were challenging the order of the cosmos appealed
to the powers of order. In Babylonia the common man made
this appeal through his own lesser "personal god." In Israel
the personal God of every family and of every man was Yahweh. And Yahweh was such precisely because he was the
God of a people, a God whose sovereignty was extended,
and whose purpose worked itself out, in the events forming
the history of that people.

If ultimate issues are located in what transpires in a supramundane realm, then an "I" finds his meaning in relation to that realm, and political, economic, and social events are transitory and without ultimate significance. But if the God is the God of a people, such realities do matter. It is impossible to talk about that people—a community, a nation, a culture—without concrete reference to those realities. If the God is the God of a people, then the "I" finds his meaning not *in spite of* the "we," but as an integral part of the "we." Thus Israel came, in often savage and offensive ways, to lament *as a "we"* situations in which the purpose and promise with which her human history had been invested by Yahweh seemed frustrated or defeated. Such laments have located the issues where God locates them, are looking for meaning for "I" where it must lie, have discerned what ultimate dilemma is. Such laments seek salvation in fundamentally biblical terms which have to do not with denial of or escape from, but rather in fulfillment of, the "we sector" of human history.

When Israel cried out she asked not for deliverance of the "I" from finitude, mortality, death. She asked for fulfillment of the promise and purpose with which God had invested her history. It is this faith that accounts for the rigorous suppression in Israel of speculation about individual, personal survival after death and of necromancy. Moreover, that faith dictated that hope of survival, when it did arise in Judaism and in Christianity, speak of resurrection of the *body*—that which tied the "I" to the "we"—and always in the context of a "general resurrection," a fulfillment of continuing history in which "I" existed only as part of "we." [53]

Although the "we" laments and the "we" thanksgivings are few in number, they afford significant insight into the nature of biblical faith.[54] The cultic background of all the laments and thanksgivings precludes argument that they are products of subjective piety. Moreover, it is a distortion of

the biblical point of view to dismiss references in the laments
to Israel's national distress as incidental and vulgar products
of nationalistic piety divorced from true religion. The biblical conviction is that the ultimate issues have to do not with
a flight of the alone to the Alone, but with real history in
which every "I" is part of the community, the continuity of
the "we." The two concluding verses of that profound confession of sin, Psalm 51, may be later additions, but they
nevertheless confirm that those who gave us the psalter saw
the hope of the "I" as bound up with the hope of the "we."
Having plumbed the depths of human distress (cf. the discussion above), Psalm 51 concludes:

> Make things good for *Zion,* as is thy will:
> Thou shalt rebuild *Jerusalem's* walls.
> (Psalm 51:18, Heb. 20.)

Similarly, Psalm 130 concludes:

> Hope, O *Israel,* in Yahweh:
> For with Yahweh is real *chesed,*
> And boundless redemption is with him.
> And he shall redeem *Israel*
> From all his sins.   (Psalm 130:7-8.)

3. *The oracle of reassurance became a prophetic form in
which Israel is directed to look to the unfolding of history
rather than to the cyclical and unseen cosmic drama for
deliverance.*[55] Such an oracle was probably a part of the
ritual in which laments were used. The priest in the Babylonian New Year ritual answered the king with, "Have no
fear. . . . The god Bel will listen to your prayer" (Pritchard,
Ancient Near Eastern Texts, p. 334), and a prophetic figure
responded to King Jehoshaphat's lament with, "Fear not, and
be not dismayed" (II Chronicles 20:15). This type of oracle
occurs, however, rarely in the laments of the Old Testament.

This is partly because the oracle was not an element in the lament proper, being rather a response to the lament, and partly because it was, even if in a somewhat formal way, a spontaneous, extemporaneous pronouncement by a prophetic figure.[56] However, the oracle of reassurance *is* found elsewhere in the Old Testament, and in circumstances that make its absence from the lament literature even more significant. It is found in prophetic literature, notably that collection of announcements of the return and restoration of Israel preserved as Isaiah, chapters 40-55.

The words of reassurance of the priest to the Babylonian king are part of the annual ritual for the New Year festival. That festival fell in the spring, when the floods in Mesopotamia receded, having made possible, but not having destroyed the possibility of, another agricultural year. The community had witnessed and participated in the dramatic conflict between the forces of order and the forces of chaos of which the cosmic myth spoke. The great festival celebrated the triumph of order, and of the god who accomplished it. It is in that context that the king's ritual humiliation and lament took place. And after the priest has reassured the king, the solemn robing and enthronement of the monarch re-enacts the victory of the god of order in the cosmic struggle. In other words, the oracle of reassurance is rooted in the heavenly drama of which the myth spoke. Just as the problems or distress that gave rise to laments were ultimately located in the divine realm, so the work of reassurance—and this would be true whatever the occasion— could be validated only by reference to that realm.[57]

It is that form, characterized by the pronouncement "Fear not" and the promise of divine intervention, that is echoed by the prophetic voice in Second Isaiah.[58] Isaiah, chapters 40-55, is addressed to Israel after the collapse of the Davidic kingdom in 587, when she had learned in exile to lament as "we." [59] The reassurance is not spoken in a historical vacuum. It is spoken against the background of the conquest of the Babylonian empire, beginning around 540 B.C., by Cyrus and the Persians. Cyrus was able to topple Babylonian power easily by claiming he was the agent of the gods, sent to restore the cults and repatriate the exiles destroyed and deported by Babylonia. The prophetic voice in Isaiah, chapters 40-55, has, therefore, two points to make. First, it is proclaimed that Yahweh is now making it possible for a restored Israel once again to be witness of his sovereignty—a new exodus is to take place. Second, it is *only* Yahweh who can have sent Cyrus, for he is the only God who has characteristically acted in the concreteness of historical event. The claims made by Cyrus are claims that make sense only in terms of the record of Yahweh. The double-edged content of this prophecy and its employment of the form of an oracle are reflected in these lines:

So has Yahweh who made you declared,
    For the one who formed you in the womb is going to help
    you:
"Fear not, O my servant Jacob,
    My favorite whom I have chosen:
For I am going to pour water where it is parched,
    Streams on the dry ground;
I am going to pour my spirit on your descendants,
    Am going to bless your progeny. . . ."
So has Yahweh, Israel's King, declared—
    Yes, Israel's redeemer, Yahweh of hosts:
"I am the first, and I am the last:
    Other than me there is no god.
Who is like me? Let him make a pronouncement,
    Let him explain what is happening, set it forth for me!
Who has in the past made pronouncements about what happens?

>Let them tell us what is now coming to pass!
>Tremble not, fear not!
>Have I not always made pronouncements, told you?
>   And you are my witnesses!
>Is there a god other than me?
>   There is no [other] refuge—
>   I know none.   (Isaiah 44:2-3, 6-8.)

Historical deliverance is the subject of this oracle of reassurance, a *modus operandi* characteristic only of Yahweh. The form of the oracle is used to direct men's eyes to the unfolding of history as a drama of redemption, not to a drama outside of and only reflected in their life. Men's hope is directed to the fulfillment of their own history, not away from it so as to deny and devalue it. Again Israel employs a form, cast in the idiom of her cultural milieu, to make clear that Yahweh *is* God. But that *Yahweh* is God fundamentally alters the content previously contained in the form. The God who *is* God has once again transferred the drama of existence from heaven to earth.[60] Thus an examination of Israel's appropriation and modification of the lament and its motifs has yielded the same distinctive analysis of ultimate issues and the same unique point of view we reached in discussion of the hymnic motifs.

This does not imply, however, that Israel arrived at a neat, doctrinaire answer that denied and throttled the longings of finite man of which the lament was and is a profound expression. Appreciation of the forms and motifs of Israel's songs demonstrates how profoundly the Old Testament upholds the validity of the lament, even as it profoundly alters the underlying point of view. The Book of Job exemplifies this both in its form and in its content. Aside from *what* is said in that book, *how* it is said is subtle and profound. While the friends of Job offer doctrinaire explanations, based precisely on issues we have explored, Job does not reply to them in

kind. Job *laments*, cries out to God, employs all the elements
of the lament, even phrases normally reserved for imprecation of enemies in his anguished indictment of God.[61] When
the friends' doctrinaire explanations are exhausted, sound as
they may have been in theory, God answers him who persisted in his lament. The character of Yahweh may have
transformed the motifs of laments, but it did not deny the
validity of the human longing voiced in the laments. What
was said *about* God, unique as it was and is, did not annihilate the need of man to cry out *to* him. Thus God's final
words to Job's friends: "My wrath is kindled against you
. . . for you have not spoken of me what is right. . . . Go
to my servant Job . . . and he shall pray for you, for I will
accept his prayer" (Job 42:7-8). The book, read in the light
of its cultural context, contrasts the presumptuousness of
"speaking about" with the integrity of "speaking to," and
thus profoundly values the form of lament Israel shared with
her neighbors. Psalm 51 puts it succinctly:

> A broken, crushed heart, O God,
> Wilt thou not despise.
> (Psalm 51:17, Heb. 19.)

4 God as the Source of Wisdom: Torah and Piety

This chapter addresses itself to a consideration of the motif which heavily influenced the piety and theology of later Israel—wisdom. For present purposes, wisdom is extremely important because of its centrality in the point of view of those who collected and preserved the psalter in its final form. We shall trace how this motif, appropriated from the culture of the ancient Near East, was transformed by Israel.

THE ORIGIN AND NATURE OF WISDOM

The Hebrew word for wisdom (*chokmah*) carries no theoretical or abstract connotations; nor is it the equivalent of "thought" or "philosophy." Its meaning is conveyed in this typical verse: "And every woman who had *ability* [literally, 'wisdom of heart'] spun with her hands" (Exodus 35:25). Reference to a concordance discloses that *chokmah* is used often to denote technical skill, and in other contexts "experience" or "shrewdness" in practical and political affairs. The same is true of its cognate, which serves as the adjective "wise" and as the noun "wise one" (*chakam*). It is in this sense that the word "wisdom" is employed in Old Testament and other Semitic literature even when it denotes profundity of knowledge and/or discernment, as in the familiar, "The fear of Yahweh is the beginning of wisdom" (Proverbs 9:10;

Psalm 111:10; cf. Job 28:28). As fingers that spin or hands
that fashion wood or metal (cf. Isaiah 40:20) are "wise," so
wisdom about life is practical, nonspeculative.

A key word in the vocabulary of wisdom is *mashal*, usually translated "proverb." *Mashal*, as the Revised Standard
Version demonstrates, has more varied meanings than "proverb." It can be translated "discourse" (Numbers 23:7), "by-
word" (Job 17:6), "parable" (Psalm 78:2), "taunt" (Isaiah
14:4), or "allegory" (Ezekiel 17:2), depending on the nature
of the pronouncement to which it refers. *Mashal* actually refers to a form of words, short or long, prose or poetry, descriptive or allusive, in which some attribute of the givenness of life is verbalized and manifested for what it is. A
mashal is the product of attentive, shrewd, perceptive (*chakam* embraces all three) observation of life. It is the product
of imagination, economy, skill (*chokmah* embraces all three)
in the use of words. A *mashal* vividly depicts reality, sets it
before man clearly, so that it can be accepted for what it is,
and be dealt with prudently. "Wisdom" that leads to the
formulation of a *mashal*, that enables man to grasp reality,
is not proficiency at abstract thought. It is not analogous to
intuitive speculation or mystical vision. Rather, it is analogous to the ability of a weaver, the skill of a craftsman, the
practical cunning of a politician.[1]

In Israel, as generally in the ancient Near East, wisdom
and wisdom literature had two sources within the culture. In
the first place, it derived from the folk culture, finding expression in the sayings and maxims circulated in everyday
life: "So it became a *mashal*, 'Is even a Saul among the
prophets?'" (I Samuel 10:12). The unexpected, even the
ridiculous, in human experience found economic illustration
in a folk tale or parable. Imagine a circle of men gathered at
a village gate in the evening to review events of the day and
evaluate them by reference to folk wisdom handed down

through the generations, someone now and then coining a new *mashal* to cover a new situation, all the members of the village contributing to it so that it embodied their collective wisdom.[2] In such circles it was recognized that age confers richness of experience, and the elders of the village were honored for this, but understanding was honored in whomever it was found. Certain members of the village were specially designated "wise."

In the second place, there were professional wise men attached to the courts of kings, those who could write, who kept the royal records and who were perhaps the equivalent of our civil service. It was one of their functions to propagate that wisdom necessary to the maintenance of order and stability in life. They were charged with the education of young men in the royal court, with instructing potential rulers in the practical sagacity requisite to success in human affairs. For this purpose, they recorded, codified, and transmitted maxims of conduct and practical wisdom.[3] They also collected examples of situations in which wise men deported themselves with wisdom.[4] Such wise men attained a place of honor in Israel when Solomon established his Near Eastern court. For that reason, Solomon became the traditional patron of wisdom for Israel, and the wisdom literature claimed him as its fountainhead.[5]

Wisdom literature, popular and courtly, was rooted in two anterior convictions. One was a confidence about order in the cosmos and in human existence. In Egypt, source of much wisdom literature, that order was designated by the word *ma 'at*, variously translated "right," "just," "true," "in order," "good." Something of its meaning is conveyed in this passage (*ma 'at* here is rendered "justice"):

If thou art a leader commanding the affairs of the multitude, seek out for thyself every beneficial deed, until it may be that thy [own] affairs are without wrong. Justice is great, and its ap-

propriateness is lasting; it has not been disturbed since the time
of him who made it, [whereas] there is punishment for him who
passes over its laws. It is the [right] path before him who knows
nothing. Wrongdoing has never brought its undertaking into port.
[It may be that] it is fraud that gains riches, [but] the strength
of justice is that it lasts, and a man may say: "It is the property
of my father. . . ." [6]

The orderly nature of experience endures—"it has not
been disturbed since the time of him who made it"; it can
be transmitted from generation to generation by sound instruction—"it is the property of my father." Confidence in
the order of life is inherent in the practical affairs of men;
it is not a philosophical concept or an ideal. In Hebrew
terms, it is precisely the function of *mashal* to reveal the
nature of the order that is given. A man who defies or denies
the established order is characterized as a "fool." Tamar does
not counter the advances of her half-brother with moralistic
pleading. She says simply, "You would be as one of the fools
in Israel" (II Samuel 13:13—the Revised Standard Version's
extraneous use of the adjective "wanton" injects a moralistic
tone not implied in the Hebrew). Israel can dismiss unbelief
with a directness that excludes pietistic passion: "It is a fool
who thinks there is no God" (Psalms 14:1; 53:1).

Wisdom also involves a realistic awareness of the limits of
human power and understanding. Ancient Near Eastern cultural wisdom is not religious or theological. Indeed it is sometimes skeptical, elevating that order discerned by shrewdness in practical affairs above fluctuating speculation about
the gods. It is characterized by a consciousness of, and an
acceptance of, the boundaries through which human per-
ception cannot penetrate. This realism, as opposed to cyni-
cal agnosticism, is responsible for the profound wisdom recorded in Ecclesiastes. Its lovely poem on the times and
seasons in life (3:1-8) is a model of wisdom, a *mashal* (or

series of them) on the fitness of a variety of temporal events and episodes. Wisdom lies in recognizing and accepting each "time" for what it really is. "He (God) has made everything beautifully appropriate in its own moment; he has even put into man's mind a consciousness of the wholeness of time of which the moments are a part, but not so as to make it possible for man to descry the totality of God's action from its beginning to its end" (Ecclesiastes 3:11).[7] Thus does the Preacher proclaim that human wisdom is able to make sense of the successive moments of life, and also discern in that succession a totality (more the sense of the Hebrew word than "eternity") which has its own meaning. But, and this *is* wisdom, the perspective of mortal man—bounded, as it is, by birth and death—is too confined to admit a grasp of the overarching purpose of God. Such realism, an astringent corrective to self-righteous, overconfident belief, is by no means incompatible with faith.

During the period of the Israelite monarchy, as during the era of the tribal confederation by which it was preceded, wisdom does not seem to have been a formative theological factor. It did, however, pervade the cultural atmosphere, and is not absent—in nontheological form—from the songs preserved in the psalter. Psalm 49, for example, celebrates an intractable order belying human pretension:

> Here this, O all peoples!
>   Lend an ear, all who live in this age,
> Both men of low estate and men of parts,
>   Rich and poor alike!
> My mouth shall speak wise things;
>   My mind's efforts [result in] understanding.
> I am stretching out my ear for a *mashal*,
>   Working at the riddle before me with lyre music.
>   (Psalm 49:1-4, Heb. 2-5.)

These lines, which open the psalm, are steeped in the wisdom tradition. The singer seeks to formulate a *mashal* in which an aspect of truth may be set forth. He uses music as a means of unloosing inspiration. The poem proper consists of two stanzas, each containing eight cola the last of which, the refrain, is a *mashal:*

(Stanza 1)
Why should I be afraid in bad times,
  When the iniquity of those as human as I am surrounds me—
The ones who trust in their wealth,
  Who praise themselves for the abundance of their riches?
Surely no man can come close to ransoming himself,
  Can pay to God the price of ransoming himself—
For the ransom of one's life is so costly
  That [everything accumulated] through all of time is not enough—
So that he should continue to live forever,
  Should not see the grave.
For it is manifest that even wise men die,
  Together with the foolish and stupid do they perish,
    And leave their wealth to others.
Some may think their houses everlasting,
  That their dwelling places [will stand] through all generations,
    Have given their own names to the earth:
But man may not take shelter in wealth,
  The *mashal* on him is that he is like the beasts that perish.

(Stanza 2)
This is the fate of those who have foolish confidence,
  The latter end of those pleased with their own pronouncements:
Like sheep are they destined for Sheol;
  Death is their shepherd;
And they descend straight to the grave;

Their form is destined to waste away;
  Sheol shall be their permanent home.[8]
Do not be afraid when some man becomes rich,
  When the wealth of his house multiplies.
For when he dies he can take none of it with him;
  His wealth will not follow him on his downward journey.
Yes, though he bless his lot in this life,
  Praises it because things went well with it,
He will follow the generation of his parents
  Who shall never at all see light.
Man may not take shelter in wealth,
  The *mashal* on him is that he is like the beasts that perish.
                                        (Psalm 49:5-20, Heb. 6-21.)

This typical wisdom poem has no religious or theological point to make. Its point is merely to assess the realities of life clearly so that they will be seen and accepted for what they are. It is not distinctively Israelite in its point of view; it could have come, in fact, from Egypt or Mesopotamia.

WISDOM THEOLOGY IN ISRAEL

Wisdom, though a pervasive element in both the popular and court life of Israel, does not appear to have played a formative role in the proclamation of who Yahweh was or in the formulas by which he was addressed by his people. It *is* implicit in the thought and vocabulary of the Old Testament, but did not provide the motifs for Israel's enunciation of her faith in the premonarchical or Davidic periods.[9] As a consequence of an upheaval as disruptive of Israel's life as the Philistine incursion into Palestine, wisdom became, with the Mosaic covenant and ancient Near Eastern cosmology, a formative element of biblical theology.[10]

The fall of Jerusalem to Babylon in 587 B.C. revoked the claim that Yahweh exercised rule over the cosmos from the

sacred city through the authority and conquests of the Davidic monarch. The empirical order of the *mythos* was abol-
ished. Israel found herself in a situation comparable to that
which had prevailed after the Philistine annihilation of the
covenant confederation and before the establishment of the
Davidic monarchy. The *mythos* could be recounted only in
the past tense. No visible, political order could be pointed
to as vindication of Yahweh's rule. The "we" upon whom
Yahweh had conferred responsibility for their own destiny
were consigned to sing about that destiny in the form of the
lament:

> Beside Babylon's streams,
>   There do we dwell; yes, we weep
>   As Zion occupies our thoughts.
> On the poplar trees there
>   Have we hung our lyres.
> In such a situation have our captors
>   Demanded of us a song,
> And our oppressors expressions of joy:
>   "Sing one of the songs of Zion for us!"
> How can we sing Yahweh's praise
>   On foreign soil?   (Psalm 137:1-4.)

Israel finds herself beside *Babylon*'s streams. The Hebrew
word for streams is the same as that for "river" in Psalm 46.
"The River: its streams make joyous the sacred city" (Psalm
46:4, Hebrews 5). How can Yahweh's praise be sung when
cosmic sovereignty seems to be exercised from alien soil by
rulers anointed by other gods? Events have exploded the
mythos within which Yahweh had been acclaimed for four
hundred years. These events were the source of the "exile"
motif still central to Jewish theology and piety.

It is true that the last chapter of the story ended by exile
had been prophetic proclamation that the collapse of the
Davidic order was ordained by Yahweh in furtherance of his

purpose in history. Remembrance of what Yahweh had wrought through David out of the ruins of the old covenant confederation lent credence to that prophetic proclamation. The messianic expectation of postexilic Judaism had its roots in that remembrance and in the prophetic interpretation of Israel's national tragedy culminating in the events of 587.[11] Expectation, however, was repeatedly frustrated. Despite the triumphant prophecies preserved in Isaiah, chapters 40-55, no highway appeared in the desert as a result of Cyrus's conquest of Babylon in 538 B.C. Despite the promise and exhortation of Haggai and Zechariah during the upheavals in the Persian empire in 522, Zerubbabel failed to resurrect the Davidic order. Despite the efforts of Nehemiah and Ezra to restore the Temple and to reform the community, Israel found herself, as the fourth century began, in a limbo, able to be affirmative only about her remembered past and her apocalyptically anticipated future.[12]

It was as a *mythos* for such an ambiguous historical situation that the wisdom motif, an element of the culture of which she had been and was still a part, came to be appropriated by Israel. Yahweh's character and purpose were no longer manifest in Israel's history nor in the conquest of the powers of chaos through his earthly vicegerent. His purpose could now, however, be discerned in that order underlying the everyday life of man to which wisdom pointed and to which the *mashal* gave expression. Exilic and postexilic Israel found a viable theological idiom in the traditions of wisdom. Collections of maxims from the wisdom schools, particularly those associated with Solomon and subsequent royal courts at Jerusalem, acquired new significance, and were assembled into one comprehensive collection bearing Solomon's name and known to us as the Book of Proverbs. As the earlier sections of Israel's canon of sacred writings— the Law and the Prophets—were dominated by motifs of the

Mosaic and Davidic eras, so the third and later section of
the canon—the Writings—was dominated by the wisdom
motif of the exilic and postexilic era.[13] So it was that the
psalter came to manifest in its final form traditions of wisdom
that afforded postmonarchic Israel its theological *mythos*.

How wisdom (*chokmah*) became invested with particular
theological significance is made clear in various passages in
the Old Testament in which wisdom is praised, and ultimately personified as the vehicle through which Yahweh
communicates with men. This development took place in no
neat chronological sequence, and the speculation involved
was flexible, continuing even into the Christian era.[14]

Job, chapter 28, is a poem artificially intruded into its context. Though in its present form given a particular twist by
the addition of the final verse (28), the poem is essentially
a meditation on the mysterious elusiveness of wisdom. The
opening verses are a beautiful description of how the technical skill of man unlocks the secrets of the earth, penetrating
its depths and uncovering its riches (Job 28:1-11). This,
however, is by way of prelude to the basic assertion of the
poem:

> But [as for] wisdom, where is it to be found?
> And where is understanding located?
> Man is not acquainted with the way to it,
> And it is not found in the land of the living.
> (Job 28:12-13.)

Wisdom, the principle (person?—"it" is feminine in Hebrew) underlying and enabling the achievements of man, is
a reality the totality of which is not available to man. This is
similar to the spirit of Ecclesiastes 3:11: a gentle, realistic
skepticism about the human capacity to penetrate ultimate
wisdom. There is One, however, who does comprehend the
totality of wisdom:

God understands the way to it,
   Is acquainted with where it is located.
Yes, he is the one who can look out on the very ends of the
earth,
   Can see everything under the heavens,
So that he determined the force of the wind,
   And meted out the waters by measure.
When he carved out channels for the rain,
   And a way for the water to fall from thunderclouds,
Even then did he see it [wisdom], and make it a part of
things,
   Establish it, and make it accountable to himself.

(Job 28:23-27.)

Wisdom, discerned by man in only a segmented way, is in
its totality not only known by God but is, in fact, his creation
and agent. ("God" and not "Yahweh" is used in this late
poem because by that time "God" has come to mean "Yahweh.") Wisdom has displaced the covenant motif and the
mythological motifs as a *mythos,* and is seen as the product
of Yahweh's creative activity, as a vehicle of his sovereignty
over life. Wisdom, the servant of God, is accessible to man
only through God. The last verse of Job, chapter 28, probably
a later addition to the poem, gives voice to a logical consequence of the poem proper, and it elucidates a central theme
of later Israel's piety and theology:

And he [God] said to man:
"Behold, the fear of Yahweh, that is wisdom,
   And turning from evil is understanding."

(Job 28:28.)

Wisdom is identified with Israel's revealed knowledge of
Yahweh; his "godness" is cast in terms of the wisdom traditions.

Wisdom as the medium through which God makes contact
with man and by which he orders the world is almost per-

sonified in Job, chapter 28. The "it" though ambiguous, could
be rendered "she."

The personification of wisdom is complete in Proverbs,
chapters 8 and 9, which probably represent the compilers'
preface to the collections of wisdom recorded in chapters 10
through 31.[15] Wisdom herself speaks, making unmistakably
clear her function in Yahweh's creation and her relationship
to the men who dwell in it:

Yahweh created me as the first step in his plan,
    Before any of his primeval deeds was done.
At the very beginning of time it was I who was established,
    At the first, before ever there was an earth.
When there was no primeval ocean was I born,
    When there were no springs flowing with water.
Before the mountains had been put in place,
    Before there were hills was I born.
Even before he made the earth and its wide spaces,
    Or any of the soil covering the continents,
When he put the skies in place, I was there,
    When he set bounds around the primeval ocean,
When he molded the clouds in the sky,
    When he put pressure behind the fountains of the prime-
    val ocean,
When he laid out a channel for the sea
    So that the water would not spread farther than was his
    will,
    When he surveyed the foundations of the earth,
Then was I alongside him as a little child,
    Then was I his delight every day,
Playing before him every moment,
    Playing in his habitable world,
        And my delight came to be in mortal men.
                                        (Proverbs 8:22-31.)

The cosmology of the poem obviously derives from the
old myth ("primeval ocean," etc.), but a new primacy is

given to wisdom. She is the first product of Yahweh's creative activity. She is antecedent to any other force in the cosmos. She is Yahweh's first born in whom he takes great delight, and she takes like delight in the sons of men.[16] The universe can be trusted and is pervaded by a wisdom that is benevolent and well disposed toward the human community.

Wisdom has, however, a counterpart. In Proverbs, chapter 7, the praise of personified wisdom is preceded by the description of another kind of female figure. The pervasiveness of the "evil woman" in the wisdom writings, as in the conclusion to chapter 7, documents that the "evil woman" was more than a harlot. Indeed the Revised Standard Version's translation of 7:5 to the contrary not withstanding, the Hebrew words in that verse in no way imply that the woman in question is a harlot. She is the opposite of wisdom. The wiles of the harlot are her weapons in the battle for the allegiance of men to whom wisdom offers true and significant life. An issue is joined. It involves man's destiny:

> Say to wisdom, "My sister art thou,"
>   And designate understanding as your close of kin,
> In order to protect yourself from the Alien Woman
>   And from that barbarous one who mouths smooth words.
>   (Proverbs 7:4-5.)

The ensuing lines describe the antagonist of wisdom enticing a "young man without sense" into her clutches with the bait of sexual pleasure (vss. 6-20). The real issue, however, emerges in the closing lines:

> She seduces [a man] with her limitless persuasiveness,
>   With her slick words does she lure him off the right track.
> Running after her with no caution,
>   He goes as an ox does to the slaughter,
> Or [he's like] a stag held with ropes

Until an arrow can get to his vital parts.
Like a bird rushing into a snare,
    He knows not that he will pay with his life.
So now, my son, listen to me,
    Take note of the words that I speak.
Let not your mind wander into her ways,
    Stray not into her paths.
For a multitude of victims has she brought down,
    And numberless is the total she's slain.
Her house is the road to Sheol,
    The descent to the chambers of death.

                        (Proverbs 7:21-27.)[17]

There is a conflict in which man is involved. But it is much less crass, more sophisticated, and man's role in it is more significant than in the conflicts of the older *mythos*. His reason plays a part. A choice lies before him. He can learn. And the reason he can learn, the meaning of his efforts to do so, lies in wisdom. Through her Yahweh himself is at work to give human life meaning and order. Her high place in the cosmos is indicated by her possession of a temple with seven pillars (Proverbs 9:1). Her persistent exhortation is made through the inclination to right behavior, is *there* in life:

Does not wisdom call,
    And understanding sound her voice?
On the high places beside the road,
    At the crossroads she takes her stand;
Next to the gates leading into the city,
    At the very threshold of the portals she cries loudly:
"To you, O men, do I call,
    My cry is to all the sons of men. . . .
With me are counsel and effectiveness,
    With me discernment and strength.
By me do kings reign,
    And rulers decree what is righteous.

> By me do princes exercise their authority,
>   And nobles become righteous rulers.
> I love those who love me,
>   And whoever seeks me finds me."
>   (Proverbs 8:1-4, 14-17.)

It was of great significance both for the nature of later Judaism and for the way Israel's Scriptures came to be used by Jew and Christian alike that the *mythos* provided by wisdom was neither rooted in historical event nor capable of being "historicized" as the cosmic myth had been. The wisdom mythos addressed itself primarily to the individual and to his conduct of his own life. To the members of the "we" who lamented the disaster of 587 B.C. it offered no hope of the restoration of the social, communal, historical continuum to which Israel's view of life had previously been attached. It offered a view of life and of the issues involved in life in which attention was focused on the individual and his action and decision, and on the connection between them and God. As a counterpart to the doctrine of God it offered a doctrine of *man* rather than a doctrine of the significance of the *human enterprise. Knowledge* leading to the good life rather than *confidence* in the human enterprise was the substance of the wisdom *mythos*. Individual well-being rather than hope for the outcome of the historical venture was its goal.[18] The door was open for religion to separate itself from social and political realities. Abraham and Moses and David became models of the wise life, teachers of wisdom, rather than participants in the continuum of history through which past and future were related to the present so as to give it meaning.[19]

The character of Israel's faith had changed, the meaning of its past had changed, as is seen in a passage from Ecclesiasticus which illustrates how wisdom assumed theological primacy in Israel. In a soliloquy (similar to Proverbs, chap-

ters 8 and 9) wisdom herself speaks, explicitly associating
her function in the universal order with Israel's role as enunciated in the historical traditions:

> I came forth from the mouth of the Most High,
>> And like a mist covered the earth.
> I established my residence in the heights,
>> And a cloudy pillar was my throne.
> The vault of heaven have I alone circuited,
>> And in the depths of the abyss have I walked.
> In the sea's watery substance as well as all the earth's dry
> soil,
>> Yes, in every people and nation have I property rights.
> Among them all I sought a resting place,
>> Someone's territory in which I might lodge.
> Finally the Creator of all gave order concerning me,
>> The One who also created me designated a permanent
>> spot for my tent.
> For he said, "With Jacob take up residence,
>> And in Israel take possession of your inheritance."
>> (Ecclesiasticus 24:3-8.)

This passage expands upon the speculation on the nature
and function of wisdom that is found in Proverbs, chapters
8 and 9. Wisdom pervades every corner of the cosmos, is
that in which all things are held together. Her point of contact with mankind is the people formed by Yahweh during
the events of which the older traditions speak. That is the
meaning of the enterprise of which "Jacob-Israel" is the
proper, given name. Thus is the continuing history of Israel
through the Davidic era interpreted:

> Before all time, at the very beginning, did he create me,
>> And so long as time shall last shall I never go into eclipse.
> In the sacred tabernacle did I do him homage,
>> Thus was I established on Zion.

The beloved city did he designate as my dwelling place,
   Yes, Jerusalem was the focus of my authority.
Thus did I take root in an honored people,
   Become the inheritance of those who are Yahweh's pos-
   session.   (Ecclesiasticus 24:9-12.)

Written long after the collapse of the Mosaic and Davidic orders, this poem refers to what was and to its abiding significance. Thus, when wisdom's soliloquy has reached its conclusion (Ecclesiasticus 24:13-22), the author makes it clear where wisdom is to be found in the world:

All this is the book of the covenant of God Most High,
   The *torah* decreed for us by Moses,
      The heritage of the congregations of Jacob.
Torah fills men with wisdom, [is boundless] as the river Pishon,
   As the Tigris in the time of the spring floods.
It sates them with understanding as the Euphrates [floods the ground],
   Yes, as the Jordan does at harvest time.
It makes instruction [*paideia*] shine forth as light,
   As Gihon at the time of grape harvest.
                (Ecclesiasticus 24:23-27.)

Israel is no longer defined as the conduit of an ongoing history which is the locus of God's purposeful activity. Israel, in the age of Ecclesiasticus, is the possessor of that book whose narrative and teaching contain the *mashal par excellence, the* truth about the nature of life. Wisdom is what imparts significance to those events to which Israel's narrative traditions witness, and the record of those events has become the book through which God's handmaiden, wisdom, speaks to men. Thus Israel's sacred history is explicitly associated with wisdom in chapters 10 through 19 of the Wisdom of

Solomon. To be an Israelite is no longer to stand in the historical continuum which itself is revelation and salvation. To be an Israelite is to be a student *of torah,* to practice the piety derived *from torah,* to conform one's life to *torah.*[20]

WISDOM, TORAH, AND THE PSALTER

Within this new *mythos* Israel's ancient songs were gathered, collected into what we know as the psalter. Certain songs exemplify what happened. Psalm 19, for example, differs radically from Psalm 29, a cosmic hymn, or those altered, peculiarly Israelite hymns, such as Psalms 136 and 105, in which the historical activity of God is acclaimed. Psalm 19 is understandable only in terms of the development of wisdom theology.[21] In it the cosmos, not the historical continuum, is the reflection of the activity of Yahweh, and *torah* (interpreted in the light of wisdom theology) is the basis of human understanding and piety:

The heavens are witness to God's glory,
　And his creative activity is evidenced by the firmament.
One day in succession to another proclaims it,
　One night in succession to another is a revelation of knowledge.
Though lacking the ability to proclaim it in words,
　Having no physical voice to be heard,
Their message penetrates the whole earth,
　What they have to convey reaches the world's end.
For the sun has pitched a tent in them,
　Comes forth as a bridegroom from his chamber,
　　Runs its course with the enthusiasm of a man in his prime.
From the heavens' very end does it come,
　Makes its circuit clear to their other side,
　　So that nothing escapes its heat.
                                        (Psalm 19:1-6, Heb. 2-7.)

This evidence of the wisdom by which the universe is given meaning affords a transition to verses that celebrate *torah* and the piety that leads to it:

> Yahweh's *torah* is perfect,
>> An imparter of life to man.
>
> Yahweh's perceivable signs are dependable,
>> Imparting wisdom to those ready for it.
>
> Yahweh's precepts are right,
>> The sources of a happy mind.
>
> Yahweh's commandment is clear,
>> A means of seeing things aright.
>
> The piety grounded in Yahweh is pure,
>> Something forever worthwhile.
>
> Those things ordained by Yahweh are dependable,
>> Altogether righteous.
>
> More desirable are they than gold,
>> Than a horde of pure gold;
>
> Sweeter are they than honey,
>> Than the drippings from the honeycomb.
>
> Indeed, by them is thy servant kept on the right track,
>> In obedience of them is great reward.
>
> Yet, who can detect his unknowing errors?
>> Keep me free of unconscious wrongs.
>
> Even more, restrain thy servant from willful wrongs,
>> Let them not get the better of me.
>
> So shall I be blameless and innocent,
>> Free of gross transgression.
>
> Let what I say and think be pleasing to thee,
>> Yahweh, my refuge and redeemer.
>
>> (Psalm 19:7-14, Heb. 8-15.)

The piety growing out of the *mythos* of wisdom, in which Israel's and traditions became *torah*, was responsible not only for individual poems;[22] it was responsible also for the collection of the ancient songs into the psalter to provide a handbook of prayer and meditation for the faithful. That

collection is a manual of devotion compiled in an age in
which the circumstances of history and the use of wisdom
to form a new theological idiom had given Israel a character
different from that of the covenant and monarchical eras.
The hymns and the laments, rooted in a different world
view, one that was concrete and dramatic, were employed
in a "spiritual" way. The community by which they were employed had become self-consciously *religious*. This came
about as a product of a history that could not be escaped
when wisdom was located in

> The book of the covenant of God Most High,
>   The *torah* decreed . . . by Moses,
>   The heritage of the congregations of Jacob.

History itself, however, is no longer viewed as the *mythos*,
especially not that part of it following 587 B.C.[23] History is
merely the situation in which Israel contemplates *torah*, in
which the piety of Psalm 19 could be practiced. Thus the
completed psalter opens neither with hymnic invocation nor
with thanksgivings but with this pietistic pronouncement:

> Happy is that man
> Who has not followed wicked counsel,
>   Has not acted in the manner of sinners,
>   Has not associated himself with scoffers.
> Yes, if one takes delight in Yahweh's *torah*,
>   Pores over it both day and night,
> He becomes as a tree planted by the cosmic source of water,
>   Whose fruit appears in due season,
>   Whose leaves wither not.   (Psalm 1:1-3.)

The Book of Psalms is not the hymnbook of a worshiping
community though it is based upon collections that had
served that purpose. It is meant to be used by a community
whose piety is analogous to modern, individualistic piety.
Wherever it refers to history or to the processes of nature it

refers to the outward garments of a reality only to be descried by mystical meditation one *torah*. Psalm 1 is balanced by what may have been originally the conclusion to the psalter, Psalm 119.[24] In content and in form this psalm extols Yahweh's *torah* and the value of "poring over it day and night." The author praises *torah* explicitly *and* in the discipline to which he subjects himself in the construction of his poem. He creates a poem of twenty-two stanzas, each containing eight couplets. He frames his message so that each couplet in a given stanza begins with the same letter, these letters proceeding consecutively from the first stanza to the last through the twenty-two letters of the Hebrew alphabet. Furthermore, God is addressed or referred to in every couplet in the psalm, and every couplet mentions *torah* either explicitly or by use of one of nine synonyms which Hebrew has for it. The total effect is impressive, if monotonous, but the poem is a remarkable example of the devotion of Israel in the era when wisdom became theological *mythos* and *torah* the devotional content of Judaism. This kind of piety is responsible for the psalter in the form in which we have it, as is seen, for example, in the artificial division of the material into five "books" obviously meant to conform to the five books of the Torah (Pentateuch), each of which was provided with a doxology (Psalms 41:13; 72:18-19; 89:52; 106:48; the whole of Psalm 150—verse numbers as in the English text).

Thus did the songs of Israel arise out of the ethos of the premonarchical covenant community and out of the ethos of the Davidic kingdom and, in the course of history, come to be related to the situation in which Israel found herself in the exilic and postexilic era. Once again a motif available in the culture of which Israel was a part was adapted to give expression to the meaning of life under Yahweh. Once again Yahweh's sovereignty was interpreted in an idiom amenable

to the realities of a given age, however drastically the use
of that idiom may have transformed the nature of Israel's
faith. Indeed, in this latter case the faith would appear to
have been transformed even more than the idiom.

Two final observations may be advanced: First, the faith
expressed in the forms of the old tribal confederation, and
the faith of the Davidic era, associated Yahweh's sovereignty
inseparably with empirical history. That history ended with
the conquest of Israel and her absorption into the Assyrian
and Babylonian empires, and the new situation prevailed
through the Persian and Macedonian eras (it was not significantly interrupted by the brief Maccabean resurgence). The
prophetic promise by which the collapse of the Davidic order had been accompanied was gradually transformed into
terms consonant with reality; apocalyptic hope itself became
a factor of wisdom-*torah* theology and piety.[25] After 587 the
only empirical history to which faith and theology could appeal was past history. A medium other than that history itself had to be found to relate faith significantly to existen-
tial circumstances. This explains both the rise of futurist eschatology in Israel and the appropriation of wisdom-*torah*
theology that could lead to a Philo's interpretation of Israel's
Scriptures in terms of Greek ontological speculation.[26]

Second, radically though the employment of the wisdom
motif as a theological idiom did transform the character of
Israel's faith, it was nevertheless responsible for the preservation of the traditions and writings produced by that faith
which might otherwise have become, through historical irrelevance, forgotten and lost. We have Israel's songs only
because they were collected into a manual for use by those
whose piety was informed by the wisdom-*torah* theology.
There can be no doubt that biblical faith is historically
oriented, conceives history as the medium of God's revelation and purposeful activity. There is equally no doubt that

the preaching and presence of Jesus of Nazareth occasioned a recovery and a resurgence of historically oriented biblical faith in Israel.

Precisely the distinctive character of the Christian *mythos* itself precludes ideological denigration or dismissal of the wisdom-*torah* theology and the influence it had, not least in the preservation and collection of Israel's sacred songs. The era in which the wisdom motif provided the idiom in which Yahweh continued to be confessed as sovereign Lord of all things is itself an important part of the history about which biblical faith requires an affirmation.

5 Yahweh's Songs in an Alien Age

Modern readers and users of Israel's songs are not members of a tribal confederation defining itself against a prevailing culture, as was the situation of premonarchical Israel. Such a condition may exist in some measure among certain "younger churches," or among churches behind the Iron Curtain. But even in those situations the pervading culture —secular, scientific, technological—derives through the intellectual history of Europe in part from Jerusalem and in part from Athens. Even where it is necessary, today, to take a position *vis à vis* the pervading culture, that culture is one whose history and character cannot be dissociated from its origins in the Christian tradition. The Canaanite city-states have, as it were, become one "post-Christian," world-encompassing society.

Nor is the contemporary user of the psalms exposed to a culture whose *mythos* even resembles that confronted by Israel when David brought her into the "mainstream" of ancient Near Eastern culture. After the collapse of Aristotelian physics in the late Middle Ages, the cosmos was swept clean of gods and demigods, of the unseen hands and souls once believed responsible for the movements of heavenly bodies and other natural phenomena. Yahweh's deposition of the other gods, locating determinative drama in the events of human history, has succeeded so completely that today it is difficult to define him as God in terms that are congruous with secular civilization. The *mythos* of Davidic Israel, climaxed in the triumphant lyrics of Isaiah, chapters 40-55, proclaimed the absolute and unique claim of Yahweh to "godness." This claim has been so successfully carried into modern culture, by the preaching of the gospel of God in Christ, that "godness," is questioned as a category containing any meaning at all.

Modern man is similarly uncomfortable with the *mythos* provided by wisdom in exilic and postexilic Israel. We have seen how contrary the character of that *mythos* really was to the heritage it was employed to preserve. It is comparably antipathetic to modern culture, characterized as it is by the absence of any prevalent metaphysical presuppositions. The secular mood of the modern world (and its conscious philosophy) admits no overarching assumptions about the nature of reality such as are proposed by the wisdom *mythos*. Formulated in a prescientific culture, the wisdom *mythos* cannot be the context within which the Bible is read and interpreted for the modern world. The two philosophies predominant in the twentieth century are not congenial to the *mythos* provided for theology and piety by wisdom. The one rejects any statement or assumption not empirically verifiable, denying the validity of all abstraction, and thoroughly excluding such a personification as wisdom. The other rejects any concept of reality that postulates an underlying essence or an ultimate reality, rooting its thought and commitment entirely in concrete, human existence. However one may judge the two philosophies, they are certainly not consonant with the wisdom *mythos*.

THE PROBLEM STATED

Precisely the accomplishments of those mature methods of study by which the psalms "come alive" on their own terms make it clear that their presuppositions, their world

view, their outlook, are vastly different from our own.[1] The
difficulties are not those usually attached to the psalms. The
national laments do involve the frustrations and aspirations
and the restricted outlook of a particular, bygone political
entity, but that is not the crucial problem. Many psalms are
informed by a spirit of vindictiveness and imprecation alien
to our habits of prayer and worship, but that is not the crucial problem either. The crucial problem pervades all the
psalms, as much when we sing, "O come, let us sing unto the
Lord. . . . For the Lord is a great God, and a great King
above all gods," as when we encounter the concluding verses
of Psalm 137, or "Wilt thou not slay the wicked, O God?"
The crucial problem is posed as much by the cosmic imagery
of Psalm 46 as by the curse which is the substance of Psalm
129. The crucial problem, even more an obstacle to commitment when we are unaware of it, lies in the vast gulf between the world view of Israel and our own world view. Is
the God dramatically proclaimed in the language of the
psalms the God of a world that no longer speaks that language? If he is, is it not an obstacle to comprehension that
we persist in that language? Does it not verge on dishonesty
to avoid particular passages that distress us, thereby lulling
ourselves into ignorance of the heritage we have and its conflict with modern views?

Neither the "apologetic" nor the "reductionist" exegesis
of the psalms will suffice. The former seeks to ignore the
gulf, speciously suggesting that yearning for God is identical
in any time and in any place. "Apologists" rely on allegori-
cal and typological interpretation, proposing that—usually
their use by Christ is stressed—the psalms of Israel have
some intrinsic merit possessed by no other prayers or songs.
Even the most scathing of imprecatory psalms, even the most
self-righteous of them, are, this view argues, vehicles of self-
knowledge and self-offering.[2] The latter, the "reductionist"

exegesis, proposes that the psalms, indeed the Old Testament generally, are subject to the judgment of the Christ in whose coming they were fulfilled. The psalms are conceived as elements of our biblical heritage, but to be used only selectively, verses or, sometimes, full psalms, to be discarded if they appear incompatible with Christ's law of love.[3]

Both approaches, perhaps unconsciously, are based on assumptions not found in Israel's songs. Both approaches assume that the psalms—either in their entirety or in the parts of them acceptable for contemporary use—are devotional, reflecting what the modern mind conceives as individual "spiritual" experience. Both approaches assume that the world view, the *mythos,* of Israel's songs is that of modern man, specifically of modern "religious" man. Such is not the case. The *mythos* of the songs of Israel is rooted in that *people's* communal grasp of its relationship as a historical, political, social phenomenon to a specific, identifiable, nameable God. It encompasses that people's appropriation and adaptation of certain cultural idioms to embody its faith. It has little or nothing to do with "religion" as it is conceived in the secular, modern world. It has little or nothing to do with "religious" experience conceived as separate from and unrelated to the empirical unfolding of life in history.

The songs of Israel do not address religion as it is usually practiced in the twentieth century, nor are they compatible with modern man's characteristic view of life, its issues and its ultimate meaning. How far we are removed from the world of Israel's songs constitutes, in fact, a paradigm of the problem presented to us by all of our biblical heritage. Certainly, read in historical context, it is possible to appreciate the songs for what they are in and of themselves. But is it possible to establish a rationale for *use* of them in the contemporary world?

AN APPROACH TO THE PROBLEM

We begin with a fact: if we *are* members of the Christian community we *do use* Israels songs. That fact is presupposed by all attempts to justify use of them and all theories about how they ought or ought not to be used. A *descriptive* definition of the Christian community would certainly have to include as one of its characteristics that it is a continuing historical body in which Israel's songs are sung. The songs of Israel are a shared ecumenical heritage of otherwise grievously separated Christians. That fact is mentioned in few, if any, *doctrinal* definitions of the Church, and probably would not enter into most statements about what the Church *ought* to be, but the fact is nevertheless there. Within the divided community confessing Jesus Christ as Lord, the songs of Israel, the psalms of the Old Testament, are used in prayer and worship, and are formative of the language common to that community. Differing confessions or standards (and lack of them), as well as different abstract definitions of what membership in the Christian community is and means, cannot erase the fact that the community is a body in which the psalms of Israel have always been and still are used.

The assumption that Israel's songs must be selected and edited to conform to preconceived standards might well give way to an examination of the nature of the community by which they are used as disclosed in what it *does* rather than in how we may *think* of it abstractly. The Church, after all, like Israel, is a continuing historical community brought into being by, manifest in, and ever formed and reformed by, the givenness of concrete events. Fundamental to its life, and to the gospel it preserves and transmits, is an affirmation of just that. The gospel is not ideology but a proclamation that the movement of history is the locus of God's revelation of himself and of the activity by which his purposes inexorably move toward fulfillment. Central, therefore, to the Church's life is no set of principles, no ideology, in terms of which this or that element in her heritage and practice—or this or that situation with which history confronts her—must be justified (or perhaps found wanting). To be a Christian is to participate in an existing, concrete, historical community defined not in abstract ideas (or ideals), but in terms of past, present, and future experience. It does not primarily involve one's personal values or convictions or piety or philosophy, though it will be without integrity if there is pretense that one has altogether transcended such considerations. It does not primarily involve agreement with one's fellow Christians on some definitive statement of the Christian faith, though the integrity of the community obviously demands continual, communal wrestling with the nature of the faith.[4] It does involve a shared heritage and an affirmation about that shared heritage. It involves, among many other things, the songs of Israel.

Precisely the presence of these songs in the Christian community's life and heritage may provide a subject for meditation leading to a more mature understanding of what the Christian position really is. Precisely these songs, read on their own terms and in their entirety, may preserve us from the illusion that *we* create the gospel community or that it conforms to any or all of *our* presuppositions. Precisely these songs make it inescapable that the Christian community is not merely an association of contemporary, middle-class, Christian, American, idealistic men of good will. This is confirmed not alone by specific reference in the songs to Israel's national disasters and ambitions, nor by the imprecations so alien to us, nor the many unfamiliar turns of phrase. It is confirmed more by the basic motifs of the psalms, by the world view which they embody. We cannot read them or use

them, if we respect them enough to take them seriously, and
persist in the notion that the Christian community conforms
to our assumptions about the nature of "religious" community. We confront a vivid and wholesome reminder that the
Christian community, now historically and empirically spread
over the world, may also transcend our, and other, parochial
assumptions.

We do not here endorse some theological antiquarianism
in terms of which the songs of Israel, and any number of
other elements of the Christian heritage, are repaired to in
a precious blindness to immediate realities. Such antiquarianism approaches idolatry. The past, including our biblical
heritage, can, and often does, provide an idolatrous façade
behind which we seek to hide from reality. Affirmation of
our biblical heritage is actually a refutation and repudiation
of theological antiquarianism. The past is no static reality.
Realistically affirmed, the past is many and diverse pasts.
Affirmation of the past affirms no one idiom or *mythos*.
Affirmation of the past for Israel *and* for the Christian community affirms the call, the promise, and the covenant commitment of God as apprehended by faith. The divine call,
the promise, and the covenant commitment are never discontinuous from a succession of pasts. The unfolding of
those pasts—the past—is, however, the unfolding of what
is ever new. Indeed, newness is a central theme of biblical
witness: when the divine promise seems doomed to unful-
fillment for lack of an heir, Sarah bears Isaac in her old age;
the Lord cries through a prophet, "Remember not the former
things. . . . I am about to do a new thing"; the one in
whom the New Testament proclaims the Old fulfilled says,
"You have heard that it was said. . . , but I say to you.
. . ." The present also must be affirmed, even the present
that seems so incompatible with the heritage of Israel's
songs.

Yet, the divine call, the promise, and the covenant commitment are not capable of abstraction from that series of moments which are its share of our past. Nor, if the biblical witness is affirmed, is the character of God capable of such abstraction. God's purpose and God's character are defined for the Bible as a story is told, a history recounted, events and situations recalled. In that sense, and in no spirit of antiquarianism, the givenness of Israel's songs as part of the Christian heritage may be responsibly affirmed. The faith to which they witness, to which the Christian community has ever witnessed, frees us to accept the songs in themselves, relieves us of any need of apology for them, renders superfluous presumptuous judgment of them or justification for them. That faith frees us from idolatrous antiquarianism, from any need of pretense about them, and enables us to regard them realistically rather than romantically. That faith frees us also from a dangerous counterpart to antiquarianism: human presumption that one generation has the obligation or the capacity to define the meaning of life, or to make decision whether or not it has any meaning. That faith affirms that the heritage out of which the present has come, the movement of God's purpose in history, can be accepted in confidence and in hope.

In that sense, the fact that the Christian community *does* preserve Israel's songs must be the place where we begin to understand what they mean for our world. In that sense, exegesis of the songs may lead us to a more mature understanding of biblical faith.

THE PROBLEM IN LIGHT OF THE SONG MOTIFS

Modern study of the psalms, in the light of the culture which produced them, makes clear that they are not creations of individual poets working apart from, or in opposi-

tion to, concrete cultural and historical circumstances. "Here
the psalmist gives voice to his. . . ," or, "In these lines the
poet reveals. . . ," are not appropriate prefaces for an exegesis of the songs of Israel. Such a preface should take account of the world view, the mood, and the atmosphere of
ancient Israel. It should refer not to the frame of mind or
the spiritual condition of individuals, but to the conventions
and the idiom of a total culture. The songs of Israel must be
appreciated in a context of social realities not dissimilar to
such contemporary realities as the "organization man" and
"one world." The songs are much more than significant
documents for faith and devotion; they reflect social and
cultural and historical circumstances that, in part, parallel
the circumstances of today.

Even in her early history, when Israel defined herself and
the character of her God against the culture by which she
was surrounded, she enunciated her *mythos* (proclaiming
that *God* created that *mythos*) in language and idioms derived from that culture. To understand the form of the
covenant formulations (and the theological implications of
them), we must have reference to Hittite suzerainty treaties,
not to abstract, individual, "religious" experiences.[5] Later,
in the hymns and laments of the psalter, arising out of the
experiences of the Israelite monarchy during its identification with the politics and culture of the ancient Near East,
it is the totality of that culture and its *mythos* that supply
the substance of Israel's devotion and worship.

Study of such songs leads us inevitably to the archives
of ancient Ugarit, to sociological analysis of life in the Nile
valley, and to contemplation of the political structure of
Mesopotamian society. It leads us to take up tools of understanding and appreciation suitable for elucidating literary
and social and cultural realities. It forces us to conclude (as
does study of any element of our biblical or ecclesiastical

heritage) that there has never been a period in which faith and devotion existed in a pure form, unaffected by, or divorced from, the contingent realities of historical circumstances.

Such study of scripture, in other words, enables us to be affirmative about our own history, about our secular culture, about the issues posed for faith by the development of new methods for study of the psalms. Such study recalls us to the biblical proclamation that God has located the drama of existence in man's history in this world. The songs of Israel offer us renewed confidence in the certain unfolding in all history, including our own, of God's purpose.

Study of the songs of Israel further makes it clear that proclamation of God's work is tied to no particular cultural idiom, to no specific ideology, to no particular *mythos*. We have seen that the psalter reflects the use by Israel of many extraneous idioms and modes of expression. We might proceed to trace the use and interpretation of Israel's songs through the rabbinic and patristic and medieval and modern worlds. There was never a time when devotion was practiced in some pure form unrelated to a particular culture. There was never a time when pure biblical theology—or another pure theology—existed independent of "pagan" intellectual motifs. The living God cannot be acclaimed without reference to human experience. His character may be compromised or distorted on account of the inadequacy of a particular cultural idiom, but he remains the living God in every age and in every circumstance. The songs of Israel confirmed this again and again. Israel did not abandon him in her monarchical age, but hailed him as conqueror of the pagan pantheon, nor did she consign him to the ruins of the Davidic kingdom, but heard wisdom proclaim him as her procreator.

If it is true that the community of witness in pre-Christian

history employed many idioms to acclaim God, passing
through two crises of cultural collapse, and that the songs
of Israel are our legacy of that experience, it is also true
that the language of proclamation was not fixed for all time
and the activity of God concluded with the last page of the
New Testament. The first five centuries or so of the life of
the new Israel, the Christian Church, are precisely the story
of how that community strove to acclaim her God as God,
and Jesus as Lord, in the idiom of Hellenistic culture, an
idiom as different from that of the earliest Christians as
ancient Near Eastern cosmological motifs were from the
covenant motif. So, if today it is apparent that during the
past four or five centuries the idiom of Hellenistic culture—
in which the gospel has long been explained and proclaimed
—has fallen into desuetude, we are not without precedent
in our efforts to adjust. The songs of Israel are our precedent.
They are evidence that the witnessing community has sur-
vived crises as traumatic as that which now envelops us.
They offer us no solution of our problem more practicable
than was available in the time of David, or after the fall of
Jerusalem to Babylonia, or when the gospel began to include
a Gentile world in the community of witness. They do offer
a reminder that our predecessors found that the Lord's song
could be sung in alien situations, and that these very situations could provide the words and the music for the song.
To sing the songs of Israel is to discover a heritage of assurance.

Study of the songs of Israel also confirms that the significant work of God and the issues of existence are located
squarely in specific, particular, concrete events of history. In
the movement of Israel's life from Abraham to Moses to
David, God was reducing creation to order. In the events
hailed by prophets as the work of God, an oracle of reas-

surance was delivered to finite, lamenting man. In the *Torah* account of Israel's story, wisdom was made available to man.

Our examination of each of these motifs of Israel's songs has led us back to the original covenant *mythos*. The covenant is not, however, basic to Israel's life and outlook as a static concept, an abstract doctrine, a set code.[6] It is, rather, the normative expression of a conviction that God has invested a specific history with that meaning which other religions and cults have located outside the human enterprise. Israel's songs reflect how, in a living way and in varying living situations, loyalty to Yahweh as sovereign Lord led the community of Israel to proclaim her covenant *mythos*. Precisely because the songs reflect differing times and idioms, they provide more tangible knowledge of Israel's faith than do the writers of the Pentateuch. What was basic to Israel's faith might well be urged as a basis for our own: a bold proclamation that all other gods are deposed and that ultimate meaning is not unrelated to the ongoing life of men under the God who invests man's life with significance.

It was precisely to that conclusion that some in Israel came once again when the series of events over which "Jesus is Lord" must be inscribed filled the void inhabited by the wisdom *mythos,* rendering that *mythos* superfluous along with its predecessors, fulfilling the prophetic promise in totally unexpected ways. For the earliest generation of Christians, Israel's songs ceased to be mere repositories of *torah,* and became once again expressions of the substance of history. Peter's Old Testament scholarship leaves something to be desired, but his use of the following royal song to clarify gospel events was typical of the use that Israel frequently made of elements of her culture:

> The Lord said to my Lord, Be seated at my right hand,
> Until I make thine enemies a footstool for thy feet.

Let all the house of Israel therefore know for certain that God has made him both Lord and Messiah, this Jesus whom you crucified.

(Acts 2:34-36, quoting Psalm 132:1.)

According to the New Testament, we live today in that era of which Peter speaks, and in which God, in Jesus, has once again located ultimate meaning in concrete history now embracing all the world. Expressed in the idiom of times past, and without *specific* direction for our situation, Israel's songs introduce us into the tradition in which Peter's affirmation makes sense. *That* tradition affirms that God is known for who he is, precisely when we confront and grapple with the problems which this book has endeavored to define.

Author's Notes

Introduction: METHOD AND APPROACH

1. On the use of the psalms down through the ages, cf. Prothero, *The Psalms in Human Life*, and Lamb, *The Psalms in Christian Worship*.

2. Cf. Duhm's commentary. Informed by the same kind of interest, if much more conservative in their results, are the commentaries of Kirkpatrick and Buttenwieser.

3. In spite of his interest in the theory of a covenant festival as expounded in the introduction to his commentary, cf. the expositions of the various psalms by Weiser.

4. Cf. Albright, "The Psalm of Habakkuk," and Cross, "Notes on a Canaanite Psalm in the Old Testament."

5. Cf. Grobel, "Form Criticism" in vol. 2 of *Interpreter's Dictionary of the Bible*, and Koch, *Was Ist Formgeschichte?*

6. Gunkel first applied the form-critical method to Genesis in his most important commentary on that book. *The Legends of Genesis* is an English translation of the introduction to the commentary. His commentary on the psalms was published in 1926. The real description of his method is found in his *Einleitung in die Psalmen*, completed after his death by Begrich, and published in 1933. In English, cf. his "The Religion of the Psalms" in *What Remains of the Old Testament?*, and "The Poetry of the Old Testament" in *Old Testament Essays*. James's *Thirty Psalmists* utilizes Gunkel's method.

7. However, there is wide diversity in classification, as well as significant disagreement at many points. Gunkel was responsible for introducing the basic method and for the most commonly accepted designations of the various types of psalms. For a survey of work done, cf. Aubrey Johnson's "The Psalms" in *The Old Testament and Modern Study*.

8. *Einleitung*, p. 9.

9. E.g., the Ugaritic literature. Cf. Kapelrud's article, "Ugarit," in *IDB*, as well as his book on the subject.

10. Cf. pp. 1-31 of the *Einleitung*.

11. On what follows, cf. pp. 32-415 of the *Einleitung*, and pp. ix-x of the commentary.

12. *Psalmenstudien I-VI* were published 1921-1924. Cf. now in English Mowinckel's substantial *The Psalms in Israel's Worship*. Leslie's *The Psalms* is a very readable semicommentary in which Mowinckel's views are quite generally adopted.

13. Cf. pp. 13-15 of *The Psalms and Israel's Worship*. Chaps. 1 and 2 of that work are Mowinckel's argument for his method.

14. His description of the festival is found in *Psalmenstudien II*, pp. 44-145. Cf. *The Psalms in Israel's Worship*, pp. 15-22 and chap. 5.

15. The Babylonian creation epic in which those events are described may be found in Pritchard's *Ancient Near Eastern Texts*, pp. 60-72 or Thomas's *Documents from Old Testament Times*, pp. 3-16. Cf. also Heidel, *The Babylonian Genesis*.

16. Gaster is a proponent of such a view. Cf. his *Thespis*, particularly the summary of this thesis on pp. 17-19.

17. In Mesopotamia the spring equinox was looked upon as the beginning of the year because, after the floods, another agricultural season was ensured. In the Palestinian area, however, the fall equinox was thought of as the beginning of the year because the fall rains ended the summer drought in that area, making another agricultural year possible. Thus Israel, having taken ever the Babylonian calendar during the exilic period, celebrates the New Year at the beginning of the seventh, rather than the first, month in her calendar (Tishri, falling in September or October).

18. Cf. the temple program for the New Year festival in Babylon in Pritchard, *Ancient Near Eastern Texts*, pp. 331-334.

19. Other aspects of Mowinckel's work on the psalms will be referred to later in this book. For a reconstruction of the annual festival much like, but significantly different from, that of Mowinckel, cf. Aubrey Johnson, *Sacral Kingship*.

20. The basic work in this is Martin Noth, *Das System der zwölf Stämme Israels*. Mowinckel also had a hand in this area of Old Testament studies— cf. his *Le Décalogue*. For quite different approaches to Israel's early history in which the theory of the league (amphictyony) is accepted, cf. the histories of Israel by Noth and John Bright. Eichrodt's theology is based on the covenant concept as early and basic. More will be said of all this in chap. 1 below.

21. Cf. the introduction to Weiser's commentary on the psalms.

22. Cf. his treatment of the origins of the Penateuch on pp. 81-99 of his *The Old Testament: Its Formation und Development*. For a more positive assessment of the work of the Yahwist as a writer, cf. von Rad, *Das formgeschichtliche Problem des Hexateuch*, or the introduction to von Rad's *Genesis*.

23. Cf. pp. 52-91 of his commentary on the psalms.

24. Cf. pp. 35-52 of his commentary on the psalms.

25. His *Gottesdienst in Israel* has appeared in two editions, the second of which is a greatly revised and expanded work treating more aspects of Israel's cult than the first which concentrated on the feast of tabernacles. His commentary is part of the *Biblischer Kommentar Altes Testament*, edited by Noth.

26. Cf. his remarks on pp. 13-14 of the first edition of *Gottesdienst*. His approach is outlined most thoroughly in the first chapter of the second edition.

27. All this is summarized on pp. 67-77 of the first edition of *Gottesdienst*. Cf. pp. 220-234 of the second edition.

28. Here Kraus follows closely Noth's "Gott, König, und Volk."

29. Cf. his *Königsherrschaft Gottes.*

30. This is true even of the enthronement songs, which he locates in the cult in the time between the first return and the period of Nehemiah and Ezra.

31. The first edition of his *Gottesdienst* is concerned solely with this question, while the second includes discussion of other cultic occasions.

32. A good survey of work to 1950 is found in Johnson's essay in *The Old Testament and Modern Study.*

33. Cf. pp. xxxvii-lvi of Kraus's commentary, and pp. 52-91 of Weiser's. Both Mowinckel's *Psalmenstudien* and his *The Psalms in Israel's Worship* assume Gunkel's form-critical outline; cf. the tables of contents.

34. Thus I do not agree, as will become clearer in chap. 1, with the position of Weiser which, it seems to me, forces everything into one mold much more than do the positions of some often attacked for overpressing a "divine kingship" interpretation.

Chapter 1: GOD AS OVERLORD

1. I have substituted the proper divine name, "Yahweh" for "God," which is found in the text. Psalms 42 through 83 form the "Elohistic Psalter" in which someone seems fairly systematically to have replaced "Yahweh" with "God" at some point—the Hebrew word for "God" being *Elohim.*

2. The fundamental characteristic of Hebrew poetry is a parallelism of thought within units of two or three lines. I have adopted the term "colon" for such a unit, and the term "stich" for a line within a colon. When I translate poetry, I indicate a colon by indenting its successive lines. On the various kinds of parallelism, cf. T. H. Robinson, *The Poetry of the Old Testament,* chap. 2.

3. The Hebrew of this and the preceding colon is hard to translate because of the ambiguity of "moment" and "unending." The idea is that the result of Yahweh's accomplishments in the shortest time would last for all time.

4. Thus the approach here is different from that of Mowinckel to this type of poem. He makes "prophetic psalms" one element in the enthronement festival (*The Psalms in Israel's Worship,* pp. 53-73).

5. The two preceding paragraphs skim over many historical problems. How Israel came into existence and the relation of her earliest period to the finished Old Testament traditions are much debated questions. For various approaches to these questions, cf. the early chapters of the histories of Bright and Noth, Newman's *The People of the Covenant,* and Mendenhall's "The Hebrew Conquest of Palestine." Smend's *Das Mosebild* is a survey of scholarly trends.

6. Cf. the treaties translated in Pritchard, *Ancient Near Eastern Texts,* pp. 199-206. A complete survey of the relevant texts as well as of modern treatments of them and their relation to the Old Testament will be found on pp. 19-28 of Baltzer *Das Bundesformular.*

7. In what follows I am dependent on the analysis of Baltzer, *op. cit.*, pp. 20-28. Cf. also the important work of Mendenhall, *Law and Covenant*, pp. 32-35, and Korosec, *Hethitische Staatsverträge*, pp. 12 ff.

8. Here it is interesting to note the passage in Enoch 100:10-13, cited by Baltzer on p. 34.

9. Cf. William J. Hinke, *A New Boundary Stone of Nebuchadrezzar I from Nippur* (Philadelphia, 1907), p. 58.

10. Cf. Baltzer, *Das Bundesformular*, pp. 48-87, and Muilenburg, "The Form and Structure of the Covenantal Formulations."

11. For a treaty between the Egyptians and the Hittites of which the copies of both parties are still extant, cf. Pritchard, *Ancient Near Eastern Texts*, pp. 199-203.

12. This will be treated in chap. 2.

13. Cf. von Rad's treatment of Deuteronomy in *IDB*.

14. Cf. my *God and History in the Old Testament*, and the closing pages of chaps. 2 and 3 of this book.

15. Thus I am much less confident than Weiser (cf. the introduction to his commentary on Psalms) of the possibility of reconstructing the festival, and I want to stress that I am now talking about the premonarchical period, not something continuing down through the era of the kingdom.

16. Cf. the early chapters of Bright's and Noth's histories. An analogy to what happened over the course of time might be found in the history of the United States in which the descendants of those who came to American shores, only much later adopt as their own and participate in the *mythos* of which the pilgrims and Paul Revere are a part.

17. Mendenhall, "The Hebrew Conquest of Palestine." On the period in question, cf. Campbell, "The Amarna Letters and the Amarna Period," and Greenberg, *The Hab/piru.*

18. Cf. the "Book of the Covenant," Exodus 20:22-23:19; the Deuteronomic Code, Deuteronomy 12-26; the "Holiness Code," Leviticus, chaps. 17-26.

19. On this office, cf. Kraus, *Gottesdienst*, pp. 59-66 (first edition), chap. 3 (second edition); Muilenburg, "The Form and Structure of Covenantal Formulations"; Newman, "The Prophetic Call of Samuel." Given the function of the office of providing a new Moses in successive generations, I would contest Grether's distinction between the "legal" and the "prophetic" word in the Old Testament (cf. his *Name und Wort Gottes*).

20. But I would disagree with Reventlow's attempts to make it the explanation of the conception of their office held by *all* the prophets (cf. his works cited in the Bibliography). My own judgment is that another tradition than that of the covenant mediator begins to be used to explain the prophetic office as Israel begins to be drawn into the Assyrian-Babylonian sphere in the eighth century, that it is southern in origin, that it first appears in Micaiah ben Imlat (I Kings, chap. 22), and is basic to the traditions of the books of Amos, Micah (chaps. 1-5), and Isaiah. Thus it is not correct to treat these prophets as essentially reformers (*contra* Albright, *From the Stone Age to Christianity*, pp. 309-314, and Bright, *History of Israel*, pp. 247-248), for they adopted a new idiom—that of the "divine assembly"

—to explain prophetic activity. On distinguishing form critically between descriptions of prophetic calls falling into two types (and, I would say, arising from two sources of tradition), cf. Zimmerli's commentary on Ezekiel, pp. 16-21.

21. On the *ribh*, cf. Gunkel, *Einleitung*, pp. 361-367; Huffmon, "The Covenant Lawsuit in the Prophets"; G. E. Wright, "The Lawsuit of God." On the basis of the traditio-historical distinction made in the note immediately preceding, I would question Wright's ready combination of *ribh* and "divine assembly" motifs and would go along with Huffmon's questions in this area.

22. Admittedly the translation of the last stich is free and rather unusual. But the meaning of the word usually translated "humbly" is obscure, and the point of the passage seems to be that covenant loyalty to Yahweh is more than cultic (even covenant-cultic), and has always involved seeing Yahweh's hand in historical events. In the eighth century, from which these words come, his hand must be seen in the Assyrian invasions as much as it was in the events of the past to which the poem alludes earlier. For not seeing this, Israel stands condemned under the covenant.

23. It appears also in Isaiah 1:2-3 and Hosea 4:1-3.

24. Thus do motifs coming from elsewhere than the covenant tradition appear even in a song rooted in that tradition. It is this kind of thing that makes it difficult to follow Weiser's attribution of all the motifs of the psalter to the covenant cult.

25. Aubrey Johnson renders the word with "devotion," and *chasid* with "devotee" or "votary": cf. *Sacral Kingship*, p. 19. On *chesed*, cf. Snaith, *The Distinctive Ideas of the Old Testament*, chap. 5.

26. Cf. n. 17 above.

27. On the "holy war," cf. von Rad, *Der heilige Krieg*. Mendenhall's theory about the conquest (n. 17 above) may provide a way of resolving the debate arising out of von Rad's insistence that the holy war was always defensive. At any rate, it could be waged against threats from within Israel as well as from without (cf. Judges, chaps. 19-21).

28. I believe there is a great deal to be said for Lods's analysis of the sources of the early chapters of I Samuel on traditio-historical as well as literary-critical grounds. Cf. his *Israel*, pp. 352-356.

29. Noth conjectures that, in addition to belonging to the twelve-tribe Israelite league with its center in central Palestine, Judah was the dominant element in a six-tribe league with its center at Hebron. Cf. *Das System*, pp. 107-108, and pp. 181-182 of his history. Cf. also, Newman, *The People of the Covenant*, pp. 111-112.

30. A lot lies between the lines of II Samuel 5:1-3. While, to the writer, David is "king," that word is never used of his office by the "elders of Israel," who seem to be hedging the office about with conditions ("King David made a covenant with them") in order to avoid what had happened under Saul. Thus later, in I Kings, chap. 12, David's successor Rehoboam has one view of the monarchy, while the successors of those elders hold quite another.

31. Cf. Alt, "Das Grossreich Davids," and pp. 191-199 of Noth's history.

32. In II Samuel 15:1-6, Absalom is not merely appealing to the peo-

ple's dislike of red tape, but is contrasting the state of affairs under the Jerusalem monarchy with the older way of life and basing his appeal on the ideals of the tribal league. Likewise the cry, "To your tents!" used both in the revolt of Sheba (II Samuel 20:1) and in the secession of the northern tribes under Jeroboam (I Kings 12:16) may be some kind of rallying cry of the old league. On what may have been the pre-Israelite traditions of Jerusalem by which Israel was affected in the Davidic era, cf. Johnson, *Sacral Kingship*, pp. 27-46.

Chapter 2: GOD AS COSMIC KING

1. In spite of Frankfort's criticisms of "patternism" in *The Problem of Similarity in Ancient Near Eastern Religions*, the prologue and epilogue of *The Intellectual Adventure of Ancient Man*, a mine of information for what we are getting at in this chapter, imply that the various parts of the culture had things in common. The drawback of the latter valuable book is that it does not treat Canaanite culture. For this, cf. Kapelrud, *The Ras Shamra Discoveries and the Old Testament*, and Gray, *The Legacy of Canaan*.

2. Cf. the introduction to *The Intellectual Adventure of Ancient Man*, particularly pp. 4-8.

3. For Egypt, cf. *The Intellectual Adventure*, pp. 43-49; for Mesopotamia, pp. 137-148. Cf. the works of Kapelrud and Gray (n. 1 above) for Canaan.

4. This point is made about Egypt in Frankfort, *The Intellectual Adventure*, by Wilson on p. 50. For a valuable summary of the long history of the whole area, cf. Bright's history, pp. 17-59.

5. The Babylonian epic may be found in Pritchard, *Ancient Near Eastern Texts*, pp. 60-72, and Thomas, *Documents from Old Testament Times*, pp. 3-16. The Baal myth is on pp. 129-142 of Pritchard, and pp. 128-133 of Thomas.

6. Cf. Jacobsen, "Primitive Democracy in Ancient Mesopotamia," and the same author in Frankfort's *The Intellectual Adventure*, pp. 125-184.

7. The Baal myth does not explicitly deal with the creation of the earth, ending with the building of Baal's house, but it does make it clear that the processes of nature that ensure life on earth are made possible by Baal's victory.

8. Cf. the discussion of what myth is and means in Frankfort, *The Intellectual Adventure*, pp. 6-10.

9. Cf. McCown, "City," in *IDB*.

10. On temples and their significance, cf. Wright and Freedman, *The Biblical Archaeologist Reader*, I, pp. 145-200. Cf. also the works of Patai, Simon, and Wensinck listed in the Bibliography.

11. Cf. in particular lines 45-65 of tablet vi of *Enuma elish*. This is the significance too of the building of a house for Baal in the Ugaritic myth. What lies behind the latter is the main subject of Obermann, *Ugaritic Mythology*.

12. Cf. the Sumerian king-list in Pritchard, *Ancient Near Eastern Texts*, pp. 265-266.

13. Cf. Frankfort's *Kingship and the Gods*, the subtitle of which is, "Ancient Near Eastern Religion as the Integration of Society and Nature."

14. In the Baal myth, cf. lines 104-105 of tablet v of II AB.

15. Cf. pp. 25 and 64 in Frankfort, *The Intellectual Adventure*.

16. Cf. the approach of Gaster in his *Thespis*.

17. Cf. Johnson, *Sacral Kingship*, pp. 27-46, and the literature cited there. Cf. also, Ahlström, "Der Prophet Nathan und der Tempelbau."

18. Cf. Johnson, *op. cit.*, pages cited just above in n. 17, and the histories of Israel by Bright and Noth. Note Genesis, chap. 14 and Joshua 10:1-27. The note in Judges 1:8 is anachronistic.

19. For *Elyon*, cf. Genesis 14:18-22; Deuteronomy 32:8; Psalms 46:4; 47:2 etc. (numbers of verses as in English text). For *Zedek*, cf. Psalm 85:10 (where *Shalom*, a form of *Shalem*, also occurs). On all this cf. Johnson, *Sacral Kingship*, pp. 31-46. On *Elyon*, cf. Pope, *El in the Ugaritic Texts*, pp. 55-58. It should be noted that the title of Baal, "*aliyan*," is not the equivalent of *elyon*.

20. Cf. the very brief account in II Samuel 5:6-10 and the commentaries *ad loc.*

21. There is dispute over this. Johnson's position, pp. 28-30 of *Sacral Kingship*, would seem to me to be cautiously sound. Ahlström, "Der Prophet Nathan und der Tempelbau," is more emphatic.

22. The question of the origins and history of the various priesthoods in Israel is a complicated and debated one. That Zadok somehow represents a new element at the time of David's occupation of Jerusalem, however, seems fairly clear. It is of significance that later Solomon banishes the house of Abiathar, leaving the Jerusalem cult to the house of Zadok.

23. Cf. Pedersen, *Israel III-IV*, p. 686.

24. See chap. 1, n. 32.

25. On the reasons for "epiphany" instead of the usual "array" or "splendor" as a rendering of *hadarah*, cf. Kraus's commentary *ad loc.* Here is a splendid example of how the Ugaritic literature can help us with Hebrew vocabulary. A cognate of the same word occurs at the end of vs. 4, where I have rendered it "theophany."

26. Here, as was the case with Psalm 81, the tenses of the verbs must be taken seriously. In this verse a set of generalizations about the theophanic power of Yahweh in the thunderstorm is followed by a description of the fact wrought on Lebanon by it, lightning having split the giant cedars there.

27. Vs. 7 of the psalm has been omitted here simply because of the problems it presents to meter and versification. It obviously refers to lightning, and must reflect a verse mutilated in transmission. This reasoning seems better than postulating some original connection between it and vs. 4b.

28. Vs. 9 presents problems. As will be seen below, I prefer the interpretation that makes the first line refer to "hinds," even if "oaks" (the words are from the same root) is a better parallel to "forests." The line about "forests" is, at any rate, too short metrically. It will be maintained below that the last line of vs. 9 ("in his temple . . .") is a fragment. Thus there are double grounds for postulating corruption of some kind in

the verse, due either to mistakes in transmission or to a desire to cover up a reference to pagan mythology.

29. Cf. May, "Some Cosmic Connotations of *Mayim Rabbim*, 'Many Waters.'"

30. This is why I prefer "hinds" to "oaks." The progress of the hymn seems to be from victory over the god of watery chaos, to victory over death, to miraculous fertility.

31. For different translations of the same lines, cf. Ginsberg in Pritchard, *Ancient Near Eastern Texts*, p. 135, and Gaster, *Thespis*, p. 197.

32. Gaster, *op. cit.*, p. 445. His own translation runs:
> [The assembly of the deities acclaims Him,]
> And in His palace all of it recites the Glory.

33. Cf. Cross, "Notes on a Canaanite Psalm in the Old Testament" and the other works referred to there. Kraus gives a Babylonian parallel in his commentary, p. 235. Note how Psalm 29 is repeated in essence in Psalm 96:7-9.

34. That this is the way to state the connection between a psalm such as 29 and Israel's older traditions would seem to be indicated by its obvious connections with the Baal myth. To connect it with the covenant tradition and the Sinai theophany as Weiser does (cf. his commentary *ad loc.*) is to avoid the obvious.

35. The quotations in the paragraphs that follow are from various Old Testament hymns. To the list could be added Psalms 8, 19, 96, 98, 100, 111, 114, 117, and 145-150.

36. Cf. *Einleitung*, pp. 66-67.

37. Cf. Mowinckel, *The Psalms in Israel's Worship*, vol. 1, p. 93.

38. Cf. Kraus, p. 702 of the commentary.

39. On this hymn, cf. chap. 3 of Watts, *Vision and Prophecy in Amos*.

40. Kraus, for example, dates Psalm 29 early in spite of the position he takes on the dates of the enthronement songs. Cf., on the one hand, his commentary on Psalm 29 and, on the other, his *Königsherrschaft Gottes*. On the debate referred to in this paragraph, cf. the introduction to the latter book.

41. So, among the interpreters of this material, Gordon and Driver vs. Gaster.

42. Other enthronement songs are Psalms 47 and 99.

43. Again, "Yahweh" for "God." Cf. chap. 1, n. 1.

44. Cf. Isaiah 14:12-15, where the same phrase as is found in Psalm 48 is used in vs. 13. Thus would the "foe from the north" in Jeremiah have had fearful connotations.

45. On the rendering of the last line, cf. Johnson, *Sacral Kingship*, p. 78. His whole treatment of Psalm 48, on pp. 77-81, is suggestive, and the present discussion relies heavily on it.

46. There are textual problems in these and the following lines. Cf. Kittel's *Biblia Hebraica* and the various commentaries.

47. Cf. Johnson, *Sacral Kingship*, p. 81, on the last line. It should be noted that individual, personal survival of death is not implied.

48. Again, "Yahweh" for "God." Cf. chap. 1, n. 1.

49. The insertion of the refrain here would seem to be justified by the clearly discernible three-stanza structure of the poem. Cf. the various commentaries *ad loc.*

50. Cf. Johnson, *Sacral Kingship,* pp. 8-10, and the works of Patai and Wensinck listed in the Bibliography. Cf. also the imagery in Ezekiel 47:1-2; Zechariah 14:8; Revelation 22:1-2.

51. The line literally speaks of "a highway in their hearts." Cf. Johnson, *Sacral Kingship,* p. 95, and the Revised Standard Version.

52. Gunkel holds Psalm 122 to be the only complete example of a pilgrimage song (*Einleitung,* pp. 309-311). I would conjecture that the origin of the "songs of ascent" (Psalms 120-134), as a collection, lies in their use at pilgrimages.

53. Cf. Kraus, p. 111 of the commentary.

54. Gunkel also lists Psalms 12, 14, 24, 75, 82, 85, 95, 121, 126, and 134 as liturgies. Psalm 76 is another song of Zion.

55. Thus songs characterized by a mixing of forms (cf. Psalms 9-10, 36, 52, 77, 90, 94, 108, 115, 119) may be due to liturgical use as well as to later authorship. It is not necessary to divide such songs into two or more pieces. Psalm 27, treated in the next chapter, is a fine example.

56. Literally vs. 6b says, "seekers thy face Jacob." I have taken this to mean "seekers of thy face (like) Jacob," rather than "seekers of thy face, O Jacob." But either of the latter could carry the sense I seek to bring out in my translation.

57. As examples, cf. Johnson, *Sacral Kingship,* pp. 63-65; Kraus, *Psalmen,* pp. 197-205; Mowinckel, *The Psalms in Israel's Worship,* pp. 174-181.

58. Cf. Rost, *Die Überlieferung des Thronnachfolge Davids.*

59. Cf. the Abimelech story in Judges, chap. 9, and the "early source" of I Samuel.

60. Cf. Johnson, *Sacral Kingship,* pp. 118-120; Crim, *Royal Psalms,* pp. 71-75.

61. Cf. von Rad's interpretation of the Yahwist in *Das Formgeschichtliche Problem* and in the introduction to his *Genesis.* While his theory may have to be modified in the direction of Noth's *Überlieferungsgeschichte des Pentateuch,* Weiser (*The Old Testament,* pp. 81-99) and Speiser (*Genesis,* xxxvii-xliii) surely underestimate the effects of "the crisis of the monarchy."

62. The same thing is true of the Isaiah tradition and the priestly stratum of the Pentateuch.

63. For a thorough investigation of the relation of kingship to eschatological messianism, cf. Mowinckel, *He That Cometh.*

64. A full list of the royal psalms includes 2, 18, 20, 21, 45, 72, 89, 101, 110, 132, 144.

65. The suffix in Hebrew is feminine. The ark is clearly feminine in I Samuel 4:17 and II Chronicles 8:11, in spite of the fact that the form of the word is masculine. I have, on the basis of this, read the first word of vs. 7 as a *hiphil* with a feminine suffix.

66. Cf. the excursis on pp. 879-883 of Kraus's commentary.

67. Cf. *Enuma elish* vi, 45-65 and II AB v-vii.

68. Cf., in contrast, the bragging account of Shalmaneser III of the battle

of Karkar, which he actually left, not to turn westward again! Pritchard, *Ancient Near Eastern Texts*, pp. 278-279.

69. Cf., on the divine assembly, H. W. Robinson, "The Council of Yahweh"; Cross, "The Council of Yahweh in II Isaiah"; Muilenburg's commentary on Second Isaiah, pp. 422-423.

70. Again, "Yahweh" for "God." Cf. chap. 1, n. 1.

71. Marduk, e.g., was not the first or only hero of *Enuma elish*. On how the Baal myth reflects some kind of conflict, cf. Pope, *El in the Ugaritic Texts*, p. 94.

72. All this *contra* the position of Albright, *From the Stone Age to Christianity*, pp. 271-272. Cf. Wright, *The Old Testament against Its Environment*, pp. 30-41.

73. How exciting such a cry would be, and how much it is rooted in the idiom of the culture, is seen in the significance of "take possession." In Deuteronomy 32:8-9 it is used in a context in which the assignment of *Israel* as Yahweh's possession is spoken of with the implication that other gods were to take possession of other peoples.

74. It is interesting to note that in the 1928 American version of the Book of Common Prayer, Psalm 95, the *Venite* in Morning Prayer, was revised into a cosmic hymn again by the removal of its concluding verses and the substitution for them of the end of Psalm 96.

75. On the legends, cf. Gunkel, *Einleitung*, pp. 323-327, who also holds that they were never an independent type of song.

76. Cf. von Rad's treatment of these passages in his *Genesis*, and Napier, "On Creation Faith in the Old Testament."

77. Pannenberg (cf. Bibliography) represents an interesting and important attempt to carry the implications of all this into theology.

Chapter 3: GOD AS SAVIOUR

1. As I see it, our knowledge of the world of the Old Testament makes it no longer possible to hold that the laments are late in origin, reflecting the trials of postexilic, more individualistic Jewish piety. As much as he is responsible for revolutionizing the study of Israel's song, Gunkel tends to treat the laments with modern piety too much in mind. Not willing to be as precise as Mowinckel on the issue involved, I would refer here to *Psalmenstudien I* and chapters 7 and 8 of *The Psalms in Israel's Worship* (cf. also vol. 2, pp. 250-251, n. xxvii of that work). Mowinckel definitely moves away from being overprecise in the later work. Weiser ties it all in too neatly with his covenant festival.

2. For this analysis and the basic outline of the following discussion, I am dependent on Westermann's important study, "Struktur und Geschichte der Klage."

3. The translation is that of Stephens in Pritchard, *Ancient Near Eastern Texts*, pp. 383-385.

4. There are problems in these lines; cf. the commentaries and the different solution of the translation in the Revised Standard Version.

5. For what is involved in rendering the line in this way, cf. Albright, *Archaeology and the Religion of Israel*, p. 198, n. 49. This psalm is full of allusions to the realm of the dead as pictured in Canaanite mythology. Cf. II AB viii, 8-9 (p. 135 in *Ancient Near Eastern Texts*).

6. On the whole question of life after death in the Old Testament, cf. Martin-Achard, *From Death to Life*.

7. Again, "Yahweh" for "God." Cf. chap. 1, n. 1.

8. Jacobsen stresses the way in which the social order mirrored the cosmic order in his treatment of Mesopotamian culture in Frankfort, *The Intellectual Adventure*.

9. Pritchard, *Ancient Near Eastern Texts*, p. 385.

10. *Ibid.*, p. 385. On enemies in the Babylonian laments, cf. Widengren, *The Accadian and Hebrew Psalms of Lamentation*, pp. 174-238.

11. Kraus's treatment of the subject in excursis 2 in his commentary (pp. 40-43) is to be recommended, although, in terms of his own conclusion, he is too critical of Mowinckel. Cf. also Gunkel, *Einleitung*, pp. 196-211.

12. Hans Schmidt found the origin of the enemies in such persons. Cf. *Das Gebet des Angeklagten* and his commentary. He is closely followed by Leslie, cf. pp. 315-260 of *The Psalms*.

13. Cf. also Psalms 5:10; 25:19-20; 58; 88.

14. Mowinckel has laid great stress on this. Cf. *Psalmenstudien I*.

15. Mowinckel traced the individual laments to the lament of a king in which demonic enemies came to be historicized as national enemies, although he did not hold that all laments in their present form view the enemies in such a way. Birkeland would hold that the enemies are all enemies of *Israel*, cf. his *Die Feinde des Individuums* and *The Evildoers in the Book of Psalms*.

16. The last two lines are difficult. I suspect they are a figure referring to adolescence, the point being that the wicked should be swept away before reproducing themselves:

Before their vessels experience any heat,

Like thornbushes, like milkweed, may he sweep them away.

17. Blank, "Men against God."

18. For a comprehensive treatment of the whole subject, cf. Gunkel, *Einleitung*, pp. 218-223.

19. Cf. Smend, "Über das Ich der Psalmen."

20. The traditional position was questioned, in such a way as to reopen discussion, by Balla, *Das Ich der Psalmen*. Cf. Gunkel, *Einleitung*, pp. 173-175, who follows Balla.

21. Schmidt would also hold this in his own way. Cf. n. 12 above.

22. The pioneer work was Mowinckel's *Psalmenstudien I*, pp. 76-133. The most thoroughgoing royal-communal interpretation is Birkeland's (cf. Bibliography). Cf. also Engnell, *Studies in Divine Kingship*. Mowinckel's later and more modified view is found in *The Psalms in Israel's Worship*, vol. 1, pp. 225-246; vol. 2, pp. 1-25. Weiser's interpretation is communal, but connected with the covenant festival; cf. his commentary, pp. 68-71.

23. Pritchard, *Ancient Near Eastern Texts*, p. 334.

24. Cf. Engnell, *Studies in Divine Kingship*, pp. 170, 210; Hooke,

Origins of Early Semitic Ritual; Johnson, "The Role of the King," pp. 71 ff.; Haldar, *Studies in the Book of Nahum.* Mowinckel, who roots the songs of Israel thoroughly in the cult, stoutly denies that the king ever represented Yahweh, cf. *Psalms in Israel's Worship,* vol. 1, pp. 58-60, 137-140.

25. This is the sense in which Mowinckel holds that the lament form goes back to the king's role in the cult. Cf. the previous note.

26. For a fuller description of what may have taken place on such occasions, cf. Gunkel, *Einleitung,* pp. 117-121; Mowinckel, *Psalms in Israel's Worship,* vol. 1, pp. 193-194; Widengren, *The Accadian and Hebrew Psalms of Lamentation,* pp. 20-36.

27. Thus I agree with Mowinckel in his denial that "we" or "us" is the only sign of a communal as opposed to an individual lament, but I also agree with him in questioning the excesses of Birkeland and Engnell in this direction. Even Mowinckel, though *The Psalms in Israel's Worship* modifies *Psalmenstudien,* probably goes too far in making what is described above the only source of laments. See the following section of this chapter.

28. This prayer is found in Pritchard, *Ancient Near Eastern Texts,* pp. 391-392, and Thomas, *Documents from Old Testament Times,* pp. 111-117.

29. In what follows I am very much dependent on the discussion by Mowinckel, *Psalmenstudien I,* pp. 137-157, and Gunkel, *Einleitung,* pp. 175-184. It will be evident that I am, with Mowinckel, more inclined than Gunkel to see actual cultic situations reflected in the psalms in their present form. Schimdt (cf. Bibliography) probably too narrowly locates laments in one setting, although he does have a point.

30. Again, "Yahweh" for "God." Cf. chap. 1, n. 1.

31. Cf. Mowinckel, *Psalmenstudien I,* pp. 145-149; Gunkel, *Einleitung,* pp. 177-178, 245-247; and the important article of Begrich, "Das priester-liche Heilsorakel."

32. Cf. on this, Mowinckel, *Psalmenstudien I,* pp. 148-149. My translation does not agree completely with his.

33. As we now go on to other types, it would be well to list the "I" laments here, although a definite line cannot be drawn between them and types associated with them: Psalms 3, 5, 7, 13, 17, 22, 25, 26, 27:7-14, 28, 31, 35, 38, 39, 42-43, 51, 54, 56, 57, 58, 59, 61, 63, 64, 68, 70, 71, 86, 88, 102, 109, 120, 123, 130, 140, 141, 142, 143.

34. Even in vs. 5; in this I agree with the interpretation of Psalm 23 by Terrien in *The Psalms and Their Meaning for Today.*

35. On this as the meaning of *todah,* cf. Mand, "Die Eigenstandigkeit der Danklieder."

36. Such a prayer may be found in Pritchard, *Ancient Near Eastern Texts,* pp. 380-381. Cf. Mowinckel, *Psalms in Israel's Worship,* vol. 2, pp. 41-42, 185-187.

37. On the distinction, cf. Gunkel, *Einleitung,* pp. 276-277. On the specific characteristics of the thanksgivings, cf. *ibid.,* pp. 265-284; Mowinckel, *Psalms in Israel's Worship,* vol. 2, pp. 32-42. Although Mowinckel's dismissal of Westermann, *Das Loben Gottes,* is too summary (cf. vol. 2, p. 28), I would agree with what Mowinckel says.

38. Quoted by Gunkel, *Einleitung,* p. 285. Gunkel discusses ancient

Near Eastern parallels to thanksgivings on pp. 284-290. Cf. Mowinckel, *Psalms and Israel's Worship*, vol. 2, pp. 185-187.

39. Johnson connects this psalm with a specific point in his reconstruction of the autumnal festival, and his treatment is most suggestive. Cf. *Sacral Kingship*, pp. 114-118.

40. The mention of proselytes (cf. also Psalm 115:9-11) does not necessarily indicate a late, postexilic date of origin. If the nature of ancient Israel was what Mendenhall argues for in his article on the conquest, Israel was precisely an association of proselytes from the very beginning!

41. "Yah" is a variant of "Yahweh" used very much in this psalm.

42. Given the connotation of "favorite" in "right hand" (Cf. Muilenburg, "The Birth of Benjamin"), it is tempting to render the community's cry, "Yahweh's king is . . ."

43. On the gates, cf. Johnson, *Sacral Kingship*, p. 117, n. 2. The term is obviously connected with the fact that those who have been vindicated by Yahweh's action are qualified to offer *todah*.

44. For a striking development of this, cf. the title essay in Reinhold Niebuhr, *Beyond Tragedy*.

45. Again, "Yahweh" for "God." Cf. chap. 1, n. 1.

46. The last two lines are obscure, though the general meaning is clear. Cf. the commentaries.

47. "Yahweh" for "God" in the first line. Cf. chap. 1, n. 1. On the reasons for "my sacrifice" cf. commentaries. This may be the last verse of the psalm in its original form.

48. The traditional "penitential psalms" are 6, 32, 38, 102, 130, 143 in addition to 51. Only 51 and 130 are really laments for sin.

49. On this point cf. Gunkel, *Einleitung*, p. 123, and Mowinckel, *Psalms in Israel's Worship*, vol. 1, pp. 194-195.

50. Here again, I would agree with Mowinckel's position as opposed either to Gunkel's or to the more extreme cultic approach. The ambiguity is seen in the "I" sometimes present in the "we" laments (44:4,6,15; 60:9; 74:12—English verse numbers), and would seem to indicate that the "we" psalms represent the modification of a form which is itself also communal, if singular.

51. Cf. the Sumerian and Babylonian king-lists, and the Egyptian attitude toward the pharaoh. I Samuel, chap. 1, may represent a suppressed apotheosis of kingship in Israel, given the fact that the play on Samuel's name really has to do with "Saul."

52. Psalm 80 may have originated in the north—after 722 B.C.? A look at the commentaries will show how the "we" laments are usually dated late.

53. On the question of life after death in the Old Testament, cf. Martin-Achard, *From Death to Life*. For a stimulating view of the consequences of this, cf. Owen, *Body and Soul*, and for an exposition of how it affects culture, cf. van Leeuwen, *Christianity in World History*.

54. Psalms 44, 60, 74, 79, 80, 83, 125, 137 are "we" laments. Psalms 124 and 129 are "we" thanksgivings.

55. Cf. Westermann on this—*Das Loben Gottes*, pp. 47-48. Cf. the im-

portant work of Begrich on this—"Das priesterliche Heilsorakel," and pp. 6-19 of his *Studien zu Deuterojesaja.*

56. On the question of cultic prophets, cf. Johnson's work on the subject.

57. In the article mentioned in n. 55 above, Begrich deals with Babylonian examples.

58. Isaiah 41:8-13,14-16; 43:1-3a; 51:7-9; 54:4-8. Cf. also Jeremiah 30:10; 46:27-28.

59. The importance of lament in the prophetic interpretation of things is brought out in Gottwald, *Studies in the Book of Lamentations.*

60. This kind of thing was and is both the glory and the problem of the Christian gospel which maintains that *the* fulfillment came in Jesus, while history still continues. Pannenberg (cf. Bibliography) is a most satisfying approach to an Old Testament student.

61. On this cf. the important and suggestive work of Westermann, *Der Aufbau des Buches Hiob.*

Chapter 4: GOD AS THE SOURCE OF WISDOM

1. On wisdom and its ways and expressions, cf. Blank in *IDB* and Irwin in *Interpreter's Bible.* Above all, cf. von Rad, *Theology I,* pp. 418-453.

2. Cf. Köhler, *Hebrew Man,* pp. 99-107.

3. Thus the various collections in the Book of Proverbs. Cf. the commentary of Fritsch and the various introductions to the Old Testament. For other such collections in the culture of which Israel was a part, cf. Pritchard, *Ancient Near Eastern Texts,* pp. 412-430.

4. Cf. the account of Solomon's wisdom in I Kings 3:16-28; 10:1-10, 23-25. Cf. von Rad's treatment of the Joseph stories, *Genesis,* pp. 428-434. For other such stories, cf. Pritchard, *Ancient Near Eastern Texts,* pp. 405-411.

5. Note how Proverbs, Ecclesiastes, and the Wisdom of Solomon maintain this tradition.

6. Lines 85-95 of "The Instructions of the Vizier Ptah-Hotep," by Wilson, in Pritchard, *Ancient Near Eastern Texts,* p. 413. For a discussion of how this writing, a typical piece of Egyptian wisdom literature, reveals the ethos of wisdom, cf. Wilson, *The Burden of Egypt,* pp. 91-95.

7. I have tried to do a more or less free translation that catches what this verse is really saying. Cf. Zimmerli, *Prediger,* pp. 171-173; von Rad, *Theology I,* 455-459.

8. Like many parts of this psalm, the latter part of vs. 14 (Hebrew, 15) is hopelessly corrupt, here probably due to pious alterations as the poem was transmitted. Given the eight cola structure of the first stanza, I have omitted vs. 15 (Hebrew, 16) as a pious intrusion—it would be a ninth colon in the second stanza.

9. "Davidic era" is used here to designate the period from David to the fall of Jerusalem in 587 B.C. For indications of the influence of wisdom on various parts of the Old Testament, cf. Dentan, "The Literary Affinities of

Exodus xxxiv 6 ff."; Malfroy, "Sagesse et Loi dans le Deuteronome"; Terrien, "Amos and Wisdom."

10. This is often left out of account in works arising out of the revival of interest in biblical theology characteristic of the last two or three decades.

11. The most significant study of this expectation is Mowinckel, *He That Cometh.*

12. I have sketched the attempts of later Israel to deal with this whole tragic period in chaps. 4 and 5 of my *God and History in the Old Testament.*

13. In varying ways Proverbs, Job, Ecclesiastes, the Song of Songs, and Ruth (on the reasons for the last two cf. my *God and History,* chap. 5) are to be characterized as wisdom literature. So should the apocalyptic writing Daniel, Ecclesiasticus, Wisdom of Solomon, Baruch, the Epistle of Jeremy, and Tobit. On the reasons for so classifying Daniel and other apocalyptic literature, cf. von Rad, *Theology II,* pp. 314-321.

14. The developments treated here are discussed by von Rad, *Theology I,* p. 441-453. Cf. also Rylaarsdam, *Revelation in Jewish Wisdom Literature.*

15. On the composition and prehistory of the book, cf. the various commentaries (Fritsch, Gemser, Ringgren).

16. Though the key word in the first line of vs. 30 is a riddle, and much discussed, "little child" seems to me to make more sense in the light of what follows than does "master craftsman." Where the picture of wisdom as a child (of the gods?) comes from may never be satisfactorily answered. Albright once held that underneath this passage lay a very ancient, northwest Semitic tradition of a goddess of wisdom (*From the Stone Age to Christianity,* pp. 167-170). It is more likely that the roots of the concept are to be traced to Egypt (cf. Herbert Donner, *Zeitschrift für ägyptische Sprache und Altertumskunde* [1957], pp. 8 ff.; I have not been able to see this).

17. On the meaning of the "strange woman" and of the personal association of wisdom as an ally of man against her, cf. Boström, *Proverbiastudien.*

18. Thus apocalyptic, in spite of how things might appear on the surface, is much more closely related to wisdom than to prophecy. Cf. the citation from von Rad in n. 13 above.

19. Note how participants in the ancient story are made the teachers of esoteric knowledge in the pseudepigraphical apocalyptic writings, which can be found in Charles *Apocrypha and Pseudepigrapha:* Enoch, the twelve sons of Jacob, Moses, etc.

20. *Torah* means so much more than "law" or "instruction" (or the Greek *nomos* by which it is rendered in Ecclesiasticus) that I have left it untranslated. Though embodied in the written Torah (Pentateuch), it is more than the literal words there. It is God's indication to men of the direction life should take, the thing by which everything in the universe is informed. Much of its meaning in later Jewish piety obviously comes from the wisdom tradition.

21. I do not mean to imply here that Psalm 19 is later in origin than Ecclesiasticus. The development as traced in this chapter is more paradigmatic than chronological.

22. Other wisdom poems are Psalms 1, 37, 73, 91, 112, 119, 127, 128, 133.

23. Actually, the official doctrine pushed the era of "inspiration" down to the time of Ezra.

24. I would reach this conclusion by proceeding along somewhat the same lines as Westermann, "Zur Sammlung des Psalters," and using his conclusions to support my contention that the original collection was more "individual" than communal. I would not agree with the conclusions he draws about the nature of the basic psalm types with respect to origins.

25. Cf. n. 18 above. Note how Daniel, an apocalytic writing, contains stories celebrating the loyalty of Israelites to Yahweh's *torah*. The piety behind the first part of Daniel is the same as that expressed in Psalms 1 and 119

26. On how "futurist" eschatology arose from the Davidic *mythos*, cf. Mowinckel's *He That Cometh*. I would not, however, restrict the use of eschatology as a concept to just its "futurist" form.

Chapter 5: YAHWEH'S SONGS IN AN ALIEN AGE

1. On how this dilemma is the real source of contemporary biblical theology, cf. the excellent article by Stendahl on the subject in *IDB*.

2. C. S. Lewis' *Reflections on the Psalms* is an excellent example, as is Bonhoeffer's discussion in *Life Together* (pp. 44-50). Bonhoeffer approaches a more realistic view of the type I would advocate, but is still "apologetic."

3. Such an approach is taken *de facto* in most modern ecclesiastical lectionaries and selections for responsive reading.

4. In one sense even the most confessional of churches is best defined descriptively in terms of the history of its confessional controversies and revisions.

5. Mendenhall's "The Hebrew Conquest of Palestine" is a beautiful example not only of sound historical reconstruction, but of explication of theological content. It shows how in the way advocated here what is traditionally called meditation can be related to the realities of historical method and the results of the use of that method.

6. It is for this reason that, although critical of some major points (for example, his treating of the priestly source before the prophets), I think von Rad's approach to Old Testament theology more faithful to Israel's own way of thinking than Eichrodt's.

Bibliography

ABBREVIATIONS

ATD	*Das Alte Testament Deutsch*
BA	*The Biblical Archaeologist*
BASOR	*Bulletin of the American Schools of Oriental Research*
BK	*Biblischer Kommentar Altes Testament*
HAT	*Handbuch zum Alten Testament*
IB	*The Interpreter's Bible*
IDB	*The Interpreter's Dictionary of the Bible*
JBL	*Journal of Biblical Literature*
VT	*Vetus Testamentum*
ZAW	*Zeitschrift für die alttestamentliche Wissenschaft*

(When works originally written in other languages have been translated into English, only the translation is listed.)

Ahlström, G. W. "Der Prophet Nathan und der Tempelbau," *VT* XI (1961), 113-127.
———— *Psalm 89. Eine Liturgie aus dem Ritual des leidenden Königs.* Lund: Gleerup, 1959.
Albright, William F. *Archaeology and the Religion of Israel.* Baltimore: Johns Hopkins Press, 1953.
———— *From the Stone Age to Christianity.* Garden City, N.Y.: Doubleday (Anchor Book), 1957, 2nd ed.
———— "The Psalm of Habakkuk," *Studies in Old Testament Prophecy* (ed. H. H. Rowley). Edinburgh: T. & T. Clark, 1950.
Alt, Albrecht. "Das Grossreich Davids," *Theologische Literaturzeitung* LXXV (1950), 213-220. Reprinted in his *Kleine Schriften zur Geschichte des Volkes Israel II.* Munich: Beck, 1953.

———— "Die Staatenbildung der Israeliten in Palästina," *Kleine Schriften zur Geschichte des Volkes Israel II.* Munich: Beck, 1953.

Balla, E. *Das Ich der Psalmen.* Göttingen: Vandenhoeck & Ruprecht, 1912.

Baltzer, Klaus. *Das Bundesformular.* Neukirchen: Verlag des Erziehungsverein, 1960.

Begrich, Joachim. "Das priesterliche Heilsorakel," *ZAW* LII (1934), 81-92.

———— *Studien zu Deuterojesaja.* Stuttgart: Kohlhammer, 1938. Munich: Kaiser, 1963 reprint.

Bentzen, Aage. *Introduction to the Old Testament.* Copenhagen: Gad, 1948-1949.

———— *King and Messiah.* London: Lutterworth, 1955.

Birkeland, Harris. *Die Feinde des Individuums in der israelitischen Psalmenliteratur.* Oslo: Dybwad, 1933.

———— *The Evildoers in the Book of Psalms.* Oslo: Dybwad, 1955.

Blank, Sheldon H. "Men Against God—The Promethean Element in Biblical Prayer," *JBL* LXXII (1953), 1-14. Reprinted in his *Prophetic Faith in Isaiah.* New York: Harper, 1958.

———— "Wisdom," *IDB* IV, 852-861.

Bonhoeffer, Dietrich. *Life Together.* New York: Harper, 1954.

Boström, Gustav. *Proverbastudien. Die Weisheit und das Fremde Weib.* Lund: Gleerup, 1935.

Briggs, C. A. and E. G. *A Critical and Exegetical Commentary on the Book of Psalms.* New York: Scribners, 1906-1907.

Bright, John. *A History of Israel.* Philadelphia: Westminster Press, 1959.

Buttenwieser, Moses. *The Psalms, Chronologically Treated, with a New Translation.* Chicago: University of Chicago Press, 1938.

Campbell, Edward F., Jr. "The Amarna Letters and the Amarna Period," *BA* XXIII (1960), 2-22.

Charles, R. H. *The Apocrypha and Pseudepigrapha of the Old Testament.* Oxford: Clarendon Press, 1913.

Crim, Keith R. *The Royal Psalms.* Richmond: John Knox Press, 1962.

Cross, Frank M., Jr. "The Council of Yahweh in II Isaiah," *Journal of Near Eastern Studies* XII (1953), 274-277.

———— "Notes on a Canaanite Psalm in the Old Testament," *BASOR* CXVII (1950), 19-21.

Cumming, C. G. *The Assyrian and the Hebrew Hymns of Praise.* New York: Columbia University Press, 1934.

Dentan, Robert C. "The Literary Affinities of Exodus xxxiv 6 f." *VT* XIII (1963), 34-51.

Driver, Godfrey R. *Canaanite Myths and Legends.* Edinburgh: T. & T. Clark, 1956.

Duhm, Bernhard. *Die Psalmen.* Tübingen: Mohr, 1922.

Eichrodt, Walther. *Theologie des Alten Testaments.* Stuttgart: Klatz; Göttingen: Vandenhoeck & Ruprecht, I (1957 5th ed.), II-III (1961 4th ed.). English translation of I, Philadelphia: Westminster Press, 1961.

Engnell, Ivan. *Studies in Divine Kingship in the Ancient Near East.* Uppsala: Almqvist & Wiksells, 1943.

Frankfort, Henri, *et al. The Intellectual Adventure of Ancient Man.* Chicago: University of Chicago Press, 1946.

———— *Kingship and the Gods.* Chicago: University of Chicago Press, 1948.

———— *The Problem of Similarity in Ancient Near Eastern Religions.* Oxford: Clarendon Press, 1951.

Fritsch, Charles T. "Proverbs," *IB* IV. Nashville: Abingdon, 1955.

Gaster, Theodor H. *Thespis. Ritual, Myth, and Drama in the Ancient Near East.* Garden City, N.Y.: Doubleday (Anchor Book), 1961 rev. ed.

Gemser, B. *Sprüche Salomos (HAT).* Tübingen: Mohr, 1937.

Gottwald, Norman K. *All the Kingdoms of the Earth. Israelite Prophecy and International Relations in the Ancient Near East.* New York: Harper, 1964.

———— *Studies in the Book of Lamentations.* Chicago: Allenson, 1954.

Gray, John. *The Legacy of Canaan.* Leiden: Brill, 1957.

Greenberg, Moshe. *The Hab/piru.* New Haven: American Oriental Society, 1955.

Grether, Oskar. *Name und Wort Gottes im Alten Testament.* Giessen: Töpelmann, 1934.

Grobel, Kendrick. "Form Criticism," *IDB* II. Nashville: Abingdon, 1962.

Gunkel, Hermann, and Begrich, J. *Einleitung in die Psalmen. Die Gattungen der Religiösen Lyrik Israels.* Göttingen: Vandenhoeck & Ruprecht, 1933.

———— *The Legends of Genesis.* Chicago: Open Court Publishing Co., 1901.

———— "The Poetry of the Old Testament: Its Literary History and Its Application to the Dating of the Psalms," *Old Testament Essays* (ed. D. C. Simpson). London: Griffin, 1927.

———— *Die Psalmen übersetzt und erklärt.* Göttingen: Vandenhoeck & Ruprecht, 1926.

———— "The Religion of the Psalms," *What Remains of the Old Testament and Other Essays.* London: Allen & Unwin, 1928.

Guthrie, Harvey H., Jr. *God and History in the Old Testament*. New York: Seabury Press, 1960.

Haldar, Alfred O. *Studies in the Book of Nahum*. Uppsala: Lundequistska Bokhandeln, 1947.

Heidel, Alexander. *The Babylonian Genesis*. Chicago: University of Chicago Press, 1951 2nd ed.

Hocart, Arthur M. *Kingship*. London: Oxford University Press, 1927.

Hooke, Samuel H. *The Origins of Early Semitic Ritual*. London: Oxford University Press, 1938.

Huffmon, Herbert B. "The Covenant Lawsuit in the Prophets," *JBL* LXXVIII (1959), 285-295.

Irwin, William A. "The Wisdom Literature," *IB* I, 212-219. Nashville: Abingdon, 1952.

Jacobsen, Thorkild. "Primitive Democracy in Ancient Mesopotamia," *Journal of Near Eastern Studies* II (1943), 159-172.

James, Fleming. *Thirty Psalmists*. New York: Putnam, 1938.

Johnson, Aubrey. *The Cultic Prophet in Ancient Israel*. Cardiff: University of Wales Press, 1962 2nd ed.

———— "The Psalms," *The Old Testament and Modern Study* (ed. H. H. Rowley). London: Oxford University Press, 1951.

———— "The Role of the King in the Jerusalem Cultus," *The Labyrinth* (ed. S. H. Hooke). New York: Macmillan, 1935.

———— *Sacral Kingship in Ancient Israel*. Cardiff: University of Wales Press, 1955.

Kapelrud, Arvid S. *The Ras Shamra Discoveries and the Old Testament*. Oxford: Blackwell; Norman: University of Oklahoma Press, 1962.

———— "Ugarit," *IDB* IV. Nashville: Abingdon, 1962.

Kirkpatrick, A. F. *The Book of Psalms*. London: Cambridge University Press, 1902.

Kissane, Edward J. *The Book of Psalms*. Dublin: Browne & Nolan, 1953-54.

Koch, Klaus. *Was Ist Formgeschichte?* Neukirchen: Verlag des Erziehungsvereins, 1964.

Köhler, Ludwig. *Hebrew Man*. London: S.C.M., 1956.

Korosec, Viktor. *Hethitische Staatsverträge. Ein Beitrag zur ihrer juistischen Wertung*. Leipzig: Weicher, 1931.

Kraus, Hans-Joachim. *Gottesdienst in Israel*. Munich: Kaiser, 1954 1st ed., 1962 rev. and enlarged ed.

———— *Die Königsherrschaft Gottes im Alten Testament*. Tübingen: Mohr, 1951.

———— *Psalmen (BK)*. Neukirchen: Verlag des Erziehungsverein, 1960.

Lamb, John A. *The Psalms in Christian Worship*. London: Faith Press, 1962.

Langdon, Stephen. *Babylonian Penitential Psalms*. Paris: Geuthner, 1927.

van Leeuwen, Arend T. *Christianity in World History: The Meeting of the Faiths of East and West*. Edinburgh: Edinburgh House, 1964.

Leslie, Elmer A. *The Psalms*. Nashville, Abingdon, 1949.

Lewis, C. S. *Reflections on the Psalms*. London: Geoffrey Bles, 1958.

Lods, Adolphe. *Israel from Its Beginnings to the Middle of the Eighth Century*. London: Routledge & Kegan Paul, 1932.

Malfroy, Jean. "Sagesse et Loi dans le Deuteronome," *VT* XV (1965), 49-65.

Mand, Fritzlothar. "Die Eigenstandigkeit der Danklieder des Psalters als Bekenntnislieder," *ZAW* LXX (1958), 185-199.

Martin-Achard, Robert. *From Death to Life*. London: Oliver & Boyd, 1960.

May, Herbert Gordon. "Some Cosmic Connotations of *Mayim Rabbim*, 'Many Waters,'" *JBL* LXXIV (1955), 9-21.

McCown, C. C., "City," *IDB* I, Nashville: Abingdon, 1962.

Mendenhall, George E. "The Hebrew Conquest of Palestine," *BA* XXV (1962), 66-87.

———— *Law and Covenant in Israel and the Ancient Near East*. Pittsburgh: The Biblical Colloquium, 1955. Reprinted from *BA* XVII (1954), 26-46, 49-76.

Mowinckel, Sigmund. *Le Décalogue*. Paris: Alcan, 1927.

———— *He That Cometh*. Nashville: Abingdon, 1956.

———— *Psalmenstudien I-VI*. Kristiana: Dybwad, 1921-24.

———— *The Psalms in Israel's Worship*. Nashville: Abingdon, 1962.

Muilenburg, James. "The Birth of Benjamin," *JBL* LXXV (1956), 194-201.

———— "The Form and Structure of the Covenantal Formulations," *VT* IX (1959), 347-365.

———— "Isaiah 40-66," *IB* V. Nashville: Abingdon, 1956.

Napier, B. Davie. "On Creation Faith in the Old Testament," *Interpretation* XVI (1962), 21-42.

Newman, Murray. *The People of the Covenant. A Study of Israel from Moses to the Monarchy*. Nashville: Abingdon, 1962.

———— "The Prophetic Call of Samuel," *Israel's Prophetic Heritage* (ed. B. W. Anderson and W. Harrelson). New York: Harper, 1962.

Niebuhr, Reinhold. *Beyond Tragedy*. New York: Scribners, 1937.

Noth, Martin. "Gott, König, und Volk im Alten Testament," *Zeitschrift für Theologie und Kirche* XLVII (1950), 157-191. Reprinted in his *Gesammelte Studien zum Alten Testament.* Munich: Kaiser, 1957.

――――― *The History of Israel.* New York: Harper, 1960 rev. trans.

――――― *Das System der zwölf Stämme Israels.* Stuttgart: Kohlhammer, 1930.

――――― *Überlieferungsgeschichte des Pentateuch.* Stuttgart: Kohlhammer, 1948 2nd ed.

Obermann, Julian. *Ugaritic Mythology. A Study of Its Leading Motifs.* New Haven: Yale University Press, 1948.

Oesterley, W. O. E. *A Fresh Approach to the Psalms.* New York: Scribners, 1937.

――――― *The Psalms.* London: S.P.C.K., 1939.

Owen, D. R. G. *Body and Soul.* Philadelphia: Westminster Press, 1956.

Pannenberg, Wolfhart. *Offenbarung als Geschichte.* Göttingen: Vandenhoeck & Ruprecht, 1961.

Patai, Raphael. *Man and Temple in Ancient Jewish Myth and Ritual.* New York: Nelson, 1947.

Patton, John H. *Canaanite Parallels in the Book of Psalms.* Baltimore: Johns Hopkins Press, 1944.

Pedersen, Johannes. *Israel. Its Life and Culture.* Copenhagen: Branner; London: Oxford University Press, I-II (1926), III-IV (1940).

Pope, Marvin H. *El in the Ugaritic Texts.* Leiden: Brill, 1955.

Pritchard, James B. (ed.). *Ancient Near Eastern Texts.* Princeton: Princeton University Press, 1955 2nd ed.

Prothero, Rowland E. *The Psalms in Human Life.* London: John Murray, 1913 4th ed.

von Rad, Gerhard. "Deuteronomy," *IDB* I. Nashville: Abingdon, 1962.

――――― *Das formgeschichtliche Problem des Hexateuch.* Stuttgart: Kohlhammer, 1938. Reprinted in his *Gesammelte Studien· zum Alten Testament.* Munich: Kaiser, 1958.

――――― *Genesis.* Philadelphia: Westminster Press, 1961.

――――― *Der heilige Krieg im alten Israel.* Zürich: Zwingli-Verlag, 1951.

――――― *Old Testament Theology I.* New York: Harper, 1962.

――――― *Theologie des Alten Testaments II.* Munich: Kaiser, 1960.

Reventlow, Henning Graf. *Das Amt des Propheten bei Amos.* Göttingen: Vandenhoeck & Rupprecht, 1962.

――――― *Liturgie und prophetisches Ich bei Jeremia.* Gütersloh: Mohn, 1963.

――――― *Wächter über Israel: Ezechiel und seine Tradition.* Berlin: Töpelmann, 1962.

Ringgren, Helmer. *The Faith of the Psalmists.* Philadelphia: Fortress Press, 1963.

——— *Sprüche* (*ATD*). Göttingen: Vandenhoeck & Ruprecht, 1962.

Robinson, H. Wheeler. "The Council of Yahweh," *Journal of Theological Studies* XLV (1944), 151-157.

Robinson, Theodore H. *The Poetry of the Old Testament.* London: Duckworth, 1947.

Rost, Leonhard. *Die Überlieferung von der Thronnachfolge Davids.* Stuttgart: Kohlhammer, 1926.

Rowley, H. H. (ed.). *The Old Testament and Modern Study.* London: Oxford University Press, 1951.

Rylaarsdam, J. Coert. *Revelation in Jewish Wisdom Literature.* Chicago: University of Chicago Press, 1946.

Schmidt, Hans. *Das Gebet des Angeklagten im Alten Testament.* Giessen: Töpelmann, 1928.

——— *Die Psalmen.* Tübingen: Mohr, 1934.

Simons, J. *Jerusalem in the Old Testament. Researches and Theories.* Leiden: Brill, 1952.

Smend, Rudolf. "Über das Ich der Psalmen," ZAW VIII (1888), 49-147.

Smend, Rudolf. *Das Mosebild von Heinrich Ewald bis Martin Noth.* Tübingen: Mohr, 1959.

Snaith, Norman H. *The Distinctive Ideas of the Old Testament.* London: Epworth Press, 1944.

Speiser, E. A. *Genesis* (Anchor Bible). Garden City, N.Y.: Doubleday, 1964.

Stendahl, Krister. "Biblical Theology, Contemporary," *IDB* I. Nashville: Abingdon, 1962.

Taylor, Charles L. *Let the Psalms Speak.* New York: Seabury Press, 1961.

Terrien, Samuel. "Amos and Wisdom," *Israel's Prophetic Heritage* (ed. B. W. Anderson and W. Harrelson). New York: Harper, 1962.

——— *The Psalms and Their Meaning for Today.* Indianapolis: Bobbs-Merrill, 1952.

Thomas, D. Winton. *Documents from Old Testament Times.* New York: Nelson, 1958. Published as a Harper Torch Book, 1961.

Vaux, Roland de. *Ancient Israel: Its Life and Institutions.* New York: McGraw-Hill, 1961.

Watts, John D. W. *Vision and Prophecy in Amos.* Leiden: Brill, 1958.

Weiser, Artur. *The Old Testament: Its Formation and Development.* New York: Association Press, 1961.

——— *The Psalms.* Philadelphia: Westminster Press, 1962.

Wensinck, Arent J. *The Ideas of the Western Semites Concerning the Navel of the Earth.* Amsterdam: Mueller, 1916.

Westermann, Claus. *Der Aufbau des Buches Hiob.* Tübingen: Mohr, 1956.

———— *Das Loben Gottes in den Psalmen.* Göttingen: Vandenhoeck & Ruprecht, 1961. Eng. trans., *The Praise of God in the Psalms.* Philadelphia: Fortress Press, 1965.

———— "Struktur und Geschichte der Klage im Alten Testament," ZAW LXVI (1954), 44-80.

———— "Zur Sammlung des Psalters" (a précis), *Zeitschrift der Deutschen Morgenländischen Gesellschaft* CXI (1961), 338-389.

Widengren, Georg. *The Accadian and Hebrew Psalms of Lamentation as Religious Documents.* Uppsala: Almqvist & Wiksells, 1936.

Wilson, John A. *The Burden of Egypt.* Chicago: University of Chicago Press, 1951.

Wright, G. Ernest and Freedman, D. N. (eds.). *The Biblical Archaeologist Reader I.* Garden City, N.Y.: Doubleday (Anchor Book), 1961.

———— "The Lawsuit of God," *Israel's Prophetic Heritage* (ed. B. W. Anderson and W. Harrelson). New York: Harper, 1962.

———— *The Old Testament Against Its Environment.* Chicago: Regnery, 1950.

———— *The Rule of God: Essays in Biblical Theology.* Garden City, N.Y.: Doubleday, 1960.

Zimmerli, Walther. *Ezechiel (BK).* Neukirchen: Verlag des Erziehungsverein, in process of serial publication.

———— *Prediger (ATD).* Göttingen: Vandenhoeck & Ruprecht, 1962.

Supplement to the Bibliography
October 1977

Anderson, B. W. *Out of the Depths.* Philadelphia: Westminster, 1974.

Barth, Christoph. *Introduction to the Psalms.* New York: Scribners, 1966.

Childs, Brevard. "Reflections on the Modern Study of the Psalms," in *Magnalia Dei, The Mighty Acts of God.* Ed. F. M. Cross et al. Garden City: Doubleday, 1976.

Clements, R. E. "Interpreting the Psalms," in *One Hundred Years of Old Testament Interpretation.* Philadelphia: Westminster, 1976.

Dahood, Mitchell. *Psalms I-III, Anchor Bible.* Garden City: Doubleday, 1966, 1968, 1970.

Donner, Herbert. "Ugaritismen in der Psalmenforschung," ZAW 79 (1967), 322-350.

Drijvers, Pius. *The Psalms, Their Structure and Meaning.* New York: Herder and Herder, 1965.

Gerstenberger, Erhard. "Psalms," in *Old Testament, Form Criticism,* ed. J. H. Hayes. San Antonio: Trinity Press, 1974.

Gunkel, Hermann. *The Psalms: A Form-Critical Introduction,* trans. T. Horner. Philadelphia: Fortress Press, 1967.

Hayes, John H. *Understanding the Psalms.* Valley Forge, PA: Judson Press, 1976.

Kraus, Hans-Joachim. *Worship in Israel,* trans. G. Buswell. Oxford: Blackwell, 1966.

Ringgren, Helmer. *Psalmen.* Stuttgart: Kohlhammer, 1971.

Rowley, H. H. *Worship in Ancient Israel.* Philadelphia: Fortress Press, 1967.

Sabourin, Leopold. *The Psalms: Their Origin and Meaning.* New York: Alba House, 1974.

Index of Biblical Passages

232

General Index

Abiathar, 55, 72
Absalom, 55
Ahlström, G. W., 213
Albright, William F., 207, 210, 216, 217, 221
Aliyan Baal, 64, 65, 68, 69, 72, 89
Alt, Albrecht, 19, 211
Amphictyony, see Tribal league
Amarna Letters, 210
Anat, 76
Apsee, 117
Ark, 54, 55, 73, 97, 98, 103, 215
Arunah, 72
Ashur, 70
Assembly, Divine, 64, 107, 210
Assembly of gods, 64, 75, 76, 79, 80, 84, 150
Assyrians, 9
Atheism, 115
Atonement, Day of, 137
Authorship of psalms, 3
Autumnal festival, 20

Baal, 76, 77, 80, 81, 82, 86, 91, 145; struggle with Yahweh, 129
Babylon, 16; as center of cosmos, 69
Babylonian epic of creation, 64, 70, 75; king-list 69; laments, 134, 158; literature, 9; New Year festival, 16, 70, 137; New Year ritual, 16, 86, 166; penitence in laments, 158; personal god, 164; prayer to

any god, 158; sin in lament, 159
Balla, E., 217
Baltzer, Klaus, 209, 210
Begrich, Joachim, 207, 218, 220
Bethel, 68
Biblical tradition: effect on Western culture, 32
Birkeland, Harris, 217, 218
Blank, Sheldon, 217, 220
Bonhoeffer, Dietrich, 222
Boström, Gustav, 221
Bright, John, 208, 209, 210, 212, 213
Buttenweiser, Moses, 207

Campbell, Edward F., Jr., 210
Canaanite city-kingdoms, 55; culture, 17; elements in David's court, 56; hymns, 57
Cassius, Mount, see Zaphon
Chakam, see Wise one
Chalcedon, council of, 57
Chaos, 16; watery, 65, 81, 110
Chasid, 51, 105
Chemosh, 129
Chesed, 50, 51, 85, 91, 147, 152, 153, 161
Chokmah, 171, 180; see also Wisdom
City, 67; as locus of God's rule, 88 ff
City-kingdom, 66 ff; Canaanite, 55; Jebusite, 71; polity, 30; Yahweh as God of, 73

West, see Sea

Westermann, Claus, vii, 216, 218, 220, 222

Widengren, Georg, 217, 218

Wilson, John A., 220

Wisdom, *chokmah*, 171, 180; folk, 172; literature, 13, 172, 173, *mashal*, 72; motif, 179; mythos, 179, 185; origin and nature, 171 ff.; personification of, 182; poem, 177; psalms, 22; Solomon as traditional patron, 173; songs, 13; theological significance of, 25, 180; and time, 175; and *torah*, 187 f., 192; torah theology, 192, 193; tradition, 24; writings and the "evil woman," 183

Wisdom of Solomon, 187 f., 221

Wise one, 171; professional men attached to court, 173

Witnesses (to covenant), 35

World view: Egypt, 62; Mesopotamia, 62

Wright, G. E., 211, 212, 216

Yadah, see *Todah*

Yahweh: as chief god, 83; choice of Jerusalem, 104; and covenant, 31; demand of god, 110 ff.; and the Divine Assembly, 107; emphasis on name, 79; enthronement as king, 16; epiphany of, 77; as god of city-kingdom, 73; as god of cosmos, 56, 57, 58, 74, 86; as Israel's god, 31; as king of cosmos, 90; as king of hosts, 97; kingship, 29; as name for god, 209; as overlord, 42; as personal god, 141 f.; and people, 30; struggle with Baal, 129; sovereignty of, 31, 38, 57; suzerainty of, 52, 53; theophany of, 17, 77

Yahwist, epic of, 101; theology of, 102

Yam, 81, 96, 117

Yoma, 137

Zadok, 55, 72

Zaphon, Mount, 69, 89, 90

Zechariah, 179

Zedek, 72

Zerubbabel, 179

Zimmerli, Walther, 211, 220

Zion, 94, 96, 98; bringing the ark to, 98; Mount, 90